Dumke / Abran (Eds.)
Software Measurement

GABLER EDITION WISSENSCHAFT

Information Engineering und IV-Controlling

Herausgegeben von

Professor Dr. Franz Lehner,
Universität Regensburg (schriftführend),
Professor Dr. Stefan Eicker,
Universität-GH Essen,
Professor Dr. Ulrich Frank,
Universität Koblenz-Landau,
Professor Dr. Erich Ortner,
Technische Universität Darmstadt,
Professor Dr. Eric Schoop,
Technische Universität Dresden

Die Schriftenreihe präsentiert aktuelle Forschungsergebnisse der Wirtschaftsinformatik sowie interdisziplinäre Ansätze aus Informatik und Betriebswirtschaftslehre. Ein zentrales Anliegen ist dabei die Pflege der Verbindung zwischen Theorie und Praxis durch eine anwendungsorientierte Darstellung sowie durch die Aktualität der Beiträge. Mit der inhaltlichen Orientierung an Fragen des Information Engineerings und des IV-Controllings soll insbesondere ein Beitrag zur theoretischen Fundierung und Weiterentwicklung eines wichtigen Teilbereichs der Wirtschaftsinformatik geleistet werden.

Reiner Dumke / Alain Abran (Eds.)

Software Measurement

Current Trends in Research and Practice

Springer Fachmedien Wiesbaden GmbH

Die Deutsche Bibliothek - CIP-Einheitsaufnahme

Software Measurement : current trends in research and practice
/ Reiner Dumke/Alain Abran (Eds.).

(Gabler Edition Wissenschaft : Information Engineering und IV-Controlling)
ISBN 978-3-8244-6876-8 ISBN 978-3-663-08949-0 (eBook)
DOI 10.1007/978-3-663-08949-0

Ursprünglich erschienen bei Betriebswirtschaftlicher Verlag Dr. Th. Gabler GmbH, Wiesbaden, und Deutscher Universitäts-Verlag GmbH, Wiesbaden, 1999

Lektorat: Claudia Splittgerber

http://www.gabler-online.de
http://www.duv.de

ISBN 978-3-8244-6876-8

Foreword

Software developers are faced with the challenge of making software systems and products of ever greater quality and safety, while at the same time being faced with the growing pressure of costs reduction in order to gain and maintain competitive advantages. As in any scientific and engineering discipline, reliable measurement is essential for talking on such a challenge.

"Software measurement is an excellent abstraction mechanism for learning what works and what doesn't" (Victor Basili). Measurement of both software process and products provides a large amount of basic information for the evaluation of the software development processes or the software products themselves. Examples of recent successes in software measurement span multiple areas, such as evaluation of new development methods and paradigms, quality and management improvement programs, tool-supporting initiatives and company-wide measurement programs.

The German Computer Science Interest (GI) Group of Software Metrics and the Canadian Interest Group in Software Metrics (CIM) have attended to these concerns in the recent years. Research initiatives were directed initially to the definition of software metrics and then to validation of the software metrics themselves. This was followed by more and more investigation into practical applications of software metrics and by critical analysis of the benefits and weaknesses of software measurement programs. Key findings in this area of software engineering have been published in some important books, such as Dumke and Zuse's *Theory and Practice of Software Measurement*, Ebert and Dumke's *Software Metrics in Practice* and Lehner, Dumke and Abran's *Software Metrics*.

This new book includes key papers presented at the 8th International Workshop on Software Metrics in Magdeburg (Germany), September 1998. It is a collection of theoretical studies in the field of software measurement as well as experience reports on the application of software metrics in USA, Canadian, Netherlands, Belgian, France, England and German companies and universities. Some of these papers and reports describe new software measurement applications and paradigms for knowledge-based techniques, test service evaluation, factor analysis discussions and neural-fuzzy applications. Others address the multimedia systems and discuss the application of the Function Point approach for real-time systems, the evaluation of Y2K metrics, or they include experience reports about the implementation of measurement programs in industrial environments.

This book will be of interest to software engineering researchers, as well as to practitioners in the areas of project management and quality improvement programs, for both software maintenance and software development in general.

We especially thank Mrs. Dörge and Mr. Foltin for their great works to prepare the unified layout of this book.

Alain Abran | Reiner Dumke

Table of Contents

I. Software Measurement History and Future Directions

Thirty Years of Software Measurement

Horst Zuse, Technische Universität Berlin (Germany)

1 Introduction

From our view, the year 1998 is the 30. anniversary of software measurement. It may be, that the earliest paper about software complexity was published by Rubey et al. [145] in 1968. There is no reference to an earlier publication. Boehm et al. [24], p.B-4, point out about this paper: *Many software attributes and their metrics are defined and discussed. There is a total of 57 attributes distributed among seven categories. They are related to mathematical calculations, program logic, computation time and memory usage, program modifiability, etc. The metrics are realized as formulas and are explained in detail.* Also in 1971 Knuth [95] published a paper of an empirical investigation of FORTRAN programs.

The magnitude of costs involved in software development and maintenance magnifies the need for a scientific foundation to support programming standards and management decisions by measurement. Already in 1980 Curtis [46] pointed out: *Rigorous scientific procedures must be applied to studying the development of software systems if we are to transform programming into an engineering discipline. At the core of these procedures is the development of measurement techniques and the determination of cause effect relationships.* As highlighted above, the establishment of well accepted structures of measurement in physics took a very long time. It is our impression that the same holds for software measurement. In the next sections we present an overview of software measurement from a historical perspective. A more detailed description of the history of software measurement can be found in [190].

1.1 Groundwork of Software Measurement

The groundwork for software measures and software measurement was established in the sixties and mainly in the seventies, and from these earlier works, further results have emerged in the eighties and nineties. The reasons for creating or inventing software measures is based on the knowledge that program structure and modularity are important considerations for the development of reliable software. Most software specialists agree that higher reliability is achived when software systems are highly modularized and module structure is kept simple [146]. Modularity has been discussed early. Parnas [132] suggested that modules should be structured so that a module has no knowledge of the internal structure of other modules, Myers [113] described the concept of module strength, and Yourdon discussed modularity in 1975 [177]. These factors affect cost and quality of software, as, for example, Porter et al. point out [136].

Shapiro [152] describes the change from efficiency of programs to the understandability of programs as follows: *Over the course of the 1970's. attributes other than efficiency began to dominate concern over software characteristics. Efficiency remained a legitimate concern, but it could no longer be the only concern. The vast increases in complexity necessitated a more complex value structure. A fast but incomprehensible program was no bargain: errors and maintenance difficulties rendered speedy execution far less advantageous. Tools such as structured techniques were means toward satisfying the demands of the new value structure, but difficulties arose in evaluating the results of their application. Like so much else in the developing software field, software metrics quickly settled into the motherhood and apple pie category. Everyone agreed on the importance of properties such as clarity, reliability, and maintainability for software quality but nobody was sure how to measure them. While efficiency lent itself to relatively straightforward measurement in terms of execution times, more nebulous criteria proved less obliging. Traditional measurement methods that concentrated on statistical analyses of defects and breakdowns were clearly inadequate for a medium in which many problems originated in specification and design rather than physical deterioration. The concept of a physical breakdown is a non sequitur in the realm of software. Of concern, rather, is how to determine, for instance, which design is less complex than another and thus likely to be less flawed and more maintainable. By 1978, consultant Tom Gilb could still complain in the pages of Software Engineering Notes that "quality goals are like the weather: everybody talks about them, but nobody quantifies them."*

The earliest software measure is the Measure LOC, which is discussed and used till today [131]. In 1955 the Measure LOC was used to analyze the size of the first FORTRAN Compiler developed by John Backus [14]. The size of the compiler was 25000 lines-of-code (machine instructions). It was planned to finish the compiler in six months, but it took 48 months. Already at this time software development took much longer than planned. It is not clear who mentioned the first time the Measure LOC. Grace Hopper constructed in 1953 the Compiler A-2. Maybe, that she counted LOC. It is also possible, that she counted the instructions of the program for the MARK I of Aiken in 1944. Instructions were counted in 1950 at the ETH-Zürich, where Konrad Zuse installed his Computer Z4. The scientists wrote in a paper that the Z4 accomplished 1000 instructions per hour.

In 1974 Wolverton [174] made one of the earliest attempts to formally measure programmer productivity using lines-of-code (LOC). He proposed object instructions per man-month as a productivity measure and suggested what he considered to be typical code rates. The basis of the Measure LOC [155], p.3, is that program length can be used as a predictor of program characteristics such as reliability and ease of maintenance. Despite, or possibly even because of, simplicity of this measure, it has been subjected to severe criticism. Estimated and actual source lines are used for productivity estimates, as described by Walston and Felix [170], during the proposal and performance phases of software contracts. In the sixties SLOC (source lines-of-code) were counted by the number of 80-column cards (physical lines-of-code). In 1983 Basili and Hutchens [18] suggested that the Measure LOC should be regarded as a baseline measure to which all other measures be compared. We should expect an effective code measure to perform better than LOC, and so, as a minimum, LOC offers a "null hypothesis" for empirical evaluations of software measures. The Measure LOC is mentioned in more than ten thousand papers.

The most famous measures, which are continued to be discussed heavily today, are the Measures of McCabe [107] and of Halstead [69]. McCabe derived a software complexity measure from graph theory using the definition of the cyclomatic number. McCabe interpreted the cyclomatic number as *the minimum number of paths* in the flowgraph. He argued that the minimum number of paths determines the complexity (cyclomatic complexity) of the program: *The overall strategy will be to measure the complexity of a program by computing the number of linearly independent paths v(G), control the "size" of programs by setting an upper limit to v(G) (instead of using just physical size), and use the cyclomatic complexity as the basis for a testing methodology.* McCabe also proposed the *measure essential complexity,* which may be the first measure analyzing unstructuredness based on primes. In 1989 Zuse et al. [180], [181], [182] showed that the idea of complexity of the Measure of McCabe can be characterized by three simple operations. Zuse et al. derived this concept from measurement theory.

The Measures of Halstead are based on the source code of programs. Halstead showed that estimated effort, or programmer time, can be expressed as a function of operator count, operand count, or usage count [68]. Halstead's method has been used by many organizations, including IBM at its Santa Teresa Laboratory [43], and General Motors Corporation [68], primarily in software measurement experiments. Today the most used Measures of Halstead are the Measures Length, Volume, Difficulty and Effort. Halstead died at the end of the seventies and it is a pity that he cannot defend his measures today.

In 1976 Gilb [63], [64] published a book entitled: *Tom Gilb: Software Metrics,* which is one of the first books in the area of software measures. Closely after the book of Gilb, in 1978 a remarkable book of Boehm et al. [24] followed. On p.4-1 they gave guidelines of the use of measures that are still valid today. In 1979 Belady [21] proposed the Measure BAND which is sensitive to nesting. Already in 1978 [89] published a paper where he discusses methods to measure programming quality and productivity. Interesting, among others, in this paper are his considerations of units of measures. Albrecht [9] introduced in 1979 the Function-Point method in order to measure the application development productivity.

In 1980 Oviedo [130] developed *a Model of Program Quality*. This model treats control flow complexity and data flow complexity together. Oviedo defines the complexity of a program by the calculation of control complexity and data flow complexity with one measure.

In 1980 Curtis [46] published an important paper about software measurement. Curtis discussed in the Chapter *Science and Measurement* some basic concepts of measurement. He pointed out that in a less-developed science, relationships between theoretical and operationally defined constructs are not necessarily established on a formal mathematical basis, but are logically presumed to exist. And, among others, he writes: *The more rigorous our measurement techniques, the more thoroughly a theoretical model can be tested and calibrated. Thus progress in a scientific basis for software engineering depends on improved measurement of the fundamental constructs.* Here, Curtis refers to Jones [89]. Jones [88], [89], [90] is also one of the pioneers in the area of software measurement.

Troy et al. [169] proposed in 1981 a set of 24 measures to analyze the modularity, the size, the complexity, the cohesion and the coupling of a software system. Especially cohesion and coupling are fundamental criteria of the understandability of a software system. The basic division of software (complexity) measures into inter-modular and intra-modular components and the specific conceptual measures of coupling and cohesion are based on a work of Constantine [44]. Measures for cohesion were proposed in 1984 by Emerson [56] and [57]. In 1982 Weiser presented the concept of slices [171], [172]. Based on the concept of slices measures for cohesion were discussed in 1986 by Longworth et al. [105] and in 1991 by Ott et al. [124]. However, there are some other papers which deal with the term cohesion in the context of measures like: Dhama [50], Lakhotia [100], Patel et al. [133], Rising et al. [139], Selby et al. [150], and Thuss [167]. The articles of Ott et al. [123], [124], [125], [126], [127], [128], [129] are fundamental considerations of the term cohesion by software measures.

In 1981 a Study Panel [135] consisting of people of the industry and universities (Victor Basili, Laslo Belady, Jim Browne, Bill Curtis, Rich DeMillo, Ivor Francis, Richard Lipton, Bill Lynch, Merv Müller, Alan Perlis, Jean Summet, Fred Sayward, and Mary Shaw) discussed and evaluated the current state of the art and the status of research in the area of software measures. During this panel

DeMillo et al. [49], p.81ff, discussed the problem of measuring software compared to other sciences. They discussed the problem of meaningfulness and introduced the term homomorphism. However, they did not give conditions for the use of software measures as an ordinal or a ratio scale.

1.2 Software Design Measurement

The simplest software design measure has been proposed by Gilb [64] in 1977, namely the number of modules, however, more sophisticated design measures were proposed in 1978 by Yin et al. [176] and Chapin [39]. These measures may be the first measures which could be used in the software design phase of the software life-cycle. Later, software measures, which can be used in the design phase, were proposed among others by Bowles [35], Troy et al. [169], McCabe et al. [108], Card et al. [38], Shepperd et al. [155], Ligier [103], [93], [94], and Zuse [183]. Based on the works of Stevens, Myers [113] and Constantine [161] much work has been done to create software (complexity) measures for the interconnectivity analysis of large software systems. Software systems contain multiple types of interrelations between the components, like data, control, and sequencing among others. In 1981 the *Interconnectivity Metric* of Henry and Kafura [77] was proposed. This measure is based on the multiplication of the fan-in and fan-out of modules. At the end of the eighties a modification of this measure [78] was proposed by creating a hybrid measure consisting of a intra-modular measure, like the Measures of Halstead and McCabe and the "Interconnectivity Metric". Other approaches, for example of Selby et al. [151] and Hutchens et al. [79] base on the early works of Myers [113] and Stevens et al. [161], and propose software measures based on data binding. Other works can be found in [32], [141] and [70].

Hall [66], [67] proposed in 1983/84 software complexity measures in order to analyze large systems. Although this approach is very intuitive, the measures are largely forgotten.

In 1979 Albrecht [9], [10] proposed the Function Point Method. Function points are derived from requirements specification. This method that can be used in the specification phase of the software life-cycle, today is widely used in the USA, the UK, and in Europe. In 1988 Jones [91] proposed an extension of function points to attempt to *validate* the measure for real-time and embedded applications. Jones called his extensions feature points. He introduced a new parameter, called algorithms, and reduced the weights assigned to data file parameters. In 1988 and 1991 this model was modified by Symons [162], [163]. He proposed an extension called Mark II function points to address the following difficulties which he identified with Albrecht's method: The system component classifications are oversimplified, the weights of the components were determined by debate and trail, the internal complexity seems to be rather inadequate, the 14 factors are overlapping and the range of the weights are always valid. A good overview of the Function-Point method can be found in Garmus et al. [62]. Articles considering the Function-Point Method from a theoretical view are from Abran, Paton, Robillard [2], [3], [7] and [134].

As already mentioned, in 1981 Boehm [28], [29] proposed the COCOMO (COnstructive COst MOdel) model which is based in the Measure LOC. A good overview of cost estimation models and measures is given by Kitchenham in [58], Chapter 9. There are four common methods of cost estimation: Expert opinion, analogy, decomposition and estimation equations. Very interesting is the method of decomposition: this involves either breaking a product up into its smallest components or breaking a project up into its lowest level tasks. Estimates are made of the effort required to produce the smallest components or perform the lowest level task. Project estimates are made by summing the components estimates. Other cost estimation models are the Raleigh Curve Model of Putnam [137] and the Bang Measure of DeMarco [48]. Because of the increasing diversity of software development processes, the 1990s are seeing renewed attention on developing improved cost models. The SEI started a small initiative on software estimation improvement in 1994. Of more interest is an effort lead by Barry Boehm, now at the University of Southern California, to revise and extend the COCOMO model, which has served the industry well for so long (over 15 years). The new version of COCOMO - called COCOMO 2.0 [27] - is still being developed and will address the various types of development processes mentioned earlier. COCOMO 2.0 explicitly handles the availability of additional information in later stages of a project, the nonlinear costs of reusing software components, and the effects of several factors on the diseconomics of scale. (Some of these are the turn over rate of the staff, the geographic dispersion of the team, and the "maturity" of the development process as defined by the SEI.) The model also revises some coefficient values and eliminates discontinuities present in the old model (related to "development modes" and maintenance vs. adaptation). Barry Boehm is leading a group of industrial and academic affiliates to review the revised set of COCOMO equations and to collect data to evaluate hypotheses to select the significant parameters for COCOMO 2.0. Boehm and his co-workers expect to provide the refined equations, representing an improved and calibrated cost model, in late 1996.

1.3 Standards in the Area of Software Measurement

At this time, only a few standards are existing in the area of software measurement. On the whole five standards should be mentioned here:

1. The IEEE: *Standard Dictionary of Measures to Produce Reliable Software* [80].

2. The *Guide for the Use of Standard Dictionary of Measures to Produce Reliable Software* [81].
3. The *IEEE Standard for a Software Quality Metrics Methodology,* also called IEEE Standard 1061, which was created by Norman Schneidewind.
4. The *Function-Point Counting Practices. International Function-Point User Group, Westerville, OH, USA,* [83] is a well known standard, and the MARK II Method of Symons [162].
5. The US Air Force policy on software metrics (Acquisition Policy 93M-017, February 16, 1994 [51]).

The reasons for a lack of standards is the low maturity of the area of software measurement. Unfortunately, most of the discussed software measures in the report [80] are process measures and measures for the maintenance phase of the software life-cycle. Only some software complexity measures can be found there. May be, that having established a framework for software measurement, which allows to derive hypotheses of reality, more standards can be defined. A uniform terminology and hypotheses about reality are essential in science.

1.4 Goal-Question-Metric Paradigm, User-View and Viewpoints

In 1984 Basili et al. [19], [20], [143] proposed the GQM (Goal-Question-Metric) paradigm. GQM is used for defining measurement goals. The basic idea of GQM is to derive software measures from measurement goals and questions. The GQM approach supports the identification of measures for any type of measurement via a set of guidelines for how to formulate a goal comprehensible, what types of questions to ask, and how to refine them into questions.

The idea that the use of software measures depends on the view of humans is also supported by Fenton [59], p.253, who did call it as: user-view. Zuse and Bollmann [178], [180] called this a viewpoint of complexity.

1.5 Measurement Theory and Software Measures

Measurement theory in the area of software measurement was introduced in the middle of the eighties by Zuse [178]. Based on articles of Bollmann and Cherniavsky [28], and Bollmann [29], in which measurement theory was applied to evaluation measures in the area of information retrieval systems, in 1985 Zuse [178], and Bollmann and Zuse, [30] transferred the measurement theoretic approach to software measurement. They used measurement theory, as described in the texts of Roberts [140], Krantz et al. [97] and Luce et al. [106]. In [30], [178], [179], [180], [181], and [182] the conditions for the use of software measures on certain scale levels, like ordinal, interval or ratio scale were presented. Additionally, measurement theory gives an empirical interpretation of the numbers of software measures by the hypothetical empirical relational system and conditions for concatenation and decomposition operations, which are major strategies in software engineering. Using such axiom systems qualitative models behind measures can be characterized. This concept is also applied in [181] for more than ninety software measures. In 1994 Bollmann and Zuse extended the measurement theoretic approach to prediction models and in 1994 Zuse [184], [186] presented the empirical conditions for the validation of software measures. In 1995 Zuse and Fetcke [187], [189] showed the empirical conditions behind object-oriented software measures. It could be shown that measures in the object-oriented area mostly assume different properties than software measures for imperative languages. Many software measures follow the structure of the function of belief from artificial intelligence.

Similar approaches of using measurement theory followed from 1987 by the Grubstake Group [15], [16] consisting of the scientists Norman Fenton (City University, London), Robin Whitty (CSSE, South Bank Polytechnic, London), Jim Bieman (Colorado State University), Dave Gustafson (Kansas State University), Austin Melton (Kansas State University), and Albert Baker. The Grubstake Group used measurement theory to describe the ranking order of programs created by software measures, but they did not use the extensive structure. Measurement theory is also proposed as a proper theory for software measures by Fenton [58], p.16.

1.6 European Software Measurement Projects

We now consider some projects in the area of software measurement in Europe. In 1986 in the UK a research project started (Alvey-Project SE/069) entitled: *Structured-Based Software Measurement* [11]. This project was intended to build on existing research into formal modeling, analysis and measurement of software structure. It was carried out at South Bank Polytechnic's Centre for Systems and Software Engineering in London, UK. Among others, results of this project can be found in Fenton [58]. In this project mostly software measures based on the prime decomposition were considered [58], [181], p.296.

From 1989 till 1992, the Project METKIT (Metrics Educational Toolkit 2384) [109] of the European Community was created. METKIT was a collaborative project part-funded by the European Commission under their ESPRIT Programme. An outcome of METKIT was the 1991 book of Fenton [58], [60] which gives an excellent overview of the area of software measurement. Other ESPRIT Projects dealing with software engineering measurement were: AMI from Nov. 1990-92 (Applications of Metrics in Industry), MUSIC from Nov. 1990-93 (Metrics for Usability Standards in Computing), MUSE from 1987-90 (Software Quality and Reliability Metrics for Selected Domains: Safety

Management and Clerical Systems), PYRAMID from 1990-92 (Promotion for Metrics), with the following task: Improvement of quality and productivity of European software-intensive systems development and maintenance by the use of quantitative methods, COSMOS from February 1989-94 (Cost Management with Metrics of Specification) and MERMAID from October 1988-92 (Metrication and Resource Modeling Aid).

1.7 Software Measurement in Germany

In Germany software measurement activities are on a low level. Since 1991 a software measurement group exists with GI (Gesellschaft für Informatik). The head of this group is R. Dumke from the University of Magdeburg. There are only some universities in Germany, where lectures of software measurement are offered. At the Technische Universität Berlin, P. Bollmann-Sdorra and H. Zuse offered the first lecture on (software) measurement in 1986. These lectures are continued till today and now are extended by the author to measures in the object-oriented environment. In Magdeburg, R. Dumke [52], [53], [54] teaches, among others, software measurement, and in Kaiserslautern, Dieter Rombach invests much effort to increase the quality of software in companies.

In the past, education in software measurement for companies were sponsored by Barbara Wix from DECollege, now with ORACLE. From 1989 H. Zuse gave in the scope of DECollege three times a year 3-day courses in software measurement for companies. Several companies introduced software measurement programs during the last years, examples are Siemens, Bosch, Alcatel, BMW, DATEV, etc. In 1994, the German Government announced a research program, where software measurement is an important part. The *Gesellschaft für Mathematik und Datenverarbeitung, St. Augustin (German National Research Center for Computer Science)* (GMD) also initiated some projects in the area of software measurement. Harry Sneed is one of the most engaged persons who is requiring software measurement in practice. We refer to the papers and books: [103], [156], [157], [158], [159], [160].

In November 1995, the government of Quebec, the University of Quebec in Montreal, Bell lab in Montreal, GMD, and the Technical University of Berlin organized a joint German-Quebec Workshop in Berlin in order to promote research and education in the software measurement area. However, the activities in the area of software measurement in Germany are increasing. More and more companies think about starting measurement programs, and more and more diploma theses are finished in this area.

In 1996 Dumke, Ebert, Rudolph, and Zuse [55] published the first edition of the Journal: *Metric News - Journal of the GI-Interest Group on Software Metrics. Otto von Guericke University of Magdeburg, Volume 1, Number 1, September*

1996. This journal informs researchers and practitioners about news in the software measurement area.

1.8 Research in the Area of Software Measurement in North America

Software measurement begun early in the seventies in US and Canada. In US various software measurement groups and activities were established since the mid-seventies. Since the measurement activities in US extensive, it is not possible to mention them all. Please look in the other sections of this chapter, too. In this section we will focus on some institutes that support the idea of measurement since years.

1. Many measurement programs have been established under the auspices of the Software Engineering Institute (SEI) at the Carnegie Mellon University to provide a platform from which an increased use of measurement within organizations can be promoted. In 1989, the Software Engineering Institute began an effort to promote the increased use of objective measurement in software engineering, project management, and software acquisitions. As part of this effort, the SEI Measurement Steering Committee was formed to provide technical guidance and increase public awareness of process measurements. Based on the advice of the steering committee, two working groups were created: Software Acquisition Metrics and Software Metrics Definition. This report and the methods in it are outgrowths of work initiated by the Effort and Schedule Subgroup of the Software Metrics Definition Working Group.

2. A long tradition (more than 15 years) of measurement has the NASA SEL-lab in Maryland [114], [115], [116], [117], [118], [119], [120], [121], [122]. Since 1981 the SEL-Lab published more than fifty papers together with the group of Basili at the University of Maryland. In 1990, the SEL-Lab had their fifteenth anniversary in research.

3. In Canada Bell labs (Montreal) developed the software measurement Tool DATRIX which contains a widely accepted set of software measures [47].

4. Alain Abran, Pierre Bourque, etc. - both with the University of Quebec at Montreal – since years are very engaged in the research areas of the Function-Point Methed and software measurement. They also support theoretical concepts in the software measurement area [1], [2], [3], [4], [5], [6], [7], [34].

5. At the beginning of the nineties the *Software Metrics Research Center and Laboratory at the Naval Postgraduate School* was founded. The director is Norman Schneidewind. The reasons for this center are, among others: *Software metrics is an evolving field directed toward improving the quality of*

software products and increasing the productivity of software developers and maintainers. It is one of the highest priority items in the DoD for the improvement of its software. Increasingly, the DoD is requiring the use of metrics in software development contracts. In the past twenty years there have been significant achievements in software metrics, including: development of software reliability models; development of specific metrics, which are designed to assess product quality and process productivity; and development of software cost prediction models.

6. Another major research and application area of software metrics is the application of software quality metrics to the Space Shuttle flight software by Ted Keller, Norman Schneidewind and John Munson [148], [149], [111], [112]: *This research involves the application of software quality metrics to the Space Shuttle flight software. This research is supported by NASA and IBM Federal Systems Company. We have shown that it is possible to apply metrics on large projects to control, predict, and assess software quality based on metrics collected during design. The approach we used was to validate metrics against a quality factor (discrepancy reports) in accordance with the metrics validation methodology we developed and that is included in the IEEE Standard for a Software Quality Metrics Methodology (1061).*

The statements above show that software measurement in US and Canada has a high priority.

1.9 Research in the Area of Software Measurement in Japan

It is not known very much from software measurement research in Japan. One of the few papers is the work of Azuma [12], [13] and Yamada [175] in the context of the ISO-Standard 9126. Together with this norm more than 100 software measures where proposed to quantify the software quality criteria [188].

In 1996 a paper appeared by Torii et al. [168] that describes the current state of quantitative analysis in software engineering along with the overview on software engineering papers published in Japan in the 1990s and the history of implementation and application of the GINGER system, which is a measurement based programming support system with real-time feedback. In the paper the quantitative analysis in software engineering is classified into four major groups: *Quality, Sizing, Human, and Code-level diagnosis.* Most of them take a model-based approach and include experimental projects. At this stage, *Specification-level* and *Design-level* analysis is not so common, but we believe GINGER can make it easy to quantitatively analyse products and processes at these levels with the advent of modern CASE tools.

1.10 Software Measurement in Australia

Much effort in the area of software measurement has been invested in Australia. On the one side many companies use the Function-Point Method, on the other side, object-oriented and cognitive software measures are major research topics [37], [71], [72], [73], [74], [75], [76], [84], [85], [165] and [166]. The Australian Software Metric Association (ASMA) is very active and organizes conferences every year.

1.11 Validation of Software Measures and Prediction Models

Validation of software measures is another very important topic in the area of software measurement because the acceptance of software measures in practice depends on whether the measures can be used as a predictor for a software quality attribute. Schneidewind [147] writes about measure validation: *to help ensure that metrics are used appropriately, only validated metrics (i.e., either quality factors or metrics validated with respect to quality factors) should be used.* Validation of software measures and prediction models, among others, are based on the following questions:

1. Is it possible to predict the error-proneness of a system using software measures from its design phase.
2. Is it possible to extract quantitative features from the representation of a software design to enable us to predict the degree of maintainability of a software system.
3. Are there any quantifiable, key features of the program code of a module that would enable us to predict the degree of difficulty of testing for that module, and the number of residual errors in the module after a particular level of testing has occurred.
4. Is it possible to extract quantifiable features from the representation of a software design to enable us to predict the amount of effort required to build the software described by that design.
5. What properties of software measures are required in order to determine the quality of a design.
6. Are there features in order to predict the size of a project from the specification phase.
7. What are appropriate software measures to underlie the software quality attributes of the ISO 9126 norm by numbers.
8. What are the criteria for the internal and external validation of software measures. What are the criteria for prediction models?

We distinguish between internal and external validation of a software measure [23], p.39. Internal validation considers the homomorphism, that means: does the measure measure what the user wants. External validation of a measure means whether the measure has any relationship to a software quality attribute (external variable). Internal validation of measures are considered by [154], [155] using an algebraic validation and Zuse [181] using so-called atomic modifications which can be seen as necessary conditions for the ordinal scale.

In 1993 and 1994 Bollmann and Zuse [31] and Zuse [185] considered prediction models of software measures and the validation of software measures from a measurement theoretic view, showing that the validation of software measures depends on the scale type of the external variable. The authors showed that the (basic) COCOMO model is the only one which can exist between two ratio scales (the measurement values and the external variable are considered as ratio scales). With respect to validation of software measures and prediction models Zuse et al. also showed that wholeness: *The whole must be at least as big as the sum of the parts,* is a pseudo-property without any empirical meaning. Wholeness is only a numerical modification of a measure without changing the empirical model. This result is important for the validation of measures and in the context of prediction models. The authors discussed the consequences whether the cost or time for maintenance can be determined from the components of the software system, too.

In 1993 the Standard 1061 of IEEE [82], [147] appeared which gives rules / ideas how to validate software measures. The Standard IEEE 1061 has been written by Schneidewind and covers terms like the discriminate power, tracking, validation, predictability, and consistency. Important to notice is that software measures are not validated for ever, the have to be re-validated in a continuous process. In 1993 Gustafson et al. [65] showed that the use of correlation analysis on many metrics will inevitably throw up spurious significant results.

1.12 Software Measures in an Object-Oriented Environment

At the end of the eighties software measures for object-oriented programming (OOP-Measures) were proposed. A very early investigation of OO-Measures can be found by Rocacher [142]. In 1989 Morris [110] discussed software measures for an object-oriented application. Morris defined nine measures: methods per object class, inheritance dependencies, degree of coupling between objects, degree of cohesion of objects, object library effectiveness, factoring effectiveness, degree of reuse of inheritable methods, average method complexity, and application granularity. Bieman [22] discussed software measures for software reuse in an object-oriented, environment, Lake et al. [98] discussed measures for C++ applications. Lake et al. developed a tool that computed a large number of traditional, class, and inheritance tree measures for

C++. A survey of the OOP literature suggested that extensive searching of the inheritance was common to OOP problem areas. Hence their OOP metrics were based primarily on the inheritance tree. Chidamber et al. [41], [42] evaluated different Smalltalk applications: weighted methods per class, depth of inheritance tree, number of children, coupling between object classes, number of other methods called by the methods of a class, and lack of cohesion in methods. Sharble et al. [153] discussed measures for an object-oriented design (OOD), Li and Henry [102] evaluated ADA-Programs. Kolewe [96] suggested three system level measures: number of class hierarchies, number of class clusters (interconnections between classes in a system) and association complexity. Chen and Lu [40] evaluated OO-Measures related to the OOD-method of Booch [33]. Karner [92] wrote a master thesis of measurement in an object-oriented environment. In a survey article about OOP measures, Coppick and Cheatham [45] extended Halstead's software science measures and McCabe's Cyclomatic Complexity and applied them to LISP Favors. Other papers of this area are [8], [17], [36], [86], [87], [99], [101], [138], [164], [165], [166] and [174].

Lake et al. [99] point out: *In several studies, Munson and Khosghoftaar [112] applied factor analysis to sets of traditional software complexity metrics to show that they could be reduced to at most five factors. They showed that groups of these metrics are similar in the sense that they seem to measure the same program characteristics and provide the same information. These studies support our belief that there are only a small number of OOP complexity domains.* Since 1994 two books appeared about object-oriented software measures. The first author is Lorenz et al. and the second one is Henderson-Sellers [76].

In 1995 Zuse [187], [189], and Fetcke [61] investigated the structures and the behavior of object-oriented software measures. The result is that object-oriented measures mostly do not assume an extensive structure. In order to characterize object-oriented software measures above the ordinal scale level, Zuse et al. introduced the Dempster Shafer function of belief, the Kolmogoroff axioms, and the De Finetti axioms as a basic set of axioms for object-oriented measures. The final result is a modified function of belief.

1.13 Current State of Software Measurement

It is undisputed that software measurement is an important method in order to get higher quality of software. In 1991, Dieter Rombach, who was working at this time with the Software Engineering Laboratory (SEL) in the USA, said at the Eurometrics in Paris: *we should no longer ask if we should measure, the question today is how.* Rombach [144] also points out: *Measurement is more than just an addition to current software development approaches. Instead, it provides the basis for introducing engineering discipline into software development. Engineering discipline requires that each software project consists of a planning and execution stage. Planning includes setting project goals in a measurable way, selecting the best suited development methods and tools based on available experience, and instrumenting these methods and tools so that the project goals can be monitored continuously. Execution includes collecting the prescribed data, interpreting them and feeding the results back to the ongoing project. Post-mortem, the project experience needs to be used to update current models of products, processes or qualities for future projects.*

We agree to this view.

References

[1] **Abran, Alain; Nguyenkim, Hong.**
Analysis of Maintenance Work Categories Through Measurement. Proc. of the Conference on Software Maintenance 1991, Sorrento, Italy, October 15-17, 1991.

[2] **Abran, Alain; Robillard, Pierre**
Reliability of Function Points Productivity Model for Enhancement Projects (A Field Study). Proceedings of the Conference on Software Maintenance 1993 (CSM93), Montreal, Canada September 27-30, 1993

[3] **Abran, Alain; Robillard, Pierre N.**
Function Points: A Study of Their Measurement Processes and Scale Transformations. Journal of Systems and Software, 1994, 25, pp. 171-184.

[4] **Abran, Alain**
Analyse des processus de measure des points de function. PhD. Thesis, Ecole Polytechnique de Montreal Quebec, Canada, 1994.

[5] **Abran, Alain; Maya, Marcela**
A Sizing Measure for Adaptive Maintenance Work Products. Proc. of the International Conference on Software Maintenance, Octover 17-20, 1995, Nice, France, 1995, pp. 286-294.

[6] **Abran, Alain; Desharnais, Jean-Marc**
Measurement of Functional Reuse in Maintenance. Software Maintenance: Research and Practice, Vol. 7, pp. 263-277, 1995.

[7] **Abran, Alain; Robillard, Pierre**
Function Point Analysis: An Empirical Study of Its Measurement Process. IEEE Transactions of Software Engineering, Vol. 22, No. 12, December 1996.

[8] **Abreu, F.B.**
Metrics for Object-Oriented Environment. Proceedings of the Third International Conference on Software Quality. Lake Tahoe, Nevada, October 4-6, 1993, pp. 67-75.

[9] **Albrecht, A.J.**
Measuring Applications Development Productivity. Proceedings of IBM Applications Devision Joint SHARE/GUIDE Symposium, Monterey, CA, 1979, pp.83-92.

[10] **Albrecht**.A.J.; Gaffney, S.H.
Software Function, Source Lines of Code and Development Effort Prediction: A Software Science Validation. IEEE Transactions of Software. Engineering Volume.9, No. 6, 1983, pp. 639-648.

[11] **Edited by: Elliott, J.J; Fenton, N.E.; Linkman, S.; Markham, G.; Whitty, R.**
Structure-Based Software Measurement. Alvey Project SE/069, 19A Road to Eiffel. Structured Programming, 1993, pp. 40-46.

[12] **Azuma**, M.; Sanazuka, T.; Yamagishi, N.
Software Quality Assessment Technology. COMSAC, IEEE, 1985.

[13] **Azuma, M.**
Japanese Contribution on Quality Metrics. ISO/IEC JTC/SC7/WG3, 1991.

[14] **Backus, J.W.; and Co-Workers**
Program 's Reference Manual. The Fortran Automatic Coding System for the IBM 704 EDPM, IBM Corporation, New York, 1956.

[15] **Baker, A.L.; Bieman, J.M.; Gustafson, D.A.; Melton, A.; Whitty, R.A.**
Modeling and Measuring the Software Development Process. Proceedings of the Twentieth Annual International Conference on System Sciences, 1987, pp. 23-29.

[16] **Baker, A.L.; Bieman, J.M.; Fenton, N.; Gustafson, D.A.; Melton,.A.; Whitty, R.A.**
A Philosophy for Software Measurement. The Journal of Systems and Software, Volume 12, No 3, 1990, pp.277-281.

[17] **Barns, Michael, G.**
Inheriting Software Metrics. Journal of Object-Oriented Programming, November-December 1993, pp. 27-34.

[18] **Basili, V.; Hutchens, D.**
An Empirical Study of a Complexity Family. IEEE Transactions on Software Engineering, Volume.9, No. 6, November 1983, pp. 664-672.

[19] **Basili, V.; Perricone, Barry T.**
Software Errors and Complexity: An Empirical Investigation. Communications of the ACM, Volume.27, No. 1, January 1984, pp. 42-52.

[20] **Basili, V.; Rombach, Dieter H.**
TAME: Integrating Measurement into Software Environments. TR-1764 ; TAME-TR-1-1987.

[21] **Belady, L.A.**
On Software Complexity. In: Workshop on Quantitative Software Models for Reliability. IEEE No. TH0067-9, New York, N.Y., pp.90-94, October 1979.

[22] **Bieman, J.M.**
Deriving Measures of Software Reuse in Object Oriented Systems. Technical Report #CS91-112, July 1991, Colorado State University, Fort Collins/ Colorado, USA.

[23] **Bieman, J.M.; Schultz, J.**
An Empirical Evaluation (and Specification) of the all-du-paths. Testing Criterion. Software Engineering Journal, Volume.7, No. 1, pp. 43-51, January 1992.

[24] **Boehm, B.; Brown, J.R.; Kaspar, H.; Lipow, M.; Gordon, J. M.; Merrit, M.J.**
Characteristics of Software Quality. TRW Series of Software Technology, Volume 1, North-Holland Publishing Company, Amsterdam, New York, Oxford, 1978.

[25] **Boehm, B.W.**
Software Engineering Economics. Prentice Hall, 1981

[26] **Boehm, B.W.**
Software Engineering Economics. IEEE Transactions on Software Engineering 10(1), pp. 7-19, 1984. Also in: Sheppard, Martin (Editor): Software Engineering Metrics - Volume I: Measures and Validations. McGraw Hill Book Company, International Series in Software Engineering, 1993, pp. 112-136.

[27] **Boehm, Barry; Madachy, Ray; Selby, Richard**
The COCOMO 2.0 Software Costs Estimation Model. WWW, 1995.

[28] **Bollmann, P.; Cherniavsky, V.S.**
Measurement-Theoretical Investigation of the MZ-Metric. In: R.N. Oddy, S.E. Robertson, C.J. van Rijsbergen, P.W. Williams (ed.) Information Retrieval Research, Butterworth, 1981

[29] **Bollmann, Peter**
Two Axioms for Evaluation Measures in Information Retrieval. Research and Development in Information Retrieval, ACM, British Computer Society Workshop Series, pp. 233-246, 1984

[30] **Bollmann, Peter; Zuse, Horst**
An Axiomatic Approach to Software Complexity Measures. Proceedings of the Third Symposium on Empirical Foundations of Information and Software Science III, Roskilde, Denmark, October 21-24, 1985. Reprinted in: Empirical Foundations of Information and Software Science III, Edited by Jens Rasmussen and Pranas Zunde, Plenum Press, New York and London, 1987, pp.13-20.

[31] **Bollmann-Sdorra, P.; Zuse, H.**
Prediction Models and Software Complexity Measures from a Measurement Theoretic View. Proceedings of the 3rd International Software Quality Conference, Lake Tahoe, Nevada, October 4-7, 1993.

[32] **Boloix, Germinal; Robillard, Pierre**
Inter-Connectivity Metric for Software Complexity. Information Systems and Operation Research, Volume.26, No. 1, 1988, pp. 17-39.

[33] **Booch, G.**
Object-Oriented Design with Applications. Benjamin/Cummings, 1991.

[34] **Bourque, Pierre; Cote, Vianney**
An Experiment in Software Sizing with Structured Analysis Metrics. Journal of Systems and Software, 1991, (15), pp.159-172.

[35] **Bowles, Adrian John**
Effects of Design Complexity on Software Maintenance. Dissertation 1983, Northwestern University, Evanston, Illinois.

[36] **Caldiera, G.; Basili, V.**
Identifying and Quantifying Reuseable Software Components. IEEE Software, Feb. 1991, pp. 61-70. Also in: Arnold, Robert, S.:.Software Reegineering. IEEE Computer Society, 1992, pp. 485-494.

[37] **Cant, S.N.; Jeffrey, D.R.; Henderson-Sellers, B.**
A Conceptual Model of Cognitive Complexity of Elements of the Programming. Process. Information and SoftwareTechnology, 1995, Volume.37, No. 7, 1995,.pp. 351-362.

[38] **Card, David N.; Glass, Robert L.**
Measuring Software Design Quality. Prentice Hall, Engewood Cliffs, New Jersey, 1990

[39] **Chapin, N.**
A Measure of Software Complexity. Proc of the AFIPS National Computer Conference, Spring 1979, pp.995-1002.

[40] **Chen, J.Y.; Lu, J.F.**
A new Metric for Object-Oriented Design. Journal of Information and Software Technology, Volume 35., No. 4, April 1993, pp.232-240.

[41] **Chidamber, Shyam, R.; Kemerer, Chris, F.**
Towards a Metrics Suite for Object Oriented Design. Proc. of OOPSLA, 1991, pp. 197-211, 1991.

[42] **Chidamber, Shyam, R.; Kemerer, Chris, F.**
A Metrics Suite for Object Oriented Design. IEEE Transactions on Software Engineering, Volume 20, No. 6, June 1994, pp. 476-493.

[43] **Christensen, K.; Fitsos, G.P.; Smith, C.P.**
A Perspective on Software Science. IBM Systems Journal, Volume.20, No..4, pp. 372-387, 1981.

[44] **Constantine, L.L.**
Segmentation and Design Strategies for Modular programs. In: Barnett, T.O.; Constantine, L.L. (Editors) Modular programming: Proceedings of a National Symposium, Cambride, Massachussetts., Information und Systems Press, 1968.

[45] **Coppick, J.; Cheatham, T.**
Software Metrics for Object-Oriented System. 20th Annual ACM Computer Science Conference (CSC'92), Kansas City, MO, 1992.

[46] **Curtis, Bill**
Measurement and Experimentation in Software Engineering. Proceedings of the IEEE, Volume 68, No. 9, September 1980, pp. 1144-1157.

[47] **DATRIX**
DATRIX - A Tool for Software Evaluation. Reference Guide, Version 2.3, Bell Canada, 1995.

[48] **DeMarco, Tom; Buxton, John**
The Craft of Software Engineering. Addison Wesley Publishing Company, 1987.

[49] **DeMillo, Richard A.; Lipton, Richard J.**
Software Project Forecasting. In /PERL81/, pp.77-94, 1981.

[50] **Dhama, Harpal**
Quantitative Models of Cohesion and Coupling Software. AOWSM (Annual Oregon Workshop on Software Metrics, April 10-12, 1994, Silver Falls State Park, Oregon, 1994.

[51] **Druyen, Darleen A.**
Software Metrics Policy, Acquisition Policy 93M-017. ASAF/Acquisition - SAF/AQ, Feb. 16, 1994 (see CRossTALK, April 1994).

[52] **Dumke, Reiner**
Softwareentwicklung nach Maß- Schätzen - Messen - Bewerten. Vieweg Verlag, 1992.

[53] **Dumke, Reiner; Zuse, Horst**
Software-Metriken in der Objektorientierten Software-Entwicklung. In: Editor: Prof. Lehner: Wartung von Wissensbasierten Systemen, Hänsel-Hohenhausen, Deutsche Hochschulschriften 561, 1994.

[54] **Dumke, Reiner; Foltin, Erik; Koeppe, Reinhard; Winkler, Achim**
Softwarequaltität durch Meßtools - Assessment, Messung und Instrumentierte ISO9000. Vieweg, Professional Computing, 1996.

[55] **Dumke, Reiner, Ebert, C.; Rudoph, E.; Zuse, H.**
Metric News - Journal of the GI-Interest Group on Software Metrics. Otto von Guericke University of Magdeburg, Volume 1, Number 1, September 1996.

[56] **Emerson, Thomas J.**
Program Testing, Path Coverage, and the Cohesion Metric: IEEE COMPSAC, 1984, pp. 421-431

[57] **Emerson, Thomas J.**
A Discriminant Metric for Module Comprehension. 7th International Conference on SW-Engineering 1984, pp.294-431.

[58] **Fenton, N.**
Software Metrics: A Rigorous Approach, Chapman & Hall, 1991.

[59] **Fenton, Norman**
The Mathematics of Complexity in Computing and Software Engineering. In: The Mathematical Revolution Inspired by Computing. J.H. Johnson & M.J. Looms (eds), 1991, The Institute of Mathematics and its Applications, Oxford University Press.

[60] **Fenton, N.; Pfleeger, S.**
Software Metrics- A Rigorous Approach, Thomson Publisher, 1996

[61] **Fetcke, Thomas**
Software Metriken bei der Object-orientierten Programmierung. Diploma thesis, Gesellschaft für Mathematik und Datenverarbeitung (GMD), St. Augustin, and TU-Berlin, 1995.

[62] **Garmus, David**
Function-Point Counting in a Real-Time Environment. CrossTalk, Volume 9, Number 1, January 1996.

[63] **Gilb, T.**
Software Metrics. Studentliterature, 1976.

[64] **Gilb, T.**
Software Metrics. Winthrop Publishers, Cambridge, Massachusetts, 1977.

[65] **Gustafson, David; Tan, Joo, T.; Weaver, Perla**
Software Measure Specification. Software Engineering Notes, Dec 1993, pp. 163-168.

[66] **Hall, Nancy R.**
Complexity Measures for Systems Design. Doctoral Dissertation, Dept. of Mathematics. Polytechnic Institute New York, June 1983.

[67] **Hall, N.; Preiser, S.**
Dynamic Complexity Measure for Software Design. IEEE Computer Society, 1109 Spring Street, Suite 200, Silver Spring, MD 20910, USA, 1984.

[68] **Halstead, M.H.; Gordon, R.D.; Elshoff, J.L.**
On Software Physics and GM's PL.I Programs. GM Research Publication GMR-2175, General Motors Research Laboratories, Warren, MI, 1976.

[69] **Halstead, M.H.**
Elements of Software Science. New York, Elsevier North-Holland, 1977.

[70] **Harrison, Warren; Cook, Curtis**
A Micro/Macro Measure to Software Complexity. The Journal of Systems and Software, No. 7, pp. 213-219, 1987

[71] **Henderson-Sellers, B.; Edwards, M.**
Oriented Systems Life-Cycle. Communications of the ACM, Sptember 1990, pp. 143-159.

[72] **Henderson-Sellers, B.**
Some Metrics for Object-Oriented Software Engineering. Technology of Object-Oriented Languages and Systems. TOOLS6 (eds. B. Meyer, J. Potter and M. Tokoro), Prentice Hall, Sydney, pp. 131-139, 1991.

[73] **Henderson-Sellers, B.; Tegarden, D.**
The Application of Cyclomatic Complexity to Multiple Entry/Exit Modules. University of South Wales, April 1993.

[74] **Henderson-Sellers, B.; Tegarden, D.; David, Monarchi**
Tutorial Notes on Object-Oriented Metrics. ECOOP 93, Kaiserslautern, Juli 26 - 30, 1993.

[75] **Henderson-Sellers, B.; Tegarden, D.**
The Theoretical Extension of Two Versions of Cyclomatic Complexity to Multiple Entry / Exit Modules. Software Quality Journal, 1994, pp. 253-269.

[76] **Henderson-Sellers**
Object-Oriented Metrics - Measures of Complexity. Prentice Hall, 1996.

[77] **Henry, S. M.; Kafura, D. G.**
*Software Structure Metrics Based on Information Flow IEEE Transactions on Software Engineering Volume.*7, No. 5, 1981, pp. 510-518.

[78] **Henry, S.; Kafura, D.; Mayo, K.; Yerneni, A.; Wake, S.**
A Reliability Model Incorporating Software Quality Factors. TR 88-45, 1988, Department of Computer Science, Virginia Polytechnic, Blacksburg, Virginia, USA.

[79] **Hutchens, D.; Basili, V.**
System Structure Analysis: Clustering with Data Bindings. IEEE Transactions on Software Engineering, Volume.11, No. 8, August 1985, pp. 749-757.

[80] **IEEE**
Standard Dictionary of Measures to Produce Reliable Software. The Institute of Electrical and Electronics Engineers, Inc 345 East 47th Street, New York, NY 10017-2394, USA IEEE Standard Board, 1989.

[81] **IEEE**
Guide for the Use of Standard Dictionary of Measures to Produce Reliable Software. The Institute of Electrical and Electronics Engineers. Inc 345 East 47th Street, New York, NY 10017-2394, USA IEEE Standard Board, Corrected Edition, October 23, 1989.

[82] **IEEE Computer Society**
IEEE Standard for a Software Quality Metrics Methodology. IEEE Standard 1061. IEEE Standards Office, 445 Hoes Lane, P.O. Box 1331, Piscataway, NJ 08855-1331.

[83] **IFPUG**
International Function Point Users Group, Function Point Counting Practices Manual, Release 3.0, IFPUG, Westerville, Ohio, 1990.

[84] **Jeffrey, D.R.; Cant, S.N.; Henderson-Sellers**
A Model for the Measurement of Cognitive Complexity of Software. NASA SEL-91-006, December 1991.

[85] **Jeffrey, D.R.: Berry, M.**
A Framework for Evaluation and Prediction of Metrics Program Success. In: First International Software Metric Symposium, May 21-22, 1993, Baltimore, Maryland, pp.28-39.

[86] **Jenkins, J.**
Software Metrics won't eliminate the Productivity Crisis. American Programmer, Volume.6, Feb. 1993, pp. 2-5.

[87] **Jensen, R.; Barteley, J.**
Parametric Estimation of Programming Effort: An Object-Oriented Model. Journal of Systems and Software, Volume.15, 1991, pp. 107-114.

[88] **Jones, Capers**
Program Quality and Programmers Productivity. IBM Technical Report TR 02.764, 1977, pp. 42-78. Also in: Tutorial on Programming Productivity: Issues for the Eighties, IEEE Computer Society, Second Edition, 1986.

[89] **Jones, Capers**
Measuring Programming Quality and Productivity. IBM Systems Journal, Volume 17, No. 1, 1978. Also in: Tutorial on programming Productivity: Issues for the Eighties, IEEE Computer Society, Second Edition, 1986.

[90] **Jones, Capers**
A Survey of Programming Design and Speicification Techniques. Proceedings of Specifications of Reliable Software, April 1979, pp. 91-103. In: Tutorial on Programming Productivity: Issues for the Eighties, IEEE Computer Society, Second Edition, 1986.

[91] **Jones, Capers**
A Short History of Function Points and Feature Points. Software Productivity Research Inc., Technical paper, Cambridge, Mass., 1988.

[92] **Karner, Gustav**
Metrics for Objectory. Master Thesis at the Linküping University, S-581 83 Linküping, Sweden, 1993.

[93] **Kitchenham, B.; Linkman, S.J.**
Design Metrics in Practice. Information and Software Technology, Volume 32, No. 4, May 1990.

[94] **Kitchenham, B.; Linkman, S.J.**
An Evaluation of some Design Metrics. Software Engineering Journal, January 1990, pp. 50-58.

[95] **Knuth, D.E.**
An Empirical Study of FORTRAN Programs. Software Practice and Experience, 1(2), pp. 105-133, 1971.

[96] **Kolewe, Ralph**
Metrics in Object-Oriented Design and Programming. Software Development, October 1993, pp. 53-62.

[97] **Krantz, David H.; Luce, R. Duncan; Suppes; Patrick; Tversky, Amos**
Foundations of Measurement - Additive and Polynominal Representation, Academic Press, Volume.1, 1971

[98] **Lake, Al**
A Software Complexity Metric for C++. Annual Oregon Workshop on Software Metrics, March 22-24, 1992, Silver Falls, Oregon, USA.

[99] **Lake, Al**
Use of Factor Analysis to Develop OOP Software Complexity Metrics. Annual Oregon Workshop on Software Metrics, April 10.12, 1994, Silver Falls, Oregon, USA.

[100] **Lakhotia, Arun**
Ruled-based Approach to Compute Module Cohesion. In Proceedings of the 15th International Conference on Software Engineering, pp. 35-44, 1993.

[101] **Laranjeira, L.**
Software Size Estimation of Object-Oriented Systems. IEEE Transactions on Software Engineering, May 1990, pp. 510-522.

[102] **Li, W.; Henry, S.**
Maintenance Metrics for the Object Oriented Paradigm. Proceedings of the First International Software Metrics Symposium, may 21-22, Baltimore/USA, 1993, pp. 52-60.

[103] **Liggesmeyer, P.; Sneed, H.M.; Spillner, A.(Editor)**
Testen, Analysieren und Verifizieren von Software. Informatik aktuell, Springer Verlag.

[104] **Ligier, Yves**
A Software Complexity Metric System Based on Intra- and Inter-modular Dependencies. IBM RC 14831 (#65457) 5/11/89.

[105] **Longworth, H.D.; Ottenstein, L.M.; Smith, M.R.**
The Relationship between Program Complexity and Slice Complexity During Debugging Tasks. IEEE COMPSAC, October 1986, pp. 383-389.

[106] **Luce, R. Duncan; Krantz, David H.; Suppes; Patrick; Tversky, Amos**
Foundations of Measurement. Volume 3, Academic Press, 1990

[107] **McCabe, T.**
A Complexity Measure. IEEE Transactions of Software Engineering, Volume.SE-2, No. 4, pp. 308-320, December 1976.

[108] **McCabe, T; Butler, Charles W.**
Desgin Complexity Measurement and Testing. Communications of the ACM, Volume.32, No. 12, Dec 89, pp. 1415-1424.

[109] **METKIT**
METKIT - Metrics Educational Toolkit. Information and Software Technology, Volume 35, No. 2, February 1993.

[110] **Morris, Kenneth, L.**
Metrics for Object-Oriented Software Development Environments. Massachusetts Institute of Technology, Master of Science in Management, May 1989.

[111] **Munson, J.C.; Khoshgoftaar, T.M.**
The use of software complexity metrics in software reliability modeling. In Proceedings of the 2nd International Symposium on Software Reliability Engineering. 1991, pp. 2-11.

[112] **Munson, J.; Khoshgoftaar, T.**
The Detection of Fault-Prone Programs. IEEE Transactions on Software Engineering, Volume.18, No. 5, May 1992, pp. 423-433.

[113] **Myers, G.L.**
Composite Design Facilities of Six Programming Languages. IBM Systems Journal, No. 3, 1976, pp. 212-224.

[114] **National Aeronautics and Space Administration**
Software Engineering Laboratory (SEL), Data Base Organization and User's Guide, Software Engineering Laboratory Series SEL-81-002, September 1981.

[115] **National Aeronautics and Space Administration**
Collected Software Engineering papers: Volume II. Software Engineering Laboratory Series SEL-83-003, November 1983.

[116] **National Aeronautics and Space Administration**
Measures and Metrics for Software Development. Software Engineering Laboratory Series SEL-83-002, March 1984.

[117] **National Aeronautics and Space Administration**
Investigation of Specification Measures for Software Engineering Laboratory. Software Engineering Laboratory Series SEL-84-003, December 1984.

[118] **National Aeronautics and Space Administration**
An Approach to Software Cost Estimation. Software Engineering Laboratory Series SEL-83-001, February 1984.

[119] **National Aeronautics and Space Administration**
Measuring Software Design. Software Engineering Laboratory Series SEL-86-005, November 1986.

[120] **National Aeronautics and Space Administration**
Collected Software Engineering papers: Volume V. Software Engineering Laboratory Series SEL-87-009, November 1987.

[121] **National Aeronautics and Space Administration**
Proceedings of the Fourteenth Annual Software Engineering Workshop. Software Engineering Laboratory Series SEL-89-007, November 1989.

[122] **National Aeronautics and Space Administration**
Proceedings of the Fifteenth Annual Software Engineering Workshop. Software Engineering Laboratory Series SEL-90-006, November 1990.

[123] **Ott, Linda M.; Thuss, Jeffrey J.**
The Relationship between Slices and Module Cohesion. Proceedings of the 11th International Conference on Software Engineering, 1989, pp.198-204.

[124] **Ott, Linda M.; Thuss, Jeffrey J.**
Sliced Based Metrics for Estimation Cohesion. Technical Report #CS-91-124, November 1991, Colorado State University, Fort Collins, Colorado 80523, USA.

[125] **Ott, Linda M.**
Using Slice Profiles and Metrics. during Software Maintenance. In: Proceedings of 10th Annual Software Reliability Symposium, pp. 16-23, June 1992.

[126] **Ott, Linda M.; Bieman, James**
Effects of Software Changes on Module Cohesion. Technical Report #CS-92-113, March 1992. Colorado State University, Fort Collins.

[127] **Ott, Linda M.; Bieman, James**
Effects of Software Changes on Module Cohesion. IEEE Conference on Software Maintenance, Orlando/Florida, November 1992.

[128] **Ott, Linda M.; Thuss, Jeffrey J.**
Using Slice Profiles and Metrics As Tools in the Production of Reliable Software. Technical Report #CS-92-115, April 1992, Colorado State University, Fort Collins. Also published as Technical Report CS-92-8, Dept. Computer Science, Michigan Technology University, April 1992.

[129] **Ott, Linda M.; Thuss, Jeffrey J.**
Slice Based Metrics for Estimating Cohesion. First International Software Metrics Symposium, May 21-22, 1993, pp. 71-81, Baltimore, Maryland, IEEE Los Alamitos, CA.

[130] **Oviedo, Enrique I.**
Control Flow, Data Flow and Programmers Complexity. Proceedings of COMPSAC 80, Chicago IL, pp.146-152, 1980.

[131] **Park, Robert, E.**
Software Size Measurement: A Framework for Counting Source Statements. Software Engineering Institute, Pittsburg, SEI-92-TR-020, 220 pages, May 1992.

[132] **Parnas, D.L.**
The Influence of Software Structure on Reliability. Proceedings of International Conference on Reliable Software, April 21-23, 1975, pp. 358-362.

[133] **Patel, Sukesh; Chu, William, Baxter, Rich**
A Measure for Composite Module Cohesion. 15th International Conference on Software Engineering, 1992.

[134] **Paton, K.; Abran, Alain**
A Formal Notation for the Rules of Function Point Analysis. Rapport de Recherche, Universite du Quebec a Montreal, No. 247, April 28, 1995.

[135] **Perlis, Alan; Sayward, Frederick; Shaw, Mary**
Software Metrics: An Analysis and Evaluation The MIT Press, 1981.

[136] **Porter, A.A.; Selby, R.W.**
Empirically Guided Software Development using Metric-Based Classification Trees. IEEE Software, Volume.7, No. 2, pp..46-54.

[137] **Putnam, L.H.**
A General Empirical Solution to the Macro Software Sizing and Estimating Problem. IEEE Transactions of Software Engineering, SE-4 (4), pp. 345-361, July 1978.

[138] **Rains, E.**
Function Points in an ADA Object-Oriented Design? OOPS Messenger, ACM Press, Volume.2, No. 4, October 1991,

[139] **Rising, Linda; Callis, Frank, W.**
Problems with Determining Package Cohesion and Coupling. Software Practice and Experience, Volume.22, No. 7, July 1992, pp.553-571.

[140] **Roberts, Fred S.**
Measurement Theory with Applications to Decisionmaking, Utility, and the Social Sciences. Encyclopedia of Mathematics and its Applications Addison Wesley Publishing Company, 1979.

[141] **Robillard, Pierre, N.; Boloix, Germinal**
The Interconnectivity Metrics: A New Metric Showing How a Program is Organized. The Journal of Systems and Software 10, 29-39, 1989, pp. 29-38.

[142] **Rocacher, Daniel**
Metrics Definitions for Smalltalk. Project ESPRIT 1257, MUSE WP9A, 1988.

[143] **Rombach, D.**
Benefits of Goal-Oriented Measurement. In Tutorial CSR, 7th Annual Conference on Software Reliability and Metrics, September 1990.

[144] **Rombach, D.**
Practical Benefits of Goal-Oriented Measurement. In: Fenton, B.; Littlewood, B.: SoftwareReliability and Metrics. Elevier Applied Science, 1991.

[145] **Rubey, R.J.; Hartwick, R.D.**
Quantitative Measurement Program Quality. ACM, National Computer Conference, pp. 671-677, 1968.

[146] **Schneidewind, N.F.**
Modularity Considerations in Real Time Operating Structures. COMPSAC 77, pp. 397-403.

[147] **Schneidewind, Norman F.**
Validating Software Metrics: Producing Quality Discriminators. In: Proceedings of the Conference on Software Maintenance (CSM91), Sorrento, Italy, October 1991, and in: Proceedings of International Symposium on Software Reliability Engineering, 1991.

[148] **Schneidewind, Norman F.**
Controlling and Predicting the Quality of Space Shuttle Software Using Metrics. SoftwareQuality Journal, 1995, pp. 49-68. Also in: Proceedings of the AOWSM (Annual Oregon Workshop on Software Metrics), Siver Fall State Park, Oregon, 1994.

[149] **Schneidewind, Norman**
Work in Progress Report: Experiment in Including Metrics in a Software Reliability Model. Proceedings of the AOWSM (Annual Oregon Workshop on Software Metrics), Silver Fall State Park, Oregon, 1995.

[150] **Selby, Richard W.; Basili, V.**
Analyzing Error-Prone System Coupling and Cohesion. Technical Report UMIACS-TR-88-46, Computer Science, University of Maryland, June 1988.

[151] **Selby, Richard, W.**
Interconnectivity Analysis Techniques for Error Localization in Large Systems. Annual Oregon Workshop on Software Metrics (AOWSM), Portland State University, March 22-24, 1992.

[152] **Shapiro, Stuart**
Splitting the Difference: The Historical Necessity of Synthesis in Software Engineering. IEEE Annuals of the History of Computing, Vol. 19, No. 1, 1997, pp. 20-54.

[153] **Sharble, Robert, C.; Cohen, Samuel, S.**
The Object-Oriented Brewery: A Comparison of Two Object-Oriented Development Methods. ACM SIGSOFT SOFTWARE ENGINEERING NOTES, Volume.18, No. 2, April 1993, pp. 60-73.

[154] **Shepperd, Martin; Ince, Darrel**
Algebraic Validation of Software Metrics. Proceedings of the 3rd European Software Engineering Conference, Milano, October 1991.

[155] **Shepperd, Martin (Editor)**
Software Engineering Metrics - Volume I: Measures and Validations. McGraw Hill Book Company, International Series in Software Engineering, 1993.

[156] **Sneed, H. M.**
Software Renewal: A Case Study. In: IEEE Software, Vol. 1, 3/1984, pp. 56-63.

[157] **Sneed, Harry**
Automated Software Quality Assurance. IEEE Transactions on Software Engineering, Volume.11, No. 9, September 1985, pp. 909-916.

[158] **Sneed, Harry**
Software Qualitätssicherung. Rudof Müller Verlag, Köln, 1988.

[159] **Sneed, Harry**
Economics of Software Reengineering. Software Maintenance: Research and Practice, Volume.3, pp. 163-182, 1991. Also in: Software Reegineering. IEEE Computer Society, 1992., pp. 121-140.

[160] **Sneed, Harry**
Metriken zur Aufwandschätzung von Software Projekten. Fachseminar, ORACLE Institute, Software Metriken 1994.

[161] **Stevens, W.P.; Myers, G.J.; Constantine, L.L.**
Structured Design. IBM Systems Journal, No. 2, 1974, pp. 115-139.

[162] **Symons, Charles, R.**
Function Point Analysis: Difficulties and Improvements. IEEE Transactions on Software Engineering, Volume.14, No. 1, January 1988, pp. 2-11.

[163] **Symons, Charles, R.**
Software Sizing and Estimating. MkII FPA, John Wiley, New York, 1991.

[164] **Taylor, D.A.**
Software Metrics for Object Technology. Object Magazine, Mar-Apr. 1993, pp. 22-28.

[165] **Tegarden, David, P.; Sheetz, Steven, D.; Monarchi, David, E.**
A Software Model of Object-Oriented Systems. Decision Support Systems: The International Journal, 7/1992.

[166] **Tegarden, David, P.; Sheetz, Steven, D.; Monarchi, David, E.**
Effectiveness of tradional Software Metrics for Object-Oriented Systems. Proceedings 25th Hawaii International Conference on System Sciences, HICSS-92, 1992.

[167] **Thuss, Jeffrey**
An Investigation into Slice Based Cohesion Metrics. Master Thesis, Michigan Technology University, 1988.

[168] **Torii, Koji; Matsomoto, Ken-ichi**
Quantitative Analytic Approaches in Software Engineering. Information and Software Technology, Vol. 38, 1996, pp. 155-163.

[169] **Troy, Douglas; Zweben, Stuart**
Measuring the Quality of Structured Design. The Journal of System and Software. Volume.2, 113-120, 1981, pp.113-120.

[170] **Walston, C. E.; Felix, C.P.**
A Method of Programming Measurement and Estimation. IBM Systems Journal, Volume.16, No. 1, pp. 54-73, 1977. Also in: Tutorial on Programming Productivity: Issues for the Eighties, IEEE Computer Society, Second Edition, 1986.

[171] **Weiser, M.D.**
Programmers Use Slices When Debugging. Communications of the ACM, 25(7), July 1982, pp. 446-452.

[172] **Weiser, M.D.**
Program Sclicing. IEEE Transactions on Software Engineering, SE-10, 4, July 1984, pp. 352-357.

[173] **Whitmire, Scott, A.**
Measuring Complexity in Object-Oriented Software. Third International Conference on Applications of Software Measures (ASM92), November 1992, La Jolla, California.

[174] **Wolverton, R.W.**
The Cost of Developing Large-Scale Software. IEEE Transactions on Computer, Volume.C-23, No. 6, pp. 615-636, June 1974. Also in: Tutorial on Programming Productivity: Issues for the Eighties, IEEE Computer Society, Second Edition, 1986.

[175] **Yamada, A.**
Information Technology - ISO/IEC 9126-8 Software Product Evaluation. Working Draft-Version 3.1, 1994.

[176] **Yin, B.H.; Winchester, J.W.**
The Establishment and Use of Measures to Evaluate the Quality of Software Designs. Proceedings ACM Software Quality Ass. Workshop, 1978, pp.45-52

[177] **Yourdon, E.**
Modular Programming. Techniques of Program and Structure and Design. Prentice Hall, 1975, pp. 93-136.

[178] **Zuse, Horst**
Meßtheoretische Analyse von statischen Softwarekomplexitätsmaßen. TU-Berlin 1985, Fachbereich Informatik, Dissertation im FB 20 (Ph. D. Thesis).

[179] **Zuse, Horst; Bollmann, P.**
Using Measurement Theory to Describe the Properties and Scales of Static Software Complexity Metrics. IBM Thomas Watson Research Center Yorktown Heights, RC 13504, 1987.

[180] **Zuse, Horst; Bollmann, P.**
Using Measurement Theory to Describe the Properties and Scales of Static Software Complexity Metrics. SIGPLAN Notices, Volume.24, No. 8, pp.23-33, August 89.

[181] **Zuse, Horst**
Software Complexity: Measures and Methods. DeGruyter Publisher 1991, Berlin, New York, 605 pages, 498 figures.

[182] **Zuse, Horst; Bollmann-Sdorra, Peter**
Measurement Theory and Software Measures. In: Workshops in Computing: T.Denvir, R.Herman and R.Whitty (Eds.): Proceedings of the BCS-FACS Workshop on Formal Aspects of Measurement, South Bank University, London, May 5, 1991. Series Edited by Professor C.J. Rijsbergen. ISBN 3-540-19788-5. Springer Verlag London Ltd, Springer House, 8 Alexandra Road, Wimbledon, London SW19 7JZ, UK, 1992.

[183] **Zuse, Horst**
Properties of Software Design Metrics. Proceedings of the Annual Oregon Workshop on Software Metrics, March 22-24, 1992, Silver Falls, Oregon, USA.

[184] **Zuse, Horst**
Foundations of Validation, Prediction, and Software Measures. Proceedings of the AOWSM (Annual Oregon Workshop on Software Metrics), Silver Fall State Park, Oregon, 1994.

[185] **Zuse, Horst**
Software Complexity Metrics/Analysis. Marciniak, John, J. (Editor-in-Chief): Encyclopedia of Software Engineering, Volume I, John Wiley & Sons, Inc. 1994, pp. 131-166.

[186] **Zuse, Horst**
Foundations of the Validation of Object-Oriented Software Measures. In: Theorie und Praxis der Softwaremessung (Dumke, R.; Zuse, H. ((Editors)), Deutsche Universitätsverlag DUV, Gabler - Vieweg - Westdeutscher Verlag, 1994, pp. 136-214.

[187] **Zuse, Horst; Fetcke, Thomas**
Properties of Object-Oriented Software Measures. Proceedings of the Annual Oregon Workshop on Software Metrics (AOWSM), Silver Statc Park, June 3-5, 1995.

[188] **Zuse, Horst; Drabe, Karin**
The System ZD-MIS, Internal Report, October 1995.

[189] **Zuse, Horst**
Foundations of Object-Oriented Software Measures. Proceedings of the IEEE Third International Software Metrics Symposium, March 1996, Berlin.

[190] **Zuse, Horst**
A Framework of Software Measurement. DeGruyter Publisher , Berlin, New York, 750 pages, 1998.

Function Point Evolution

Charles R. Symons, Software Measurement Service Ltd. Kent (England)

Charles Symons discusses the strengths and weaknesses of various ways of measuring "Software Size", which is a key component of performance measures and of estimating methods, namely

- Source Lines of Code,
- The "Function Point" method originally developed by Allan Albrecht of IBM, now standardised as the IFPUG 4.0 method,
- The MkII FP method, designed to overcome certain weakness of the Albrecht method, developed by the author,
- The "Full Function Point" method, developed by Alain Abran et al from Quebec, which aims to extend the IFPUG method to handle real-time software,
- The ISO standard 14143 Part 1 which establishes some principles of "Functional Size Measuremen".

Current Function Point methods for software sizing can and should be updated to meet modern software engineering needs

- re-base on modern software engineering concepts,
- generalise to be applicable in a wider range of software domains (e.g. real-time, process control, etc.),
- above all to improve and prove the accuracy of performance measurement and early life-cycle estimating,
- improved integration of early life-cycle estimating methods based on functional requirements with methods used later in the life-cycle based on components and activities.

The economic value of finding a solution to these needs would be enormous. The way forward in his view is to be found in ideas of Industrial Engineering published by Frederick Taylor in 1911. Symons proposes an "International Software Metrics Initiative" to meet these objectives.

II. Software Measurement Foundations

Metrics Validation Proposals: A Structured Analysis

Jean-Philippe Jacquet and Alain Abran, Université du Québec à Montréal (Canada)

Abstract

In the literature, the expression metrics validation is used in many ways with different meanings. This paper analyzes and compares some of the validation approaches currently proposed. The basis for this analysis is a process model for software measurement methods which identifies the distinct steps involved from the design of a measurement method to the exploitation of the measurement results. This process model for software measurement methods is used to position various authors' validation criteria according to the measurement process to which they apply. This positioning enables the establishment of relationships among the various validation approaches. It also makes it possible to show that, because none of these validation approaches proposed to date in the literature covers the full spectrum of the process of measurement methods, a complete and practical validation framework does not yet exist.

1 Introduction

Over the past twenty years, a significant number of software metrics have been proposed to better control and understand software development practices and products. Unfortunately, very few of them have been looked at closely from a measurement method perspective and it is currently difficult to analyze the quality of these metrics because of a lack of an agreed-upon validation framework.

What are software metrics and how do you determine that they are valid? A number of authors in software metrics have attempted to answer these questions [1, 2, 3, 4, 8, 9, 10, 11, 15, etc.]. However, the validation problem has up to now been tackled from different points of view (mathematical, empirical, etc.) and by giving different interpretations to the expression "metrics validation"; as suggested by Kitchenham et al: "*What has been missing so far is a proper discussion of relationships among the different approaches*" [8].

This paper analyzes and compares the validation approaches currently proposed in the literature. The basis for this analysis is the process model for software measurement methods presented in [7]. This measurement method process model identifies the distinct steps involved, from the design of a measurement method to the exploitation of the measurement results in subsequent models, such as quality and estimation models.

Our proposed process model for software measurement methods is then used to position various authors' validation criteria according to these measurement process steps. This positioning enables the establishment of relationships among the various validation approaches. It also makes it possible to show that, because none of these validation approaches proposed to date in the literature covers the full spectrum of the process of measurement methods, a complete and practical validation framework does not yet exist.

This paper is organized in the following way. In the first section, the measurement process model is presented. The second section describes the different types of validation according to which part of the measurement process it refers to: the design of a measurement method, the application of a measurement method, or the exploitation of the measurement method (in predictive systems). In sections 4, 5 and 6, validation proposals from various authors are then positioned within the framework proposed.

2 A process model for software measurement methods

The analysis proposed here is being carried out by using a process model for software measurement methods. This process model [7] specifies the distinct steps involved from the design of a measurement method to its utilization. These steps are presented in Figure 1:

- **Step 1:** Design of the measurement method: before measuring, it is necessary to design a measurement method.

- **Step 2:** Application of the measurement method rules: the rules of the measurement method are applied to software or piece of software.

- **Step 3:** Measurement result analysis: the application of the measurement method rules produces a result.

- **Step 4:** Exploitation of the measurement result: the measurement result is exploited in a quantitative or qualitative model.

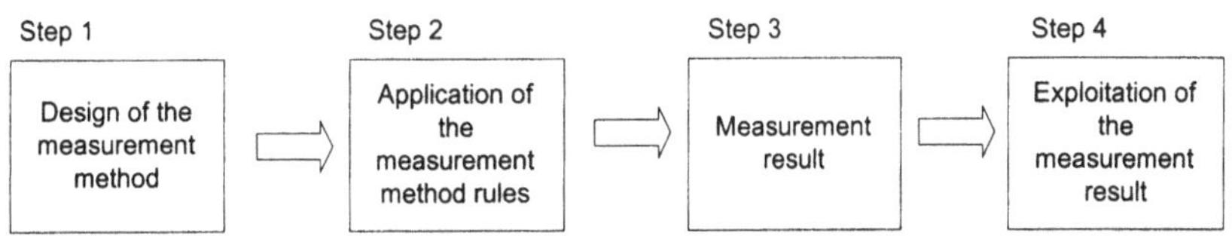

Figure 1: Measurement Process - High-level Model (Jacquet and Abran 1997 [7])

This high-level model was then refined based on an extensive literature review in the domain of scientific measurement. This literature review, from within and from outside the software engineering domain, has permitted the identification of the required substeps within each of the proposed measurement steps.

The detailed set of substeps identified is illustrated in Figure 2 and these substeps can be described as follows:

Step 1: Design of the measurement method

- **Substep 1** :

  For the initial substep, the objectives of the measurement method must be specified. Among other things, what is going to be measured (what object, what attribute, etc.) must be known precisely, what will the intended uses of the measurement method be, etc.

- **Substep 2:**

  Once the attribute (or concept) has been chosen, an (empirical) operational definition of this attribute must be given. This can easily be done for concrete attributes (such as size for a person, or size in lines of codes for software), but will be more complicated for abstract attributes (this is what Zuse calls the "*intelligence barrier*" [16]). In that case, the operational definition has to be as close as possible to the "meaning" of the attribute in order to capture it properly. Using mathematical notation (measurement theory vocabulary), the axiomization of the attribute will constitute an empirical relational set.

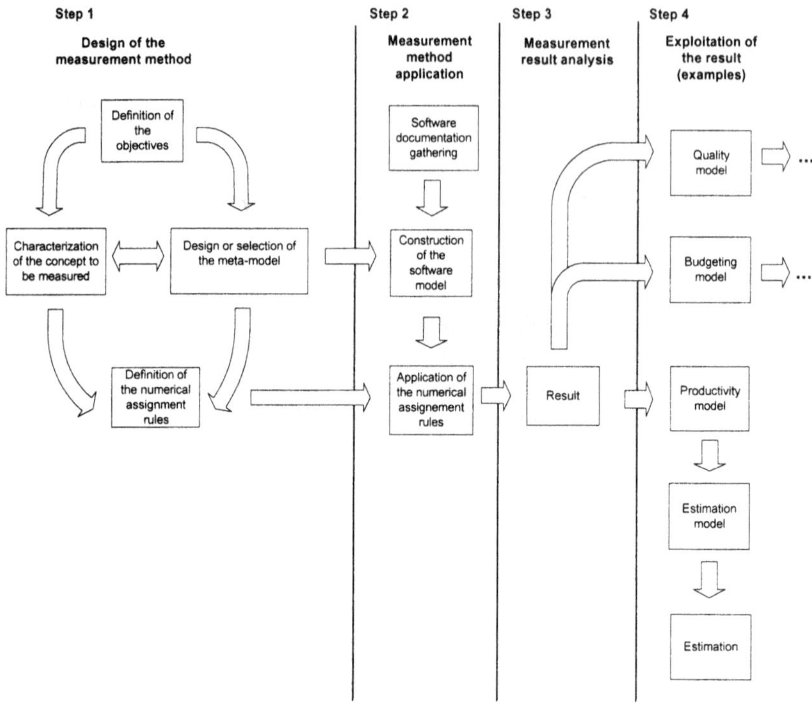

Figure 2: Measurement Process - Detailed Model (Jacquet and Abran 1997 [7])

- **Substep 3 :**

  Design or selection of the metamodel
  Software is not a tangible product. However, it can be made visible through multiple representations (e.g. for a user, a set of reports, screens etc; for a programmer, a set of lines of Code, etc.). The set of characteristics selected to represent software or a piece of software, and the set of their relationships, constitute the metamodel proposed for the description of the software to which the proposed measurement method will be applied. The metamodel must therefore describe the entity types that will be used to describe the software and the rules that allow the identification of the entity types. For example, in the Function Point measurement method (FPMM) [17], an Internal Logical File (ILF) is a piece of software of the entity type. This entity type is defined according to the FPMM's metamodel. The IFPUG manual presents a definition of this ILF entity type, as well as identifying rules to ensure that each and every ILF can be clearly recognized within software.

- **Substep 4 :**

  Definition of the numerical assignment rules
  This substep, the rules allowing assignment of a numerical value to the couple (attribute, object) measured are defined. Very often, the basis for the numerical assignment rules is the characterization of the concept and of the proposed metamodel. In mathematical vocabulary, the expression of these rules allows definition of a formal relational system.

Step 2: Application of the measurement method
This step is made up of three substeps:
- Substep 1: the gathering of the documentation necessary to carry out the application of the measurement method.
- Substep 2: the construction of the software model (for example, the various pertinent entities for the measurement method are referenced).
- Substep 3: the application of the numerical assignement rules.

Step 3: The application of the measurement method provides a measurement result.

Step 4: This result of the measurement method can be used in predictive models such as budgeting or quality models.

3 What is metrics validation?

The expression *metrics validation* has been used with many distinct interpretations in the software engineering literature, leaving readers somewhat puzzled as to which authors' proposals should be used, and under what circumstances. Rather than trying to recommend and select a single author's interpretation as the correct one for what has been referred to by various authors as "metrics validation", we will look at the validation issue using the measurement process model presented in the previous section. Therefore, rather than discussing a single validation proposal, a framework will be suggested which includes a sequence of validation procedures which should address, with different techniques, the distinct steps of the measurement process model, as presented in Figure 2:

- **Validation of the design of a measurement method.**
  This type of validation deals mainly with step 1 of our model. It consists in checking that the measurement method really measures what it is supposed to measure.

For example, Fenton [3] refers to this concept when he discusses the validation of "a software measure ", expressing it in the following way: *Validation of a software measure is the process of ensuring that the measure is a proper numerical characterization of the claimed attribute[...].*

Similarly, Zuse [16] refers to this validation concept of the design of a measurement method when he uses the expression " internal validation of a software measure": *Internal validation of a software measure means to check empirically whether the measure really captures the claimed attribute.*

- **Validation of the application of a measurement method**. This type of validation addresses both step 2 and step 3 of the measurement process model presented in Figure 2.

This type of validation aims to answer questions such as: How can one know whether the application of a specific measurement has been properly carried out? and, "What degree of confidence one can have in the result obtained by applying a specific measurement method?.

For this kind of operation, the use of the word "validation" is not unanimously accepted. Now, such validation is crucial, but, surprisingly, is scarcely discussed in the software engineering literature.

- **Validation of predictive systems.** This type of validation deals with the predictive quality of the models in which the measurement results are exploited, as illustrated in the right-hand side of Figure 2.

This is the type of validation most often discussed in software engineering. In this case, the expression *software metrics* is taken to meant a *predictive system* or *integrated in a predictive system*, but does not deal at all with the issues related to the design and application of measurement methods.

Fenton [3], for example, addresses the validation of predictive system: *Validation of a prediction system, in a given environment, is the process of establishing the accuracy of the prediction system by empirical means, i.e. by comparing model performance with known data points in the given environment.*

In the software engineering literature, the distinction between the above three types of validation is almost never explicitly stated. For example, fairly distinct validation methods are proposed for "validating metrics", but even though they explicitly refer to this same expression they do not address the same issue (validation of measurement methods and validation of predictive systems) and they do not use the same validation techniques.

In the next section we will present and discuss some work that has been carried out on each of these kinds of validation and will try to highlight and clarify the differences *between validation of a measurement method* and *validation of a predictive system*.

4 Validation of the design of a measurement method

What is a valid measurement method? This question has not been addressed directly by most authors. Some authors have, however addressed it indirectly (for example: Fenton [3], Zuse [16]) when they argue that a software measure is valid if the representation condition is verified, i.e. if a homomorphism exists between the empirical relational system (defined at the second substep of step 1 in the process of Figure 2) and the numerical relational set (defined at the fourth substep in the process in Figure 3). When they do so, they are addressing the design step of a measurement method.

The validation of the design of a measurement method should therefore deal with the establishment of relations across the following substeps: characterization of the concept to be measured and definition of the numerical assignment rules. A valid measurement method design would consist of a design for which its numerical assignment rules properly represent the empirical characterization of the measured attribute, and the validation process would consist in proving that empirical data are properly "captured" by the measurement method design.

Various authors have proposed more detailed validation criteria which address this measurement method design issue. These criteria are mostly based on checking that the representation condition is satisfied, but also that this is not a sufficient condition. For example, in Shepperd et al.'s work [12, p.75], inspired by Weyuker [13] and Prather[10], a list of axioms is proposed which must be satisfied. Some of these axioms are:

Axiom a: *It must be possible to describe, even if not formally, the rules governing the measurement method [...].*

Axiom b: *The measure*[1] *generate at least two equivalence classes.*
Axiom c: *If an infinite number of objects or events is measured, eventually two or more must be assigned to the same equivalence class, that is, you can't measure an infinite number of objects.*
Axiom d: *The metric*[1] *must not produce anomalies, that is, the metric must preserve empirical ordering. In other words, the representation theorem must hold.*

The fifth axiom deals with the representation condition but the others can be seen as complementary axioms. For example, axiom 2 is aimed at checking that the measurement method "does something", i.e. is capable of discrimination and will not assign the same value to every object. Shepperd et al. argue then that axiomization is a *vital tool* for validation because it provides, among other things, ways to establish some properties of the model, such as consistency - *so that there exists one and only one outcome for any set of inputs* - and completeness - *the axiom set is sufficiently rich and that there is no set of inputs for which no outcome is prescribed.*

This type of validation requirements reflects the fact that, even if the representation condition is satisfied, a measurement method could have undesirable properties. For example, many of these properties can manifest themselves because of the construction of the (empirical) operational definition of the concept. For example, supposing that the representation theorem has been demonstrated for a functional size measurement method, then this method will assign the same number to every software if and only if the empirical relational system asserts that every software has the same functional size. This means that this empirical relational system, and consequently the operational definition of the concept, does not characterize the attribute of functionality properly (substep 2 of step 1 in Figure 2). In that case, it cannot be said that the measurement method measures what it is supposed to measure. Consequently, validation of a measurement method also has to deal with validation of the other substeps of the design step (in Figure 2), including the characterization of the attribute to be measured.

Kitchenham et al. have proposed additional criteria in [8] which deal with the design step of a measurement method. In what they refer to as validation of a measure, they describe and discuss several theoretical and empirical validation criteria for the design of a measurement method. Among other things they propose to:

---

[1] In this text, the words *measure* and *metrics* can be understood as *measurement methods*.

- check attribute validity (substeps "definition of the objectives" and "characterization of the attribute to be measured" in Figure 2). This means, for example, checking whether or not the attribute is exhibited by the measured object. They also propose empirical methods to check whether or not the results of a measurement method capture the meaning of the attribute. Their proposed methods use measures of association and are validation methods based on the establishment of correlations between the measured attribute and results of the measurement method.
- tackle validation of the "numerical assignment". This mean requiring mathematical consistency of these rules (for both direct and indirect measures). They also propose models and methods to validate units of measure.

The set of validation criteria proposed by Kitchenham et al. addresses many of the substeps of step 1 (Figure 2). Nevertheless, there is at least one that is not well covered, one that should deal with objects (software) or, more precisely with the representation of these objects (substep 3 of step 1 in Figure 2) on which the measurement is applied. For example, for the application of the Function Point Analysis measurement method [17], the software object has to be modeled using concepts of ILF, EIF, boundary, etc.. Such a model is created using identification rules, and from that point on it allows the application of the numerical assignment rules. In other words, the identification rules have an influence on the creation of the numerical relational set and, logically, on the design of the empirical relational set as well when these rules are used in the design of the operational definition of the concept. For example, many " software metrics " definitions use terms like "process", "flows of data" without providing precise definitions for them. Perhaps the representation theorem has been demonstrated for these " metrics ", but, if the entities used in this demonstration are not properly and unambiguously defined, then what value can be credited to this demonstration?

In conclusion, one can say that in the software engineering literature, validation of the design of a measurement method has mainly been tackled from a measurement theory viewpoint: a valid measurement method is a method which verifies the representation theorem. Nevertheless, it appears that this requirement is not sufficient and some authors have proposed additional criteria. However, it seems that the validation of a measurement method has to do with the validation of an empirical relational set, and, consequently, with the validation of attributes and objects (or models of theses objects[2]) taking part

[2] In this, one can find the type of argument made by Gustafson et al. in [4] about the importance of modeling the object to be measured.

in the description of this empirical set and consequently in the measurement method. This problem does not seem to have been tackled completely and the validation criteria for this substep of the design of a measurement method are still relatively poorly covered.

5 Validation of the application of a measurement method

The second type of validation is the validation of the application of a measurement method: it deals with a specific utilization of a measurement method. Once a measurement method has been validated, it can be applied. But, after the method has been applied, how can it be ascertained that the application process has been properly carried out? What degree of confidence can one have in the measurement result, knowing that mistakes may have been made when applying the method? How can a result be formally accepted before it is used by an organization?

Even though these questions are important, they are rarely discussed in the software engineering literature.

Validation of the application of a measurement method should involve both steps 2 and 3 of the measurement process described in Figure 2:

- Validation of the quality of the implementation of the various substeps (software documentation gathering, construction of the software model, application of the numerical assignment rules) of the process of applying a measurement method.

- Validation of the correctness of the result obtained (step 3 in the process in Figure 2).

Among the very few proposals identified in the software engineering literature for the evaluation of the correctness of a measurement result, Morris and Desharnais [9] address this type of validation when they discuss the validation of Function Point measurement results. This proposal consists of two steps:

- *A priori validation : reviews all the steps and procedures of the data collection process within benchmarking data [9].* For example, a priori validation includes verification of accurate and reliable documentation and the *verification of the existence of training and/or coaching programs to ensure that the staff collecting the metrics have a solid understanding of software metrics that they collect.*

- *A posteriori validation: establishes the degree of quality of the data collected and, wherever required, will eliminate from the comparative studies the data deemed not reliable [9].* For example, a posteriori validation includes verification *that the data definitions and coding schemes are consistent across sites and over time.*

Morris and Desharnais validation proposal is fairly extensive for this type of validation but, it has been discussed only in the context of its application to the Function Point Analysis measurement method. Nevertheless, many of the criteria described in this validation method could be generalizable to other measurement methods.

6 Validation of a predictive system

The third type of validation is the validation of a predictive system. This type of validation is, in fact, the one most often discussed in software engineering and many papers have been written about validating metrics from the perspective of their use as predictive systems. A possible explanation could be that it is perceived to be more useful and easier to validate predictive systems because the properties of many external variables, such as cost, time and productivity, are better known.

Schneidewind writes that *if metrics are to be of greatest utility, the validation should be performed in terms of the quality function (quality assessment, control and prediction) that the metrics are to support* [11]. However, Kitchenham et al. disagree with Schneidewind and remark that *validating a predictive or usage model is different from validating a measure* [8]. It is then important to make a real distinction between validation of a measurement method and validation of a predictive system. For example, a predictive model using one or multiple measurement methods can be valid even thought one or more of the measurement methods are invalid. This would mean that the measurement methods and the model are self correctors (i.e. the errors of one counterbalance the errors of the other).

Furthermore, validation of a measurement method is less context-dependent than the validation of a predictive system. For example, one can validate a functional size measurement method for a type of software. Now, this measurement method can be used in a predictive system in order to predict productivity for a specific group of programmers in a specific environment. This predictive system can be validated for this context, but would have to be revalidated if used in another environment. This revalidation involves reexamination of the results of the predictive model in this new context and not the revalidation of the measurement method itself. Consequently predictive systems are validated according to a context. This type of validation should be performed every time the predictive system is used in a different context.

A great number of methods have been developed for the validation of predictive systems. Two representative examples are now briefly discussed.

Among the set of articles written about the validation of predictive systems, one of the most exhaustive is [11]. In this article, Schneidewind proposes an empirical validation method based on corroboration of the relationships among attributes in specific contexts:

Schneidewind's validation proposal for predictive systems is based on six validity criteria which are: association, consistency, discriminative power, tracking, predictability and repeatability (see [11]). For example, the repeatability criterion "*assesses whether* (a metric) *M can be validated on a sufficient percentage of trials to have confidence that it would be a dependable indicator of quality in the long run*". These six criteria support the functions of assessing, control and predicting. This proposal for this type of validation is mostly based on statistical techniques such as correlation analysis, providing specific methods to establish correlations among attributes.

Schneidewind's approach is mainly empirical, but does not refer at all to measurement theory and does not deal with measurement method concepts. On the other hand, in [16], Zuse has begun to addresses the validation of predictive systems from a measurement theory viewpoint. He proposes processes and theoretical conditions for validation of measurement methods as predictive systems.

In conclusion, one can say that the validation of predictive systems is concerned with the fourth column of the process presented in Figure 2. This kind of validation is very often confounded with the validation of measurement methods (first column of the process in Figure 2). This can be explained by the fact that many authors have not made a clear distinction between a measurement method and a predictive system.

7 Conclusion

In the software engineering literature, the expression *software metrics validation* has been used with different interpretations and most authors have not explicitly stated which step of a measurement method process their validation proposal is intended to address. Some classifications of validation studies for software metrics have been proposed in the past (see, for example, Gustafson [6]) but these classifications has been made according to different criteria and sometimes without a clear distinction being made between measurement methods and predictive models.

In this paper, a framework has been explicitly stated which characterizes three types of validation when addressing the validation issue: validation of the design of a measurement method, validation of the application of a measurement method and validation of the use of measurement results in a predictive system (see Figure 3).

VALIDATION TYPE	DESCRIPTION
Validation of the Design of a Measurement Method	This type of validation refers mainly to **step 1** of our process. In the software engineering literature, validation of the design of a measurement method has been tackled mostly from a measurement theory viewpoint: a valid measurement method is a method which verifies the representation theorem. However the validation of all the substeps of step 1 have not been addressed.
Validation of the Application of a Measurement Method.	The validation of the application of a measurement method has been rarely discussed in software engineering although this is an important issue for practitioners and for good empirical research. Morris et al. distinguishes *a priori* validation, which is related to **step 2** of the measurement process in Figure 2, from *a posteriori* validation, which is related to the **step 3** of the measurement process.
Validation of Predictive Systems	This type of validation refers to **step 4** of the process presented in Figure 2. This type of validation is very often confounded with validation of measurement methods (first column, Figure 2).

Figure 3: Validation Types

In this article, many authors have been referred to according to the validation type they refer to. A recapitulation of this classification is presented in Figure 4. It has also been illustrated that a great number of proposals to validate measurement methods are incomplete since they do not tackle the correctness of the operational definition of the attribute (and consequently the pertinence of the empirical set used) or the correctness of the object representation used by the measurement method. This problem could perhaps be addressed by investigating validation frameworks from other research fields such as the social sciences or management sciences for example.

MEASUREMENT PROCESS MODEL	AUTHORS WITH VALIDATION PROPOSALS
Step 1: Design of the Measurement Method.	
Definition of the objectives.	[8] Kitchenham et al.
Design or Selection of the Metamodel.	
Characterization of the Concept.	[8] Kitchenham et al.: for example, these authors tackle the attribute validity. [12] Shepperd, Ince, [10] Prather, [13] Weyuker: These authors propose axioms that should be satisfied. These axioms are in the main related to properties of the attribute (or concept) measured.
Definition of the Numerical Assignment Rules.	[3] Fenton, [15, 16] Zuse, [8] Kitchenham et al. [12] M. Shepperd, Darrel Ince, etc: Theses authors require that the representation condition be satisfied, i.e. that the numerical assignments rules properly characterize the attribute (concept) measured. [8] Kictchenham et al: for example, these authors tackle the validity of the measurement method unit.
Step 2: Measurement Method Application	
Software Documentation Gathering.	[9] Morris, Desharnais
Construction of the Software Model.	[9] Morris, Desharnais
Application of the Numerical Assignment Rules	[9] Morris, Desharnais

Step 3 : Measurement Result Analysis	[9] Morris, Desharnais
Step 4: Exploitation of the Results	[3] Fenton [8] Kitchenham et al. [11] Schneidewind [15] Zuse [16] Zuse

Figure 4: Validation notions and authors

Acknowledgments

This research was carried out at the Software Engineering Management Research Lab. at the Université du Quebec à Montréal. This laboratory is made possible through a partnership with Bell Canada. Additional funding is provided by the Natural Sciences and Engineering Research Council of Canada. The opinions expressed in this article are solely those of the authors.

References

[1] **A. Abran, E. Ahki**
Validation requirement for functional size measurement. Internal Report, Research Laboratory in Software Engineering, Université du Québec à Montréal, 1994.

[2] **K.G. van der Berg, P.M. van der Broek**
Axiomatic Validation in the Software Metric Development Process. in Software Measurement, Edited by A. Melton, International Thomson Publishing Compagny, p.157, 1996.

[3] **N. Fenton**
Software Metrics : A Rigorous Approach. Chapman & Hall, 1991.

[4] **N. Fenton and B. Kitchenham**
Validating Software Measures, J. of Software Technology, Verification and Reliability, vol 1, no. 2, pp. 27-42, 1991.

[5] **D.A. Gustafson, J.T. Tan, P. Weaver**
Software Metric Specification. in Software Measurement, Edited by A. Melton, International Thomson Publishing Compagny, p.179, 1996.

[6] **D.A. Gustafson, R.M. Toledo, N. Temsamani**
A critique of validation/verification techniques for software development measures. in T. Denvir, R. Herman and R. W. Whitty, eds., Formal Aspects of Measurement, pp. 145-156. Springer, New York, 1992.

[7] **J.P. Jacquet, A. Abran**
From Software Metrics to Software Measurement Methods: A Process Model. Accepted at the Third International Symposium and Forum on Software Engineering Standards, ISESS '97, IEEE, Walnut Creek (CA), June 1997.

[8] **B. Kitchenham, S. L. Pfleeger, N. Fenton**
Towards a Framework for Software Measurement Validation. IEEE Transactions On Software Engineering, Vol 21, Dec. 1995.

[9] **P.M. Morris, J.M. Desharnais**
Function Point Analysis. Validating the Results. IFPUG Spring Conference, Atlanta, April 1996.

[10] **R.E. Prather**
An Axiomatic Theory of Software Complexity Metrics. Computer Journal, 27(4):42-45, 1984.

[11] **N. Schneidewind**
Methodology for Validating Software Metrics. IEEE Transactions on Software Engineering, Vol. 18, no. 5, pp. 410-442, May 92.

[12] **M. Shepperd, Darrel Ince**
Derivation and Validation of Software Metrics. Oxford Science Publications, 1993.

[13] **E.J. Weyuker**
Evaluating Software Complexity Measures. IEEE Transaction of Software Engineering, 14(9):1357-1365, 1988.

[14] **Horst Zuse**
Foundations of Validation, Prediction and Software Measures. Proceedings of the AOSW94 (Annual Oregon Software Metric Workshop), Portland, April 20-22, 1994.

[15] **Horst Zuse**
Measurement theory and software measures. Formal Aspects of Measurement, Editors: T. Denvir, R. Herman, R. Whitty. Workshops in Computing, Springer Publisher, 1992.

[16] **Horst Zuse**
A Framework of Software Measurement. preliminary version, Oct. 96, to be published in 1997.

[17] **International Function Point Users Group (IFPUG)**
Function Point Counting Practices Manual. Version 4.0, 1994.

On the use of a Segmentally Additive Proximity Structure to Measure Object Class Life Cycle Complexity

Geert Poels, Catholic University of Leuven (Belgium)

1 Introduction

According to Whitmire [14] software is characterised by three dimensions. The data dimension refers to what the software system remembers. The function dimension relates to what a system does. And finally, the control or dynamic behaviour dimension considers the different behavioural states of software. Most object-oriented software measures focus on aspects of the data and function dimensions. For instance, Chidamber's et al. MOOSE metric suite [1] is used to measure the static structure of an object-oriented design (depth of inheritance, number of children), the structural complexity of the design (weighted methods per class, coupling between objects, response for a class), and the interaction between functions and data (lack of cohesion in methods).

Poels et al. [9] propose a measure for a specific aspect of the dynamic behaviour of objects, i.e., life cycle complexity. After creation, the methods of an object can be invoked. The effect of this method triggering is that the state of the object changes. Although the triggering of methods is decided at run-time, the invocation order is subject to constraints imposed by the problem domain. These constraints are specified in the abstract data type definition of the object. The attribute 'life cycle complexity' refers to the complexity of this specification.

In [9] a life cycle complexity measure was proposed using the so-called distance-based approach. Basically, the attribute 'life cycle complexity' is defined as the distance from the life cycle specification to some reference point, chosen by the person that performs measurement. The subjective reference point models the life cycle as if it were not complex at all. The greater the distance between the actual life cycle specification and the artificial zero complexity specification, the greater the life cycle complexity. The distance-based approach contains a constructive procedure to define a metric space that is used to represent these distances.

The main advantages of the distance-based approach are intuitiveness and flexibility. However, it was not clear how the approach fits into the representational theory of measurement. In [9] only the numerical conditions for a metric space were considered. To define a metric as a measure in the sense of measurement theory, we also need to consider empirical conditions. This is the main focus of the current paper. We show that the function defined using the distance-based approach is not merely a metric, but an additive metric.

Moreover, the approach constructs a segmentally additive proximity structure, which is exactly the empirical relational structure assumed by an additive metric. Using a theorem of Suppes et al. [12] we further show that the scale type of the life cycle complexity measure is ratio.

In section 2 we discuss the distance-based approach to software measurement in general terms, not specifically related to a particular software attribute. In section 3 the approach is applied to life cycle complexity measurement. The measurement theoretic investigation is presented in section 4. In section 5 our research is compared to related work. In particular, we focus upon the relation between proximity representations and extensive representations. Finally, in section 6 conclusions are drawn, attention is paid to the assumptions underlying our approach, and further research directions are outlined.

2 Distance-Based Software Measurement

The distance-based approach to software measurement is presented next.

1. Let P be a set of similar software products and let α be the attribute of interest. Choose a set of software product abstractions M that captures α and define a mapping abs: $P \rightarrow M$.
   As software products are human artefacts, P is finite [7] or at least countable [13]. The attribute of interest α must be an internal attribute of the software products in P [2]. A software product abstraction is a model of a software product that is used to emphasise α, while simultaneously de-emphasising other internal attributes [19]. The function abs is total, but neither a surjection, nor an injection.

2. Define a set T_e of elementary transformations on M that is constructively and inverse constructively complete.
   Elementary transformations (elementary edit operations [8], elementary modifications [16], elementary operations [19]) are atomic changes of the elements of M. Each elementary transformation $t_i \in T_e$ is a function $t_i : M \rightarrow M$. $T_e = \{t_0, t_1, \ldots, t_n\}$ is constructively complete if each abstraction $m \in M$ can be built by applying a finite sequence of elementary transformations $t_{i1}, \ldots, t_{ik}$ on an initial abstraction $m_I \in M$ [6]. T_e is inverse constructively complete if $\forall t_i \in T_e$: $\exists! \, t_i^{-1} = t_j \in T_e$: $t_j(t_i(m)) = m$, where $m \in M$.

   T_e can be used to define a metric space (M, δ). A function $\delta : M \times M \rightarrow Re$ is a metric if and only if the following properties hold [SKLC89, p. 46]:
   - $\forall x, y \in X$: $\delta(x, y) \geq 0$ *(non-negativity)*
   - $\forall x, y \in X$: $\delta(x, y) = 0 \Leftrightarrow x = y$ *(identity)*
   - $\forall x, y \in X$: $\delta(x, y) = \delta(y, x)$ *(symmetry)*
   - $\forall x, y, z \in X$: $\delta(x, y) \leq \delta(x, z) + \delta(z, y)$ *(triangle inequality)*

   If $\delta : M \times M \rightarrow Re$ is a metric, then (M, δ) is a metric space.

Let us first introduce the following definitions and notations (based on similar definitions and notations that can be found in [15]). Assume that for all $t_i : M \rightarrow M$, $t_i \in T_e$.

- Let T be a sequence of elementary transformations $t_{i1}, \ldots, t_{ik}$. A T-derivation from $m \in M$ to $m' \in M$ is a sequence of abstractions $m_0, m_1, \ldots, m_{k-1}, m_k$ such that $m = m_0$, $m' = m_k$ and $t_{ij}(m_{j-1}) = m_j$ for $1 \leq j \leq k$.
- We say that a sequence T of elementary transformations $t_{i1}, \ldots, t_{ik}$ takes $m \in M$ to $m' \in M$ if it defines a T-derivation from $m \in M$ to $m' \in M$. If T takes m to m', we denote T as $T_{m,m'}$.
- The length of the sequence T of elementary transformations $t_{i1}, \ldots, t_{ik}$ is k. If k = 0 then T is empty. An empty sequence T is denoted by $\varnothing$.
- Generally, there are different sequences to take m to m'. The set of all sequences of elementary transformations that take $m \in M$ to $m' \in M$ is denoted by $\boldsymbol{T}_{m,m'}$.
- The set of all shortest sequences of elementary transformations that take $m \in M$ to $m' \in M$ is $\boldsymbol{ST}_{m,m'} \subseteq \boldsymbol{T}_{m,m'}$.
- The sets of all sequences and shortest sequences of elementary transformations that take any $m \in M$ to any $m' \in M$ are $\boldsymbol{T}$ and $\boldsymbol{ST}$ respectively.

3. Using the following constructive procedure, define a metric $\delta : M \times M \rightarrow Re$ such that (M, δ) is a metric space.
   a) Let c be a positive real number. $\forall\, m, m' \in M, \forall\, T_{m,m'} \in \boldsymbol{T}_{m,m'}$:
      _$(T_{m,m'}) = kc$,
      where k is the length of $T_{m,m'}$.
   b) m, m' ∈ M:
      $\delta(m, m') =$ _$(T_{m,m'})$,
      where $T_{m,m'} \in \boldsymbol{ST}_{m,m'}$.

   For each pair of abstractions (m, m') ∈ M × M, the function δ returns the product of the positive real number c and the length of the shortest sequences of elementary transformations that take m to m'.

   A function δ defined with this constructive procedure satisfies the metric axioms (cf. Theorem 1 in the appendix).

4. Choose a reference model $r \in M$ that is the software product abstraction for which holds that $\forall\, p \in P$: $abs(p) = r \Leftrightarrow \alpha(p)$ is null.

   The choice of reference model for an attribute is subjective as it is based on intuitive, empirical or theoretical arguments. However, if appropriately chosen, then it can be argued that the value of $\alpha(p)$ is low when abs(p) is 'close to' r and the value of $\alpha(p)$ is high when abs(p) is 'far from' r. At this stage, we informally define $\alpha(p)$ as the dissimilarity between abs(p) and r.

The assumption that a (unique) reference model can be found is essential to the distance-based approach to software measurement. This assumption also depends upon the assumption that a suitable abstraction can be found to emphasise the attribute of interest.

5. Define a function μ : $P \rightarrow Re$ such that $\forall p \in P$: $\mu(p) = \delta(abs(p),r)$.
   The function μ will be used as a software measure for α. In section 4 it will be examined how this measure definition approach fits into the representational theory of measurement.

3 The Life Cycle Complexity of Object Classes

An object class is a set of objects with similar properties. The expression 'object class' is also used to denote the abstract data type (ADT) that specifies the object properties. Chidamber et al. [1], Fetcke [3], Zuse [18], and Zuse et al. [17] define an object class as a set of instance variables and a set of methods. These sets are actually abstractions of an object class used by the above authors for software measurement. The set of instance variables and the set of methods capture respectively the data and function dimensions of an object class. If needed, additional abstractions can be defined. For instance, Chidamber et al. [1] define for each method the set of instance variables it uses. The degree of similarity between two methods is defined as the intersection between the sets of used instance variables of the methods. The degree of similarity between two methods is used as an abstraction to measure object class cohesion.

Apart from the data and the function dimension, a third dimension of software is distinguished, i.e., the control dimension that refers to the dynamic behaviour of objects [14]. This dimension too has interesting aspects worth measuring. For instance, Poels et al. [9] introduced the notion of life cycle complexity. We briefly describe this aspect of complexity here.

Objects in a system have a life cycle. They enter into an initial state after creation. When their methods are triggered (e.g., by messages, events, etc.), they may (but must not) change state. At some moment in time, they enter an ending state when they are destroyed. The life of objects is a dynamic property. Generally, it cannot be predicted at the outset. However, constraints can be imposed on the life of objects. For instance, a constraint of the problem domain states that for the objects of some object class X, method B cannot be triggered unless method A was triggered before. As a real-world example, in a library it is required that books cannot be borrowed unless they are first catalogued. Such constraints can be statically described using some form of state modelling technique. For instance, in [11] regular expressions are used to model the life cycle of objects.

A regular expression is defined on the set of methods M_X of the object class X by means of the sequence ".", selection "+", and iteration "*" operators. For instance, if $M_X = \{A, B, C, D, E, F\}$, then the regular expression $A . B . (C + D)^* . (E + F)$ means that for each object of class X first the method A must be triggered. Next the method B is invoked. Next we have zero, one or more times the choice between triggering method C or method D. Finally, triggering either E or F ends the life of the object. As can be seen, the regular expression for the object class X specifies the constraints that are imposed on the triggering of the methods in M_X. We also say that the regular expression specifies the life cycle of the object class.

Informally, the complexity of a life cycle is a function of the constraints that are imposed on the life cycle. In fact, many different points of view on object class life cycle complexity can be expressed. One of these is presented below. Another point of view can be found in [9]. Basically, we formalise the different points of view by applying the distance-based approach to life cycle complexity measurement. This will result in a set of life cycle complexity measures, one for each point of view. The different steps of the approach are executed as follows:

Step 1: Find a suitable abstraction that captures life cycle complexity

Clearly, neither the set of methods nor the set of instance variables of an object class is an abstraction that emphasises life cycle complexity. We need some kind of state transition model like regular expressions (or Finite State Machines, Jackson Structure Diagrams, Petri-Nets, ...) to measure life cycle complexity.

Let UM be the universe of methods (or alternatively, the universe of event types that trigger these methods [11]), let R*(UM) be the set of all regular expressions that are built on UM using the ".", "+" and "*" operators, and let P be a countable or finite set of object classes. It holds for all $p \in P$ that M_p (i.e., the set of methods of class p) is a finite subset of UM (i.e., $\forall\, p \in P$: $M_p \subseteq UM$). The function abs : $P \rightarrow R^*(UM)$ maps object classes into their regular expressions:

Step 2: Find a constructively and inverse constructively complete set T_e of elementary transformations on R*(UM)

Theorem 2 (cf. appendix) states that the following set T_e of elementary transformations is constructively and inverse constructively complete:

$T_e = \{t_i\}$, $i = 0, 1, \ldots, 9$,
where $t_i(e) = e'$ is defined as:

$t_0(e) = e . x = e'$	(add right sequence method)
$t_1(e) = x . e = e'$	(add left sequence method)
$t_2(e) = e + x = e'$	(add right selection method)

$t_3(e) = x + e = e'$ (add left selection method)
$t_4(e) = (e)^* = e'$ (add iteration)
$t_5(e) = t_5(e' . x) = e'$ (delete right sequence method)
$t_6(e) = t_6(x . e') = e'$ (delete left sequence method)
$t_7(e) = t_7(e' + x) = e'$ (delete right selection method)
$t_8(e) = t_8(x + e') = e'$ (delete left selection method)
$t_9(e) = t_9((e')^*) = e'$ (delete iteration)
for $e, e' \in R^*(UM)$, $x \in UM \cup \{1\}$

The symbol "1" denotes an empty method (i.e., a method triggered by the "do nothing" event type [11]). Note that the elementary transformations may be applied on a regular expression or any part of a regular expression that is itself a regular expression.

Step 3: Define the metric space $(R^*(UM), \delta)$

a) Let c = 1. $\forall e, e' \in R^*(UM), \forall T_{e,e'} \in \boldsymbol{T}_{e,e'}$:
  $\_(T_{e,e'}) = k$,
    where k is the length of $T_{e,e'}$.

b) $\forall e, e' \in R^*(UM)$:
  $\delta(e, e') = \_(T_{e,e'})$,
  where $T_{e,e'} \in \boldsymbol{ST}_{e,e'}$.

For each pair of regular expressions $(e, e') \in R^*(UM) \times R^*(UM)$, the function δ returns the length of the shortest sequences of elementary transformations that take e to e'.

Step 4: Find a reference abstraction $r \in R^*(UM)$

This step is crucial in the distance-based approach. The choice of reference abstraction determines our point of view on object class life cycle complexity. We present one particular point of view. Another point of view can be found in [9].

The reference abstraction is the trivial life cycle defined on the set of methods of an object class. For an object class X with a set of methods M_X, the trivial life cycle is specified as the regular expression trivial(X). Suppose $M_X = \{A, B, C, D, E ,F\}$, where the method A creates an object occurrence of X, the methods E and F destroy an object occurrence of X, and the methods B, C, and D modify the state of the object occurrences of X, without destroying them or creating new occurrences. Then trivial(X) = $A . (B + C + D)^* . (E + F)$. As can be seen, the only constraints imposed by a trivial life cycle are that first occurrences must be created, next their state can be modified zero, one or more times, and finally their lives must be ended.

The life cycle complexity of an object class p ∈ P is defined as the dissimilarity between abs(p) and trivial(p).

Note that in this example the reference point is relative to the object class being measured. For each object class p ∈ P a specific reference abstraction trivial(p) ∈ R*(UM) is defined.

Step 5: Define a life cycle complexity measure

$$\forall\, p \in P:\ \mu\ (p) = \delta\ (abs(p), trivial(p))$$

Basically this means that the life cycle complexity of the object class p is measured by the length of the shortest sequences of elementary transformations that take abs(p) to trivial(p). In other words, the minimum number of elementary transformations needed to transform the actual life cycle of p into its trivial life cycle measures the life cycle complexity of p.

4 Proximity Structures

According to the representational theory of measurement, measurement is the assignment of a homomorphism from an observed (empirical) relational system (structure) into some numerical relational system (structure) [10]. A homomorphism maps a set of empirical entities into a set of numbers such that all empirical relations and operations are preserved in the numerical relational structure. A metric can be seen as a homomorphism that preserves a dissimilarity relation. Sufficient conditions for the representation of an empirical relational structure in a metric space are presented by Suppes et al. [12]. We first list these conditions (axioms) and next discuss how they apply to the distance-based approach to software measurement.

4.1 Sufficient Conditions For An Additive Metric Representation

Let M be a set (of software product abstractions) and let •≥ be a quaternary relation on A. For all m_1, m_2, m_3, m_4 ∈ M, (m_1, m_2) •≥ (m_3, m_4) denotes the observation that the dissimilarity between m_1 and m_2 is at least as great as the dissimilarity between m_3 and m_4. The relation •≥ is used to define an equivalence relation •≈ (i.e., (m_1, m_2) •≈ (m_3, m_4) ⇔ (m_1, m_2) •≥ (m_3, m_4) and (m_3, m_4) •≥ (m_1, m_2)) and a strict ordering relation •> (i.e., (m_1, m_2) •> (m_3, m_4) ⇔ (m_1, m_2) •≥ (m_3, m_4) and not ((m_3, m_4) •≥ (m_1, m_2))).

The relational structure (M, •≥) is a proximity structure if and only if the following axioms hold for all m, m' ∈ M [12, p. 161]:

P_1. •≥ is a weak order, i.e., it is transitive and strongly complete;

P_2. (m,m') •> (m,m) whenever m ≠ m' *(positivity)*;
P_3. (m,m) •≈ (m',m') *(minimality)*;
P_4. (m,m') •≈ (m',m) *(symmetry)*.

The relation •≥ is also used to define a collinear betweenness relation [12, p.164]. For m_1, m_2, m_3 ∈ M, the ternary relation $\langle m_1m_2m_3\rangle$ is said to hold if and only if for all m_1', m_2' and m_3' ∈ M:

$$(m_1, m_2) \bullet\!\geq (m_1', m_2') \text{ and } (m_1', m_3') \bullet\!\geq (m_1, m_3) \Rightarrow (m_2', m_3') \bullet\!\geq (m_2, m_3)$$

Informally, the collinear betweenness relation $\langle m_1m_2m_3\rangle$ holds if m_2 lies on an additive segment from m_1 to m_3, i.e., along the segment from m_1 to m_3 distances are additive. Hence, if $\langle m_1m_2m_3\rangle$, then $\delta(m_1, m_2) + \delta(m_2, m_3) = \delta(m_1, m_3)$. The collinear betweenness relation is needed to define a special kind of proximity structure: the segmentally additive proximity structure.

A relational structure (M, •≥) is a segmentally additive proximity structure if and only if the following axioms hold for all m_1, m_2, m_3, m_4 ∈ M [12, p. 168]:
S_1. (M, •≥) is a proximity structure;
S_2. If $(m_1, m_2) \bullet\!\geq (m_3, m_4)$, then there exists m_5 ∈ M such that $(m_1, m_5) \bullet\!\approx (m_3, m_4)$
and $\langle m_1m_5m_2\rangle$;
S_3. If $m_3 \neq m_4$, then there exist $m_0', \ldots, m_n'$ ∈ M such that $m_0' = m_1$, $m_n' = m_2$ and $(m_3, m_4) \bullet\!\geq (m_{i-1}', m_i')$, i = 1, …, n.

The above definitions are needed to discuss the following representation and uniqueness theorem, presented by Suppes et al. [12, p. 168]:
Suppose (M, •≥) is a segmentally additive proximity structure. Then there exist a real-valued function δ on M × M such that, for any m_1, m_2, m_3, m_4 ∈ M,
M_1. (M, δ) is a metric space;
M_2. $(m_1, m_2) \bullet\!\geq (m_3, m_4) \Leftrightarrow \delta(m_1, m_2) \geq \delta(m_3, m_4)$;
M_3. $\langle m_1m_2m_3\rangle \Leftrightarrow \delta(m_1, m_2) + \delta(m_2, m_3) = \delta(m_1, m_3)$;
M4. If δ' is another metric on M satisfying the above conditions, then there exist $\beta > 0$ such that $\delta' = \beta\delta$.

A proof can be found in [12, p. 171]. Informally, M_1 implies that δ satisfies $\delta(m, m') = \delta(m', m) > \delta(m, m) = \delta(m', m')$ for all m ≠ m', which requires the empirical conditions P_2, P_3 and P_4. Condition P_1 is required by M_2 if •≥ is to be preserved by ≥. Empirical condition S_2 is the segmental solvability condition, required by M_3. For any distinct m_1, m_2 ∈ M and for any nonnegative $\varepsilon \leq \delta(m_1, m_2)$, there exists a m_5 on a segment from m_1 to m_2 whose distance from m_1 is exactly ε. Condition S_3 is an Archimedean property to guarantee that (m_3, m_4) cannot be infinitely small compared with (m_1, m_2). Finally, note that M_4 states that the assumption of a segmentally additive proximity structure allows dissimilarity to be measured on a ratio scale.

We now relate this theorem of proximity measurement to the distance-based approach. First it is shown that the constructive procedure presented in the previous section results in a function δ satisfying M_1 till M_4. Next it is shown that the empirical conditions for a segmentally additive proximity structure are satisfied, at least for a specific observation criterion regarding the dissimilarity ordering $\bullet\geq$. We said that $(m_1, m_2) \bullet\geq (m_3, m_4)$ denotes the observation that the dissimilarity between m_1 and m_2 is at least as great as the dissimilarity between m_3 and m_4. We can make this statement more precise. The dissimilarity ordering $(m_1, m_2) \bullet\geq (m_3, m_4)$ is observed when the length of the sequences in $\boldsymbol{ST}_{m1,m2}$ is at least as great as the length of the sequences in $\boldsymbol{ST}_{m3,m4}$.

4.2 Numerical Conditions

According to Theorem 1 (cf. appendix), the constructive procedure presented in the previous section results in a metric space (M, δ), which satisfies M_1.

Regarding M_2, if $(m_1, m_2) \bullet\geq (m_3, m_4)$, then the length of the sequences in $\boldsymbol{ST}_{m1,m2}$ is at least as great as the length of the sequences in $\boldsymbol{ST}_{m3,m4}$. Suppose the length of the sequences in $\boldsymbol{ST}_{m1,m2}$ and $\boldsymbol{ST}_{m3,m4}$ is respectively k and k'. For a metric δ defined using the constructive procedure, it then holds that $\delta(m_1, m_2) = kc \geq k'c = \delta(m_3, m_4)$, where c is a positive real number. On the other hand, if $\delta(m_1, m_2) \geq \delta(m_3, m_4)$, then this implies that the length of the sequences in $\boldsymbol{ST}_{m1,m2}$ is at least as great as the length of the sequences in $\boldsymbol{ST}_{m3,m4}$. Hence, it holds that $(m_1, m_2) \bullet\geq (m_3, m_4)$.

Regarding M_3, we note that, for any $m, m' \in M$, the abstractions $m_0, m_1, \ldots, m_{k-1}, m_k$ of the T-derivation defined by $T_{m,m'} \in \boldsymbol{ST}_{m,m'}$ lie on an additive segment from m to m'. If any of these abstractions m_i $(0 \leq i \leq k)$ would not lie on an additive segment from m to m', then, because of the triangle inequality, $\delta(m, m') < \delta(m, m_i) + \delta(m_i, m')$. But then m_i cannot be an abstraction of a T-derivation defined by a shortest sequence of elementary transformations that takes m to m'.

Regarding M_4, assume $\delta(m, m') = \_(T_{m,m'}) = kc$, where k is the length of $T_{m,m'} \in \boldsymbol{ST}_{m,m'}$ and c is a positive real number. Let c' be any other positive real number. Then, $\delta'(m, m') = \_(T_{m,m'}) = kc'$. Both δ and δ' satisfy M_1 till M_3. For all $m, m' \in M$ it holds that $\delta'(m, m') = (c'/c)\,\delta(m, m') = \beta\,\delta(m, m')$. As $c' > 0$ and $c > 0$, it holds that $\beta > 0$. Hence, M_4 is satisfied.

4.3 Empirical Conditions

We now check each of the empirical conditions for a segmentally additive proximity structure with respect to the observation criterion for $\bullet\geq$. This procedure is somewhat analogous to the procedure used by Whitmire [14] for the length measurement of use cases (cf. infra).

The segmental solvability condition (S_2) is easily satisfied given the above interpretation of $\bullet\geq$. Suppose $(m_1, m_2) \bullet\geq (m_3, m_4)$ and let the length of the sequences in $\boldsymbol{ST}_{m3,m4}$ be k. Then, we can always find an abstraction $m_5 \in M$ such that $\langle m_1 m_5 m_2 \rangle$ and the length of the sequences in $\boldsymbol{ST}_{m1,m5}$ is k. Take any $T_{m1,m2} \in \boldsymbol{ST}_{m1,m2}$ and m_5 is the abstraction m_k of the T-derivation defined by $T_{m1,m2}$.

P_1 requires $\bullet\geq$ to be transitive and strongly complete. As T_e is constructively and inverse constructively complete, there is at least one shortest sequence of elementary transformations between each pair of abstractions. As all sequences of elementary transformations have a length represented by the natural number k, and any pair of natural numbers can be compared using $\geq$, strong completeness is shown.

For transitivity we need to show that

$$(m_1, m_2) \bullet\geq (m_3, m_4) \text{ and } (m_3, m_4) \bullet\geq (m_5, m_6) \Rightarrow (m_1, m_2) \bullet\geq (m_5, m_6).$$

Again, this is easily demonstrated. Suppose the lengths of the sequences in $\boldsymbol{ST}_{m1,m2}$, $\boldsymbol{ST}_{m3,m4}$ and $\boldsymbol{ST}_{m5,m6}$ are respectively k, k' and k". Then, $(m_1, m_2) \bullet\geq (m_3, m_4)$ implies $k \geq k'$ and $(m_3, m_4) \bullet\geq (m_5, m_6)$ implies $k' \geq k''$. As the $\geq$ relation is transitive for natural numbers, it then holds that $k \geq k''$, leading to the observation that $(m_1, m_2) \bullet\geq (m_5, m_6)$.

Next, positivity (P_2) must be shown. The length of the sequences in $\boldsymbol{ST}_{m,m}$ is always zero. No transformations are required. On the other hand, when $m \neq m'$, then at least one elementary transformation is required to transform m into m'. Hence, the length of the sequences in $\boldsymbol{ST}_{m,m'}$ is always positive. Therefore, it holds that $(m, m') \bullet\geq (m, m)$.

Minimality (P_3) is trivial. If no transformations are required to transform m into m and m' into m', then no difference in the length of the shortest sequences can be observed. Hence, $(m, m) \bullet\approx (m', m')$.

Symmetry (P_4) is satisfied as for any $T_{m,m'} \in \boldsymbol{ST}_{m,m'}$, inverse($T_{m,m'}$) $\in \boldsymbol{ST}_{m',m}$ and the length of the sequences in $\boldsymbol{ST}_{m,m'}$ and $\boldsymbol{ST}_{m',m}$ is equal. If inverse($T_{m,m'}$) would be longer than some $T_{m',m} \in \boldsymbol{ST}_{m',m}$, then inverse($T_{m',m}$) would be shorter than $T_{m,m'}$, which would imply that $T_{m,m'} \notin \boldsymbol{ST}_{m,m'}$.

The Archimedean axiom (S_3) is often the most difficult to test [14]. Informally, it implies that when m_3 and m_4 are dissimilar, this dissimilarity cannot be infinitely small as compared to the dissimilarity of other pairs of abstractions. Indeed, the smallest positive dissimilarity that m_3 and m_4 can have is when they can be transformed into each other by means of a single elementary transformation. The length of such a shortest sequence is one, which is not infinitely small as compared to any other natural number that represents the length of a shortest sequence of elementary transformations.

4.4 Measure Validation

We have shown that a dissimilarity ordering $\bullet\geq$ on M × M, constructed using a constructively and inverse constructively complete set of elementary transformations T_e, satisfies the empirical conditions S_1 till S_3 of a segmentally additive proximity structure. In other words, when we accept the above observation criterion for $\bullet\geq$, then the empirical conditions S_1 till S_3 are implicitly assumed. According to the representation and uniqueness theorem of the segmentally additive proximity structure, presented in Suppes et al. [12], the existence of a function δ on M × M that satisfies M_1 till M_4 is guaranteed. We also showed that the constructive procedure of the distance-based approach defines such a function δ. The metric δ is a measure of dissimilarity in the sense that it preserves the empirical conditions of the segmentally additive proximity structure (M, $\bullet\geq$). Moreover, according to the uniqueness theorem (i.e., M_4) it is a ratio scale measure. Admissible transformations for the ratio scale are implicitly incorporated in the constructive procedure through the choice of a positive real number c.

The function δ can also be used to measure the attribute α. Recall that, for a software product p ∈ P, α (p) was defined as the dissimilarity between abs(p) ∈ M and r ∈ M. This dissimilarity is measured by μ (p) = δ (abs(p), r). As δ is measured on a ratio scale, ratios between measurement values (e.g., μ (p) / μ (p')) are meaningful. We might for instance say that α (p) is twice α (p') when μ (p) / μ (p') = 2.

5 Evaluation

The distance-based approach to measurement is intuitive and flexible. It is intuitive in the sense that an internal attribute of a software product is defined and measured as the dissimilarity between a software product abstraction capturing the attribute and some predefined reference abstraction. The reference abstraction is the abstraction of a software product that has a null value for the attribute. The more the software product abstraction and the reference abstraction are dissimilar, the higher the value of the attribute must be. The approach is flexible in the sense that different people may chose different reference abstractions, without essentially changing the metric space that was constructed.

The approach was used in section 3 to measure the life cycle complexity of object classes. The discussion in section 4 shows that the resulting life cycle complexity measure is more than just an arbitrary mapping from a set of object classes into the real numbers. In fact, we believe that the distance-based approach fits well into the representational theory of measurement.

Some other evaluation topics are discussed below.

5.1 Related Work

In section 4 it was shown that the distance-based approach assumes a segmentally additive proximity structure. This type of empirical relational structure was used by Whitmire [14] to measure the length of use cases. The abstraction of the use case used for length measurement is a directed graph in which the nodes are software objects and the edges are message links. It is assumed that the graph has a single entry point. The length of the use case is defined as the longest geodesic from the entry point to any termination point. A geodesic in a graph is the shortest path between a pair of nodes. The length of the geodesic from node a to node b is defined as the distance between a and b. Whitmire showed that the empirical conditions of the segmentally additive proximity structure are easily assumed for distances in a directed graph.

The distance-based approach can be seen as a generalisation of Whitmire's approach. We construct a directed graph in which the nodes are software product abstractions and the edges are elementary transformations between the abstractions. The geodesics in the graph correspond to the shortest sequences of elementary transformations between software product abstractions. The length of these geodesics is used to decide upon the dissimilarity ordering between the software product abstractions. As such a segmentally additive proximity structure is constructed. An attribute is defined as a specific geodesic in the graph, i.e., the geodesic from the abstraction of the software product that must be measured to a predefined reference abstraction.

Whitmire [14] further claims that he built his ratio scale use case length measure without the use of extensive measurement. We believe this statement is not entirely correct, as will be shown next.

5.2 Proximity Representations vs. Extensive Representations

Suppes et al. [12] show that the construction of an additive metric representation is reducible to the construction of extensive measurement.

Let $(M, \bullet\geq)$ be a segmentally additive proximity structure. Define the sets N, S, and T, the concatenation operator $\bullet$, and the relation $\bullet\geq'$ as follows:

- $N = \{(m, m) \mid m \in M\}$
- $S = (M \times M - N) / \bullet\approx$
- (i.e., S is the set of all equivalence classes of $M \times M$ except the class containing the null pairs)
- $\bullet\geq'$ is the natural order on S induced by $\bullet\geq$
- For any $(m_1, m_2), (m_3, m_4), (m_5, m_6) \in S$: $(m_1, m_2) \bullet (m_3, m_4) = (m_5, m_6)$ if and only if there exists $m_7 \in M$, such that $(m_1, m_2) = (m_5, m_7)$, $(m_3, m_4) = (m_7, m_6)$, and $\langle m_5 m_7 m_6 \rangle$. Let T be the set of all pairs $((m_1, m_2), (m_3, m_4))$ for which $(m_1, m_2) \bullet (m_3, m_4)$ is defined.

It is proven in [12, p. 170] that (S, T, $\bullet\geq'$, $\bullet$) is an extensive structure with no essential maximum. The primary difference with the closed extensive structure is that the concatenation operator $\bullet$ is only closed for the elements in T. The empirical conditions for the extensive structure with no essential maximum are slightly modified from those of the closed extensive structure (cf. [5, p. 84]). But the implication is the same, i.e., it leads to the construction of a ratio scale.

The proof of the representation and uniqueness theorem for the additive metric representation relies strongly upon the reduction of the segmentally additive proximity structure to an extensive structure with no essential maximum. It was shown by Krantz et al. [5, p. 85] that if (S, T, $\bullet\geq'$, $\bullet$) is an extensive structure with no essential maximum, then there exists a function $\phi : S \rightarrow Re^+$ such that for all $(m_1, m_2), (m_3, m_4) \in S$:

$$(m_1, m_2) \bullet\geq' (m_3, m_4) \Leftrightarrow \phi(m_1, m_2) \geq \phi(m_3, m_4)$$

and

$$\text{if } ((m_1, m_2), (m_3, m_4)) \in T, \text{ then } \phi((m_1, m_2) \bullet (m_3, m_4)) = \phi(m_1, m_2) + \phi(m_3, m_4).$$

If another function ϕ' satisfies these numerical conditions, then there exists $\beta > 0$ such that, for all nonmaximal (m, m') $\in$ S, $\phi'(m, m') = \beta\,\phi(m, m')$.

It is now shown by Suppes et al. [12, p. 172] that the additive metric δ on M $\times$ M can be defined by letting

$$\delta(m, m) = 0$$

and

$$\delta(m, m') = \phi(m, m') \text{ for } m \neq m'.$$

The numerical condition M_4 (i.e., dissimilarity is measured on a ratio scale) follows directly from the corresponding property of the extensive representation by ϕ. We believe that the real difference between a proximity representation and an extensive representation is the nature of the concatenation operator. This is discussed below.

5.3 Concatenating Attributes vs. Concatenating Objects

Extensive measurement relies upon the identification of empirical concatenation operators. Some people argue that such concatenation operators do not make sense for software products. For instance, Gustafson et al. [4, p. 164] state that "In this case, a possible binary operation is the concatenation of control flow graphs.

However, this operation seems to be of limited usefulness since we rarely concatenate programs. For the notion of operations on the models to be useful, they need to match the operations performed on the original documents". However, Zuse [19, p. 298] argues that "Concatenation operators are hidden behind measures. It is not necessary that programmers concatenate objects in reality. If concatenation operations are not intuitive, then it is not our fault. They are derived from the considered measure. Important is that the condition of a closed binary operation is fulfilled. Concatenation operators are not artificial, they are simply there!"

So, from a theoretical point of view no objection can be raised against the use of empirical concatenation operators. From a pragmatical point of view, we might run into difficulties. For instance, in previous research we did not succeed in finding a combination rule related to proposed object class life cycle complexity measures and the concatenation operator || for regular expressions. The operator || is the parallel composition of two regular expressions [11]. Although || is closed, the algorithm to calculate e || e' is not simple. It requires for instance that e and e' are transformed into Finite State Machines before the parallel composition operator is applied.

Using the distance-based approach we need not to consider the concatenation of software product abstractions. The concatenation operation • of the extensive structure with no essential maximum that was obtained by reducing the segmentally additive proximity structure (M, •≥), does not concatenate the abstractions in M. It concatenates dissimilarities, which are attributes of a pair of abstractions. In fact the dissimilarities (m_1, m_2) and (m_3, m_4) are concatenated when there exists an abstraction m_7 on an additive segment from m_5 to m_6 such that the dissimilarity (m_1, m_2) is equal to the dissimilarity (m_5, m_7), and the dissimilarity (m_3, m_4) is equal to the dissimilarity (m_7, m_6). Likewise, numerical condition M_3 does not require that abstractions are concatenated. It only requires that distances on an additive segment are concatenated.

5.4 Life Cycle Complexity Measures vs. Object-Oriented Software Measures

According to Fetcke [3], Zuse [18], [19], and Zuse et al. [17] most object-oriented software measures do not assume an extensive structure. However, according to these authors, many object-oriented software measures assume the empirical conditions of the modified function of belief. These conditions make use of the object class unification and intersection operations. These operations make sense as an object class is defined as a set of methods and a set of instance variables. Unfortunately, we do not know what the regular expression of an object class looks like if it is the union (or intersection) of two other object classes. On the other hand, we showed that object class life cycle complexity can be measured with a ratio scale. The modified function of belief does not lead to the ratio scale.

6 Conclusions

In this paper we used a distance-based approach to define an object class life cycle complexity measure. The paper focused on a measurement theoretical investigation of this approach to software measurement. It was shown that our approach fits into the representational theory of measurement. The constructive measure definition procedure leads to an additive metric representation. The scale type of the resulting measures is ratio.

Throughout the paper a number of assumptions were made. Further research must examine each of these assumptions in detail. In particular we wish to investigate the consequences of violating the assumption that the reference abstraction is unique (i.e., $\forall$ p $\in$ P: abs(p) = r $\Leftrightarrow$ α (p) is null). We believe that this assumption can be loosened through the assignment of different positive real values c_i to the different types of elementary transformations in T_e. A shortest sequence of elementary transformations is then a special case of a minimum cost sequence of elementary transformations (see e.g., [15]). The assignment of different c_i values represents the difference in relative costs among the different types of elementary transformations. However, it must be carefully examined how this 'generalised' distance-based approach fits into the representational theory of measurement.

Acknowledgments

This work is supported by a doctoral research grant from the Fund for Scientific Research - Flanders (Belgium) (F.W.O.).

References

[1] **S.R. Chidamber and C.F. Kemerer**
A Metrics Suite for Object Oriented Design. IEEE Trans. Software Eng., Vol. 20, No. 6, pp. 476-493, June 1994.

[2] **N.E. Fenton and S.L. Pfleeger**
Software Metrics: A Rigorous & Practical Approach. 2nd edition, PWS Publishing Company, London, 1997, 638 pp.

[3] **T. Fetcke**
Investigations of the Properties of Object-Oriented Software Metrics. ECOOP'95 Workshop on Quantitative Methods for Object-Oriented System Development, Aarhus, Denmark, 7-11 Aug. 1995, 7 pp.

[4] **D.A. Gustafson, J.T. Tan, and P. Weaver**
Software Measure Specification. ACM Software Eng. Notes, Vol. 18, No. 5, pp. 163-168, Dec. 1993.

[5] **D.H. Krantz, R.D. Luce, P. Suppes, and A. Tversky**
Foundations of Measurement. Vol. 1, Academic Press, New York, 1971, 557 pp.

[6] **A.C. Melton, D.A. Gustafson, J.M. Bieman, and A.L. Baker**
A Mathematical Perspective for Software Measures Research. IEEE Software Eng. J., Vol. 5, No. 5, pp. 246-254, Sept. 1990.

[7] **S. Moser and V.B. Misic**
Measuring Class Coupling and Cohesion: A Formal Metamodel Approach. Proc. Asia Pacific Software Eng. Conf., Hong Kong, 2-5 Dec. 1997, pp. 31-40.

[8] **B.J. Oommen, K. Zhang, and W. Lee**
Numerical Similarity and Dissimilarity Measures Between Two Trees. IEEE Trans. Computers, Vol. 45, No. 12, pp. 1426-1434, Dec. 1996.

[9] **G. Poels and G. Dedene**
Complexity Metrics for Formally Specified Business Requirements. Proc. 8th Ann. Oregon Workshop on Software Metrics, Coeur d'Alene, Idaho, 11-13 May 1997, 11 pp.

[10] **F.S. Roberts**
Measurement Theory with Applications to Decisionmaking, Utility, and the Social Sciences. Addison-Wesley, Reading, Mass., 1979, 420 pp.

[11] **M. Snoeck and G. Dedene**
Existence Dependency: The Key to Semantic Integrity Between Structural and Behavioural Aspects of Object Types. IEEE Trans. Software Eng., Vol. 24, No. 4, pp. 233-251, Apr. 1998.

[12] **P. Suppes, D.M. Krantz, R.D. Luce, and A. Tversky**
Foundations of Measurement: Geometrical, Threshold, and Probabilistic Representations. Vol. 2, Academic Press, San Diego, Calif., 1989, 493 pp.

[13] **J. Tian and M.V. Zelkowitz**
A Formal Program Complexity Model and Its Application. J. Systems and Software, Vol. 17, pp. 253-266, 1992.

[14] **S.A. Whitmire**
Object Oriented Design Measurement. Wiley Computer Publishing, New York, 1997, 452 pp.

[15] **K. Zhang and D. Shasha**
Simple Fast Algorithms for the Editing Distance Between Trees and Related Problems. Siam J. Computing, Vol. 18, No. 6, pp. 1245-1262, 1989.

[16] **H. Zuse and P. Bollmann**
Software Metrics: Using Measurement Theory to Describe the Properties and Scales of Static Software Complexity Metrics. ACM SIGPLAN Notices, Vol. 24, No. 8, pp. 23-33, Aug. 1989.

[17] **H. Zuse and T. Fetcke**
Properties of Object-Oriented Software Measures. Proc. 7th Ann. Oregon Workshop on Software Metrics, Silver Falls, Oregon, 5-7 June 1995, 27 pp.

[18] **H. Zuse**
Foundations of Object-Oriented Software Measures. Proc. IEEE 3rd Int'l Software Metrics Symposium, Berlin, Mar. 1996, 14 pp.

[19] **H. Zuse**
A Framework for Software Measurement. Walter de Gruyter, Berlin, 1998, 755 pp.

APPENDIX

THEOREM 1

Let M be a set (of software product abstractions) and let $T_e = \{t_0, t_1, \ldots, t_n\}$ be a constructively and inverse constructively complete set of elementary transformations $t_i : M \rightarrow M$. Define _ : $\boldsymbol{T} \rightarrow Re : T_{m,m'} \rightarrow kc$, where k is the length of $T_{m,m'}$ and c is a positive real number. Define $\delta : M \times M \rightarrow Re : (m, m') \rightarrow$ _$(T_{m,m'})$, where $T_{m,m'} \in \boldsymbol{ST}_{m,m'}$. Then, (M, δ) is a metric space.

PROOF

(i) *Non-negativity*
$\forall$ m, m' $\in$ M: δ (m, m') ≥ 0 as c > 0

QED

(ii) *Identity*
$\forall$ m, m' $\in$ M: δ (m, m') = 0 $\Rightarrow$ _$(T_{m,m'}) = 0 \Rightarrow k = 0$ (as c > 0) $\Rightarrow$ m = m'
$\forall$ m, m' $\in$ M: m = m' $\Rightarrow \boldsymbol{ST}_{m,m'} = \{\emptyset\} \Rightarrow \delta$ (m, m') = _$(\emptyset)$ = 0.c = 0

QED

(iii) *Symmetry*
Let $T_{m,m'} \in \boldsymbol{ST}_{m,m'}$ be the sequence of elementary transformations $t_{i1}, \ldots, t_{ik}$ that defines the sequence of abstractions $m_0, m_1, \ldots, m_{k-1}, m_k$ from $m = m_o$ to $m' = m_k$, where $t_{ij}(m_{j-1}) = m_j$ for $1 \leq j \leq k$.
The sequence of elementary transformations $t_{ik}^{-1}, \ldots, t_{i1}^{-1}$ (notation: inverse$(T_{m,m'})$) can be used to take m' back to m.
As inverse$(T_{m,m'}) \in \boldsymbol{ST}_{m',m}$, it holds that

$$\delta(m, m') = \_(T_{m,m'}) = kc = \_(\text{inverse}(T_{m,m'})) = \delta(m', m)$$

QED

(iv) *Triangle inequality*
Let $T_{m,m'} \in \boldsymbol{ST}_{m,m'}$ be the sequence of elementary transformations $t_{i1}, \ldots, t_{ik}$ that defines the sequence of abstractions $m_0, m_1, \ldots, m_{k-1}, m_k$ from $m = m_o$ to $m' = m_k$, where $t_{ij}(m_{j-1}) = m_j$ for $1 \leq j \leq k$.
Let $T_{m',m''} \in \boldsymbol{ST}_{m',m''}$ be the sequence of elementary transformations $t_{ik+1}, \ldots, t_{ih}$ that defines the sequence of abstractions $m_k, m_{k+1}, \ldots, m_{h-1}, m_h$ from $m' = m_k$ to $m'' = m_h$, where $t_{ij}(m_{j-1}) = m_j$ for $k < j \leq h$.
Define $T_{m,m'} \oplus T_{m',m''}$ as the sequence of elementary transformations $t_{i1}, \ldots, t_{ih}$ that takes m to m" over m'.
It holds that $T_{m,m'} \oplus T_{m',m''} \in \boldsymbol{T}_{m,m''}$, but it is not implied that $T_{m,m'} \oplus T_{m',m''} \in \boldsymbol{ST}_{m,m''}$. It also holds that
_$(T_{m,m'} \oplus T_{m',m''})$ = hc = _$(T_{m,m'})$ + _$(T_{m',m''})$ = δ (m, m') + δ (m', m") = kc + (h-k)c.
Therefore, $\forall\, T_{m,m''} \in \boldsymbol{ST}_{m,m''}$:
δ (m, m") = _$(T_{m,m''}) \leq$ hc = _$(T_{m,m'})$ + _$(T_{m',m''})$ = δ (m, m') + δ (m', m").

QED

THEOREM 2

Let UM be the universe of methods. T_e is constructively and inverse constructively complete.

PROOF

The only operators allowed to build regular expressions on methods are "." (sequence), "+" (selection) and "*" (iteration). Starting from the empty method symbolised by "1", every regular expression $e \in R^*(UM)$ can be constructed using a finite sequence of elementary transformations t_i, with $i \in \{0, 1, 2, 3, 4\}$. Hence, T_e is constructively complete.

For all elementary transformations t_i and $\forall$ e, e' $\in R^*(UM)$ it holds that if $t_i(e) = e'$ then $e = t_{(i+5) mod 10}(e')$. Hence, T_e is inverse constructively complete.

QED

Attribute-Based Model of Software Size

Lem. O. Ejiogu, Softmetrix, Inc. Chicago (USA)

Abstract

Although many practitioners continue to expound KLOCs as a metric of software size, the popular consensus is that it does not address the well-known problems of software management: analysis, design, testing, maintenance, documentaion; and software certification. A principled approach built on sound theoretical foundation is critical for measuring software size. Every science has an underlying body of principles. The measurement of software size can greatly benefit from a formal component theory. One such methodology is briefly introduced below. Because of space, the reader is referred to [1, 2] for its rich feedback effects and sample worked examples.

1 Motivation and Introduction

More vibrant criticisms of the current practice of thinking and denoting the abstract phenomenon called ***Software Size*** *continue to proliferate. Recently for example, one such thought-provoking criticism (itself, the primary motivation for this article) was repeated by* Pancake [9]-- *"People have tried to come up with software metrics, and they always degenerate to lines of code which is exactly the wrong measure for OOP. You want to reduce the lines of code, you don't want to give people incentives for writing more!." Given these acid criticisms, it is realistically admissible that researchers and practitioners investigate a better approach to conceptualising, teaching, denoting, and computing software size. The KLOCs approach does not address the problems of software systems especially, with respect to* Object Oriented Technology. *Worse still, in the special area of software quality and software complexity measurements, KLOC technique complicates our measures of software systems. The reason is simple. LOC is not an attribute of software behaviour.* As the abstract discipline of the assignment of numbers to the objects of our observations, measurement must concern itself with the manifest properties of the target object. For example, nesting, size, reachability, cohesion, modularity, well-structuredness, hierarchy, etc., are ***bona fide*** fundamental candidates for software measurements. But, LOC does not measure them. On another metrical front, ***EFFORT*** is a measure of human capability; ***software has no "effort"***. Worse still, it is further known that many of the advocates and experts of KLOCs don't really believe in the logical relevancy of its applicability to software measurements. And ***Function Point,*** an estimation technique based on expert opinion has its share of acidic criticisms. It imports some factors that are strictly not components of software; and employs an unsound mathematics-- Files * Inquiries * G, etc. With ***graph-theoretic techniques***, the critics have prevailed.

Yes! An alternative and practically better model does exist in the literature of Software Engineering [2, 4]. This model based on the ***Tree Structure,*** presents software size in the language of ***component theory*** or ***Units Of Thought, UOT*** *or* units of functionality, *or just simply,* classes of objects. *It is founded on the empirical thesis that* **as the number of functions in a given software system grows/diminishes, so does its size proportionally increase/decrease.** *This concept of proprtionality determines intrinsically how to logically compute software size. It is imperative to observe* that this methodology has **completely and practically nothing outside of** ***software behaviour*****:** *storage devices,* weighting functions, complexity adjustments; no subjectivities; no ambiguities; no questionnaires, and none of the *cost-prohibitive* ***data-gathering*** that is used in this pure computation. *In addition,* ***this*** **Tree methodology** ***is perfectly independent of***

> ***programming languages;***
> ***programming methodologies;*** **and**
> ***programming environments.***

This is pure measurement.

Besides that, the model is derived as a formula using a simple mathematical notation *[1-2] that concretely describes the* **Software Refinement Process.** *And our measure must satisfy the three Mathematical Postulates of a Measure Function, viz.: -*

1. *the measure of the empty set must be zero;*
2. *the measure of a pure subset must be less than that of its superset;*
3. *the measure of a union of sets must not exceed the sum of the measure of its members.*

As **a feedback effect**, *this model can be used even at the requirements phase of the software life cycle. Why wait to measure software size after coding*? But, its greatest merit is in the design phase where it completely and exhaustively exposes the totality of the system's components. These components can be used to control software projects for: allocation, testing, task scheduling. It has other feedback effects to software development [2]:--analysis, design, coding, testing, documenting, and above all, Cost Estimation. Each of notation and feedback effect transcends the results of KLOCs thinking. Furthermore, the component theory is analogous to the modules of electronics engineering whereby each unit of thought, UOT embodies a single function. Each component or UOT defines exactly its own (mathematically) inequivalent class. This philosophy is critical to effective software design and its measurement.

2 Concept and Notation

In mastering this orientation of thinking about software size, it is imperative we realize that certain concepts that are being used with the measurement of software size have no realistic descriptive expressivity about ***software behavior***. Software is abstract even when crafted on physical devices. For instance, a disk or tape is not part of, or component of software. These are ***physical storage devices*** for software; and must not be included in measuring software size. In [2], we defined the new term, software completely and exclusively in terms of ***bits and bytes***.

The rational starting point for understanding software size is ***the Software Refinement Process***. As the fundamental underlying principle behind every known software development methodology, it is justifiably the practical theoretical point to focus the investigation of *software behavior*. *And* in order to advance this investigation, we will introduce an ***effective formal notation*** to portray the software refinement process in consistency with the hierarchical decomposition advocated by structured programming theory. The derivation of this process conclusively vindicates that software size can be best conceived as the summation of the inherited but discrete complexes/components of nodes/classes.

In [2; section 1.5], an extensive summary was presented on the inexorable influence of ***formal notations*** for the rapid advancement of the sciences especially, mathematics. This traditional elucidation of a perplexing problem towards formal application has become very critical for the science of software metrics if it is to free "software engineering" from ordinary craft and art to a scientific discipline. This is the popular anticipation of the advocates. The obstacle arises from the traditional perception of software as masses of Lines-Of-Code. This obstacle has greatly diminished the potentials for software measurements. But, viewed as models of ***input/output, i.e., as COMPONENTS***, the realistic solution is illuminatedly resolved.

In the language of units-of-thought, the notation, Δ denotes an arbitrary component of software module/system (inclusive). In the language of systems, it is called the ***COMPLEX***; in the language of abstraction, it is called ***the OBJECT***; in the language of trees, it is called the ***NODE***. Henceforth, any two of the ***three*** will be used synonymously. *In the philosophy of object oriented thinking, t*his concept of software size is the ideal in software design. Now, our primary goal will be to exploit this notation to formally generate ***a tree structure*** in consistency with the paradigm of ***hierarchical abstraction*** of software refinement process whereby the tree structure results from the ***hierarchical ordering of the nodes***. With this formal organization, the task of computing software size reduces naturally to merely counting the nodes of the tree; every software module is finite. Essentially, this tree diagram simply plays the equivalent role of traditional architectural designs. The engineer must see form and function in some unified pattern.

The notation, Δ was first introduced in [3] for the purpose of formalizing the hierarchical decomposition. Since then, it has been successfully tested [1, 2] and applied to advance the research, development, modeling, and application of formal software metrics. When properly realized, this notation can technically become the intellectual device for *controlling software productivity*, an idea/tool whose time is overdue. Its ramifications to the developments of several other models of formal software metrics [2] have really been serendipitous. An effective notation is the inspiration for scientific advancement of ideas. Every science must have its own method of investigation.

According to this philosophy, the initial problem serves as the ***root node*** of the module/system (itself represented as the ***Delta Notation*** without subscripts and superscripts). And the ***iteration*** of the refinement process begins here in total and complete consistency with the advocacy of the theory of structured programming [1, 2, 3]:

- ***first,*** refine the root node to obtain all its explosion numbers or child nodes at level, L = 1;
- ***second,*** refine *EACH* node at level 1 to obtain its explosion numbers on child nodes at level, L = 2;
- ***third,*** repeat this for every child node at level 2 to obtain its child nodes at level, L = 3;
- ***subsequently,*** continue this *iteration* until every node at level L = K is refined completely to irreducibility (i.e. , to prime nodes or leaves/leaf) at level L = K + 1.

  Symbolically, continuing our formal notation, we have:

  at level, L = 1; an arbitrary node is $\Delta_p^{<0>}$;

  at level, L = 2; an arbitrary node is $\Delta_q^{<0,p>}$;

  at level, L = 3; an arbitrary node is $\Delta_r^{<0,p,q>}$;

  ;

  ;

  at level, L = K; an arbitrary node is $\Delta_j^{<U>}$;
  for p, q, r, j = 1, 2, ..., K; and
  <U> = <0, p, r, ..., v>.

The complete form, $\Delta_j^{<U>}$ which traces the origination of each node together with its explosion number denotes an arbitrary component of software [module/system]. It is crystal clear that according to this notation, every node *representation* is *UNIQUE; and can be conveniently addressed/documented as such. This is a strong feedback effect to software productivity. Observe that we have here obtained a mapping* of our software onto some tree.

In applications, any given node may be used to generate an L-level/Height/Depth tree using the closed form [1, 2]:

$$\mathbf{T_L = \{[\ \Delta_j^{<U>}\ ]\ \mid\ 1 \leq |<U>| \leq L;\ j = 1, 2, ..., k\};}$$

where |<U>| means the cardinality of the sequence, <U>. The signature, **<U>** is called the node's ***Trace of Hierarchy, TOH.*** It traces the genealogy/ancestry of the node.

In summary, a node refines into K (hereditary) child nodes; each j of K is called an ***explosion number***; K = max{j} is called its ***twin number*** [1, 2, 4]. The root's twin number will be specially exploited in the computation of software size. This ***formal ordering*** of the nodes (fig. 2.1) gives the system a logical structure that enhances ***the working*** and ***teaching*** and ***measuring*** of software systems. Contrary to conventional KLOC thinking, software is not a mass of codes; the proper hierarchical organization or integration of software components spells better management.

The simple derivation of this tree together with its several applications and feedback effects advances software metrics to a science. Fenton and Whitty [6] independently observed it in their ***Prime Decomposition Theorem*** and Fenton concludes [5; p. 177]-- "We will now show that this tree is all we need to define a very large class of interesting measures.". **In another perspective, Fenton [6; p. 190] supports the proposal to measure software size in terms of nodes--** "*Size*: which may be measured as *number of nodes, ..*".

3 Computations of Software Size

Presently in industry and research, software size is not known or even computable until after the coding sub-phase long after several surgical operations have been performed on the software module (and the result of this measurement has remained the acidic ferment of criticisms). The negation of this practice is one primary triumph of this application, the delta notational methodology. An added advantage of this goal is that we can henceforth compute software size at the initial phase of the SLC, the Requirements Definition. At this phase, the application of units-of-thought can best define the logical path to effective software development and maintenance. But first, the following four definitions set the standard for meaningful computations/measurement of software size based on the properties of software behaviour.

Definition 3.1: Node/Object/Complex/Unit-of-Thought

A node or object or complex or UOT is an *independent but internally consistent* sequence of instructions [BITS and BYTES] of software module/system (inclusively).

The notion of "independence" implies meaningful entity-hood. (A node/object/complex/UOT is often a noun or noun phrase implying some functionality about the object.

Familiar examples are:-- DO-------CONTINUE, DO------END; BEGIN------END; PROCEDURE, FUNCTION, PACKAGE, SUBROUTINE, MODULE, METHOD, SECTION, PARAGRAPH; {...... }, etc., etc.

Definition 3.2: A Module

A *module* is an independently compilable sequence of complexes (*modified from Myers [7]).*

Definition 3.3: Module Size

The size of a module is defined as the total number of components or nodes/objects or units-of-thought refined out of its root node (and this excludes the root node). The unit of measure is NODE.

However, researchers in software metrics are currently not addressing this physical necessity theory of measurements called **units and dimensions** *or* **units of measure***; a practice that implies incomplete result and/or inadequate knowledge.* The idea of "units of measure" establishes our intuitive persuasion of the metrical denomination of shape or mold or "embodiment"-- linearity, fluidity, liquidity, weight, area, etc.

Definition 3.4: System Size

The size of a system, is defined as the total number of constituent modules within the system and excluding the root node *(a System is a combination of modules).* The unit of measure is m*odules.*

Example 3.1: MODEL FORMULA FOR COMPUTING SOFTWARE SIZE

As promised earlier, we now show how to exploit the root's twin number to compute software size (fig. 2.1). The ***UOTs*** *or objects of refinement are naturally distributed along the various* ***topological legs of nesting*** *(a topological leg of nesting is a genealogical ordering of nodes also, called the* **Trace of Hierarchy, TOH***).* For each such topological leg, we obtain a simple count of its nodes. The complete iteration leads to the computable (can be automated) model formula:

$$\textbf{Software } \textit{Size}, S_z = \sum_{i=1}^{T} \sum_{j=1}^{l} \sum_{k=1}^{n} U_{ijk}.$$

where ***n*** = *number of nodes per nesting;*
l = *level/Height/Depth of nesting;*
t = *twin number of the root node; and*
l = *|<u>| - 1.*

"CLEARLY, A SIMPLE FUNCTION IS BOUNDED AND MEASURABLE." [7; p. 155].

FUNCTION NOTATION CONVENTION IN TM: We here remind the *reader that the above result is a simple mapping*

$$\mu : E ===> R = (R, *, +),$$

the real number system where $E = (Xn_j , T)$*, the set of node-attributes of tree,* ***T*** *(has several attributes). Our mapping becomes the* ***ASSIGNMENT***

$$S_z <=== \mu\ (E = \{Tree\ Nodes\}) = (R, *, +);$$

here our identified empirical elements are the n_j *,* T*. In short, E carries the message of relevant Software Behaviour. This is the strategy/practice adopted throughout TM.*

Example 3.2: SOFTWARE SIZE/MASS @ CODING

The generalized model formula in example 2.1 (given for the primary purpose of formalization) simply requires counting the nodes on each topological leg of the root node. Empirically, we can state with some demonstrative proof, the theorem:

THEOREM 3.1 [NODES/OBJECTS OF A CODED MODULE]:
Every coded version of a well-structured *software module/system has some representative tree structure. (See [2] for derivation; see also, EXAMPLE 3.2 of [1]).*

LESSON: *Poorly Structured systems are difficult to measure.*

Now that we have measured, "we know" [Clarke Maxwell]. As a coclusion, let's now demonstrate Fenton's assertion [5; p. 177] viz. "We will now show that this tree is all we need to define a very large class of interesting measures.", by introducing the measure of ***Structural Complexity,*** S_c [1, 2, 4], another member of the classes of software complexity:

$$S_c \Leftarrow\!\!== \mu\ (E = \{H, t, M\}\ , T) = (R, *, +) \textbf{ becomes:}$$
$$S_c = \mu\ (H, t, M) = H * t * M;$$

where H = Height/Depth of the tree = max{L}; and M = Monadicity (the total number of leaves of T); where we have by experience, interpreted the phenomenon of Structure Complexification multiplicatively. The rationale is that increasing any of H, t, M empirically ***complexifies*** the task of the programmer; and conversely. This is the true meaning of ***Software Behaviour***. We choose the ***unit of measure, Plexigram.*** *S_z has the physical expression of numerousity; and S_c* has that of "weight"; (in fact, Dr. H. D. Mills once wrote that "complexity has weight"). Observe that although, each of S_c and S_z is a category/class of software complexity S_c is computationally multiplicative; while S_z is additive. **Who says *S*oftware *C*omplexity is additive?**

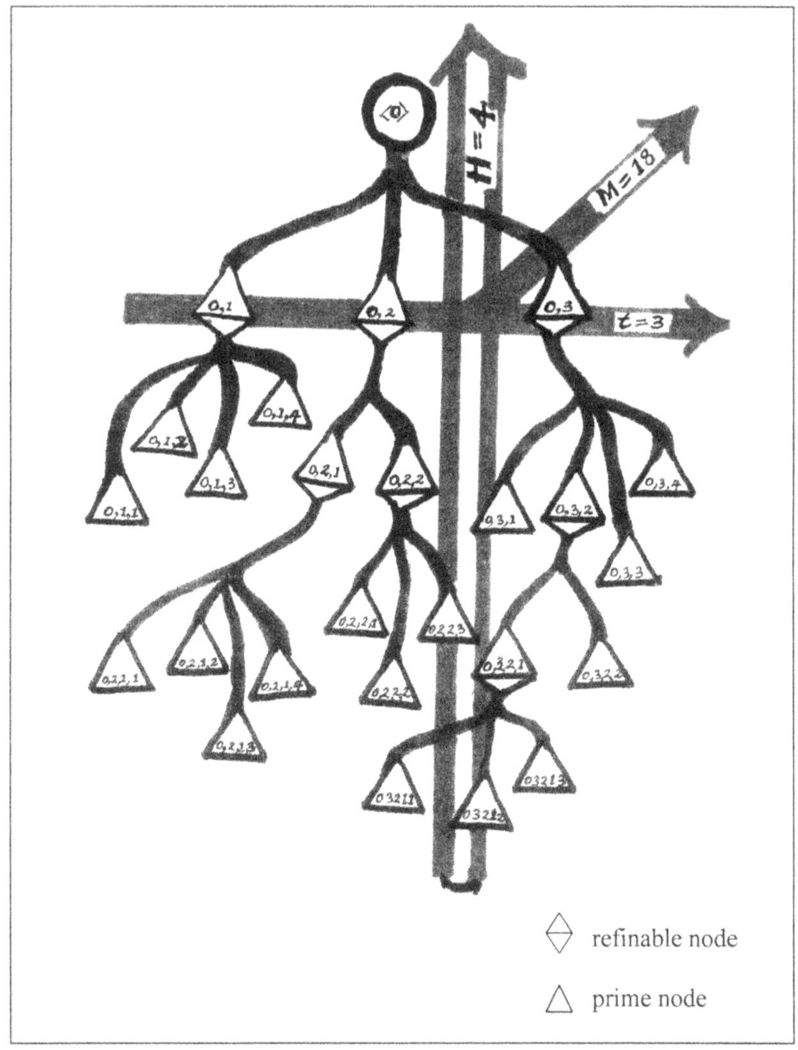

Figure 2.1: Hierarchical Mapping of Module Components Onto Tree Nodes.
© Softmetrix, Inc., 1998

References

[1] **Ejiogu, Lem O.**
Beyond Structured Programming: An Introduction to the Principles of Applied Software Metrics. in vol 11 #1, 1990 Journal of Structured Programming, Springer-Verlag, New York, Berlin.

[2] **Ejiogu, Lem O.**
Software Engineering with Formal Metrics. QED Publishing Group/John Wiley & Sons, New York, NY, 1991.

[3] **Ejiogu, Lem O.**
Effective Structured Programming. Petrocelli Books/TAB Books, Blue Ridge, Pa., 1983.

[4] **Ejiogu, Lem O.**
A *Simple Measure of Software Complexity*. in IN-DEPTH/11 - 16 of COMPUTERWORLD, April 2, 1984. **REPRINTED IN:** (ACM) SIGPLAN NOTICES vol 20 #3 (1985); and (ACM) PERFORMANCE EVALUATION vol 13 #1 (1985).

[5] **Fenton, Norman E.**
Software Metrics: A Rigourous Approach. Chapman & Hall, London, 1991.

[6] **Fenton, N. E. and Whitty, R. W.**
Axiomatic Approach to Software Metrication Through Program Decomposition. Computer Journal vol29 #4 (1986); 329-339.

[7] **Munroe, M.E.**
Introduction to Measure and Integration. Addison-Wesley Publishing Co., Reading, Ma, 1953, 1959.

[8] **Myers, Glenford J.**
Composite/Structured Design; Van Nostrand Reinholdt, New York, NY, 1978.

[9] **Pancake, Cherri M.**
The Promise and the Cost of Object Technology: A Five-Year Forecast. in Communications of the ACM vol 38 #10 (Oct1995).

APPENDIX

1. **FUNDAMENTAL THEORETICAL PRINCIPLES OF FOUNDATION FOR TM:**
    1. **GOOD NEWS=> *The language of Structured Programming is Metrication. This is the first observation – practicality of metrication.***
    2. ***PRINCIPLE OF PURITY*** [Independence of EXTERNALS]: TM imports nothing outside of Software Behaviour-- files, weighting functions, no data gathering, no questionnaire, etc.
    3. ***Independence of Programming Determinisms:--*** *programming languages; programming methodologies;* and programming environments.
    4. ***Scientific Principle: In the sciences, the Tree Structure is a*** **"UNIVERSAL PRINCIPLE".**
    5. ***Software Engineering Principle-1:*** *The* ***Software Refinement Process*** is itself the very fundamental underlying principle behind every software project development. It is a ***"UNIVERSAL PRINCIPLE"***.
    6. ***Software Engineering Principle-2:*** **The Hierarchical Decomposition *PRINCIPLE*" of Structured** Progrmming is also, a "*UNIVERSAL PRINCIPLE.*

    NOTE/cf: COMPLEXITY reflects the intrinsic attributes of behaviour incarnate within a system; and QUALITY reflects the elegance built into the system by the designer/programmer.

2. **FEEDBACK EFFECTS OF** TM:

    Simplifies Software Measurements via, CLASSIFICATIONS of:

    1. **SOFTWARE COMPLEXITY** (becomes imperative and self-evident) The Tree Methodology, ***TM*** measures some of them directly: Size; Structural; Psychological; Reachability; Cost; Hierarchy; Twinning; Nesting; Computational; etc.; AND
    SOFTWARE QUALITY (designer's perfection of excellence):
    Entropy; Stability; Refinement; ....;
    Structuredness/modularity, ...);
    Reliability (sub-classes: ....);
    Testability (sub-classes: Test/Path Coverage .);
    Maintainability (sub classes: duration, efficiency, ...)
    Cohesion (sub-classes: function, module, ...);
    Coupling (sub-classes: data, function, module,);
    ....; etc.; etc.; ....).
    Feedback Effect as introduced by TM is the sub-conscious goal behind the critical search for Software Metrics-***the improvement of***

the software process. What is a metric if it is just a number? The purpose of a metric is not the creation of numbers; but, the improvement of the things we do. For example, adherence to node inequivalence can reduce (functional) Cohesion; yet another feedback is in Program Slicing (for compiler designers and testers).

2. ***The Empirical Benefit to Software Maintenance: We can very easily ADD/DELETE a node TO/FROM this tree, T without perhaps, affecting others. The Reachability metric can reconstruct structure.***
3. Software Capability Measurement becomes a science [Permits statistical computations; Not included here, per se; but, to be introduced in Forthcoming Work];
4. Software Certification finally becomes a practical goal.

Multidimensional Software Performance Measurement Models: A Tetrahedron-based Design

Luigi Buglione, Università di Roma (Italy) and
Alain Abran, Université du Québec à Montréal (Canada)

Abstract

*This work presents an improved version of an open multi-dimensional model of performance, called **QEST** (**Q**uality factor + **E**conomic, **S**ocial and **T**echnical dimensions) [8]. Performance is defined here as productivity adjusted by quality, both of which can be represented from multiple viewpoints. The QEST model integrates into a single representation three dimensions, each one represented by a productivity measurement value derived from an instrument-based measurement process, which value is then adjusted by a perception-based measurement of quality achieved. Both components of performance, that is productivity and quality, take into account the same three distinct viewpoints of performance:*

- ***economic dimension**, the perspective is the managers' viewpoint, with particular attention paid to cost and schedule drivers;*
- ***social dimension**, the perspective is the users' viewpoint, with particular attention paid to the quality in use drivers;*
- ***technical dimension**, the perspective is the developers' viewpoint, with particular attention paid to technical quality.*

1 Introduction

Measures are increasingly being recognized as fundamental to adequately assessing current software practices and software products and to setting realistic targets when designing improvement programs.

The focus of this work is software products, which are to be measured and assessed through a three-dimensional measurement model with the ability to handle independent sets of dimensions without predefined weights.

Such a generic three-dimensional structure will allow organizations to choose the components of each dimension according to their own needs and will give them the ability to select relevant measures and to implement them. This type of model will be referred to here as an *open multi-dimensional model of performance.*

The paper is subdivided into three parts:

- a descriptive part, presenting the conceptual aspects of this open model, including its structure and components;
- a mathematical part, presenting the mathematical expressions for tetrahedron-based geometrical figures;
- a procedural part [2], with the description of the steps required to implement the model in a specific environment.

2 Measurement of performance

In a competitive market period such as the current one, company competitiveness strongly depends on myriad types of factors such as the capability to react on time to customers' requests and the minimization of costs of goods and services offered. Monitoring these factors and their impact on the development process is increasingly critical. Therefore, measuring performance levels becomes a key component for improving the planning, monitoring and delivery of goods and services, as well as for the design of improvement programs.

Performance is not a single one-dimensional concept: it is not enough to meet a specific target in an unconstrained environment. It is a multidimensional concept that must integrate multiple viewpoints, most of which are present simultaneously in the software development process, such as:

- the **E**conomic one, represented by the managers' viewpoint;
- the **S**ocial one, represented by the users' viewpoint;
- the **T**echnical one, represented by the developers' viewpoint.

Performance models in the software engineering literature mostly take into consideration the first and third of the viewpoints listed above, and handle them separately. Because of a growing involvement of users with computer technologies, the second viewpoint should also be taken into account in software assessment, thereby adding complexity to performance measurement when three dimensions have to be taken into account simultaneously. If the three dimensions can be handled concurrently in an integrated mode, then such types of models can more adequately represent performance measurement.

In the literature survey, three studies were identified as dealing with multidimensionality in software performance measurement, although sometimes from distinct perspective of performance, as well as three distinct approaches:

- in Gonzales [11] a **vectorial approach** is proposed to measure software complexity, always considering a 3D space; the three *dimensions* are given by Length, Time and Level for each of the three complexity domains

(Syntactical, Functional, Computational) with a list of predefined and non-normalized complexity factors and measures;

- in Hatfield [12], the measurement of product performance is defined as the single viewpoint related to product assessment (asset / customer-project / strategic management) as a *dimension*, but it represents the 3D concept through a **cube** and uses only a single non-normalized measure per dimension;
- in Donaldson & Siegel [10], *n* different normalized measures are used to define the "product integrity value" (and not the single interest group) as a *dimension* using a vectorial approach, representing the concept in a 2D space through the use of **Kiviat graphs**.

The model proposed in this paper to combine these assessments from the three dimensions within a single value to determine performance is referred to as the **QEST model** (**Q**uality, and **E**conomic, **S**ocial and **T**echnical productivity).

The QEST model proposes the use of a certain number of measures not predetermined by the model itself (not as in Gonzales and Hatfield) and expresses the performance measuring concept with a 3D construction (rather than a 2D one, as in Donaldson & Siegel), and with a pyramidal representation (3 sides - 3 viewpoints) rather than a cubic one (4 sides - 3 viewpoints, as in Hatfield); QEST proposes a geometrical representation of performance with the same number of sides as the number of viewpoints considered.

Another unusual feature of the QEST model is the following: the measurement of performance (**p**) is given by the *integration* of an instrument-based measurement process (expressed in the model by the component **RP** - *Rough Productivity*) with a perception-based measurement process based on the subjective perception of quality - and expressed in the model by the component **QF** - *Quality Factor*).

In summary:

Performance = Productivity and Quality

Performance = PR and Q

Performance measurement = (Instrument-based measurement of Productivity) and (Perception-based measurement of Quality)

3 The structure of the QEST model

The QEST model provides a multi-dimensional *structured shell* which can then be filled according to management objectives in relation to a specific project, and can therefore be referred to as an *open model.* This section presents the design of this *open model* for the measurement of software project performance, making it possible to handle the multiple and distinct viewpoints already discussed, all of which exist concurrently in any software organization.

The basic purpose of the structured shell of the open model is, as stated above, to express performance as the combination of the specific measures (or sets of measures) selected for each of the three dimensions, these values being derived from both an instrument-based measurement of productivity and a perception-based measurement of quality.

A three-dimensional geometrical representation of a tetrahedron was selected as the basis of the model and is illustrated in Figure 1.

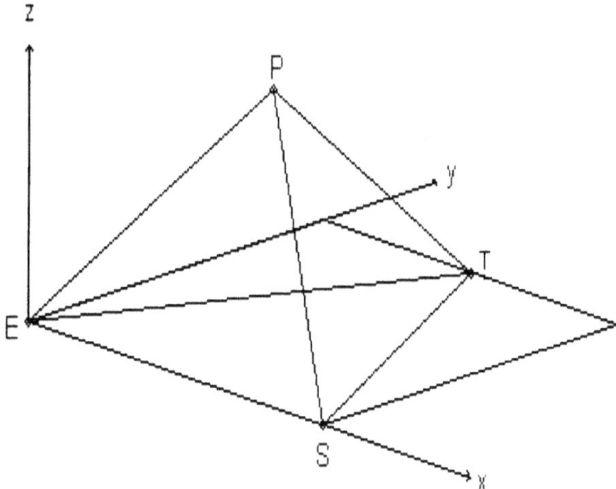

Figure 1: Regular tetrahedron with E, S, T dimensions as base axes and performance P as vertex

This open model can be represented as a *regular tetrahedron* in a three-dimensional space where[1]:

- the three dimensions (E, S, T) in the space correspond to the pyramid base corners and the convergence of the sides, the P vertex, which describes the top performance level;

[1] To obtain a less complex geometrical formula, the ES line on all Figures is put on the X axis, which is just one of the possible positions it can assume in a 3D space. The other sides of a tetrahedrom being at 60 degrees, the other sides will not be on the y or z axes. Knowing the geometrical relations between measures in a regular triangle with sides of unit length, it is possible to obtain the other point coordinates easily. Note that H point represents the center of the base of the regular tetrahedron, expressed in Figure 3.

- when the three sides are of equal length, the solid shape that represents this three-dimensional concept is therefore a pyramid with its triangular base and sides of equal length (*tetrahedron*).

This pyramid-type representation imposes the following constraint: the sides must be equal, and this is achieved through giving equal weights to each of the three different dimensions chosen – and with sides of length exactly equal to 1 (*regular tetrahedron*); in this way, the dimensions are represented through a normalized value between 0 and 1 for each of them on a ratio scale, for ease of understanding.

For any specific project, its value on each dimension is given by the weighted sum of a list of *n* normalized measures having been selected as representative of each of the three viewpoints. The selection of the specific measures within each dimension is an implementation issue.

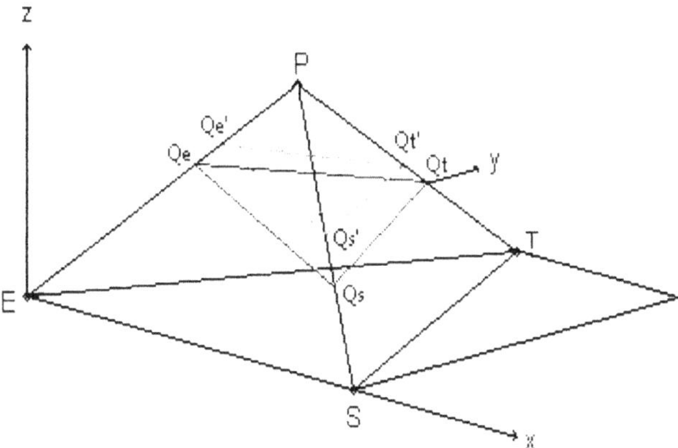

Figure 2: (Qe,Q s,Q t) and (Qe',Q s',Q t') plane sections

The values of the three dimensions, shown in Figure 2 as (Qe, Qs, Qt), each placed on its tetrahedron side, describe a sloped plane section in the space and return the three-dimensional productivity measurement.

The three-dimensional measure of quality (QF) represents a three-dimensional weighting factor of the productivity measurement representation. From a geometric viewpoint, it is representable through an upward or downward translation of the (Qe, Qs, Qt) section describing the new (Qe', Qs', Qt'), if the project quality characteristic value is greater or smaller than a predetermined quality target for each dimension. The determination of specific target values is again an implementation issue.

Refer to the new sloped section for every calculation.

According to some notions in analytic geometry [6, 19], it is possible to determine the equation of the (*Qe'*, *Qs'*, *Qt'*) sloped section, the one referred to as the arithmetic sum of the productivity and quality measurement.

Consider the economic dimension, for example. The formula for determining the translated point will be $\boxed{e' = e + QF}$, where e is the Economic Productivity value and QF the Quality Factor.

After (e, s, t) index calculation and knowing the E, S, T, P coordinates:

$$E = (0,0,0); S = (1,0,0); T = \left(\frac{1}{2}, \frac{\sqrt{3}}{2}, 0\right); P = \left(\frac{1}{2}, \frac{1}{2\sqrt{3}}, \frac{\sqrt{6}}{3}\right); H = \left(\frac{1}{2}, \frac{1}{2\sqrt{3}}, 0\right)$$

Expressing (e, s, t) coordinates in the 3D space with Qe, Qs and Qt as follows:	and (e', s', t') coordinates with Qe', Qs' and Qt' in the same way:
$\begin{cases} Qe = E + e \bullet \overrightarrow{EP} = \left(\frac{1}{2}e, \frac{1}{2\sqrt{3}}e, \frac{\sqrt{6}}{3}e\right) \\ Qs = S + s \bullet \overrightarrow{SP} = \left(1 - \frac{1}{2}s, \frac{1}{2\sqrt{3}}s, \frac{\sqrt{6}}{3}s\right) \\ Qt = T + t \bullet \overrightarrow{TP} = \left(\frac{1}{2}, \frac{\sqrt{3}}{2} - \frac{t}{\sqrt{3}}, \frac{\sqrt{6}}{3}t\right) \end{cases}$	$\begin{cases} Qe' = E + e' \bullet \overrightarrow{EP} = \left(\frac{1}{2}e', \frac{1}{2\sqrt{3}}e', \frac{\sqrt{6}}{3}e'\right) \\ Qs' = S + s' \bullet \overrightarrow{SP} = \left(1 - \frac{1}{2}s', \frac{1}{2\sqrt{3}}s', \frac{\sqrt{6}}{3}s'\right) \\ Qt' = T + t' \bullet \overrightarrow{TP} = \left(\frac{1}{2}, \frac{\sqrt{3}}{2} - \frac{t'}{\sqrt{3}}, \frac{\sqrt{6}}{3}t'\right) \end{cases}$

Then, starting from the generic equation of a plane in a 3D space:

$$\Pi: \begin{vmatrix} X - x_1 & Y - y_1 & Z - z_1 \\ x_2 - x_1 & y_2 - y_1 & z_2 - z_1 \\ x_3 - x_1 & y_3 - y_1 & z_3 - z_1 \end{vmatrix} = 0$$

it is possible to obtain the sloped section equation:

$$X\frac{(s't' - s' - e't' + e')}{\sqrt{2}} + Y\left(\frac{(s' - 2e's' + e' - 2t' + s't' + e't')}{\sqrt{6}}\right) + Z\frac{(3 - 2e' - 2s' - 2t' + e's' + e't' + s't')}{2\sqrt{3}} + \frac{(e's' + e't' - e' - e's't')}{\sqrt{2}} = 0$$

The sloped section coefficients are therefore:

$$\begin{cases} a = \dfrac{(s'\,t' - s' - e'\,t' + e')}{\sqrt{2}} \\ b = \dfrac{(s' - 2e'\,s' + e' - 2t' + s'\,t' + e'\,t')}{\sqrt{6}} \\ c = \dfrac{(3 - 2e' - 2s' - 2t' + e'\,s' + e'\,t' + s'\,t')}{2\sqrt{3}} \\ d = \dfrac{(e'\,s' + e'\,t' - e' - e'\,s'\,t')}{\sqrt{2}} \end{cases}$$

With this 3D representation (the sloped plane), it is possible to determine and represent performance considering at least three distinct geometrical concepts:

- the **distance** between the center of gravity of the tetrahedron base and the center of the plane section along the tetrahedron height – the greater the distance from zero, the higher the performance level. The inclination angle of the section also represents here additional information about dimensions.

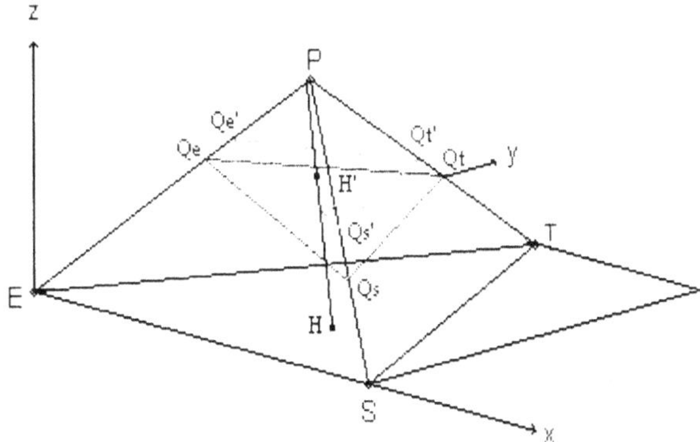

Figure 3: HH' distance

Z is the height of the intersection point between Π plane and the perpendicular straight line to the P vertex. Substituting X and Y values with those of the P point, it is possible to obtain Z as follows:

$$Z = \frac{1}{c}\left(-\frac{a}{2} - \frac{b}{2\sqrt{3}} - d\right)$$

where *a, b, c, d* are the generic coefficients of the sloped section equation.

In the end, this Z value must be translated into the corresponding percentage term. In fact, the height of a regular tetrahedron is equal to $\sqrt{6}/3$, and so the final formula for expressing the *p* index through the distance *g* is the following:

$$p = \frac{g}{\sqrt{6}/3}$$

- the **area** of the sloped plane section – the smaller the area, the higher the performance level. Additional information is also given by the inclination angle of the plane, indicating the best and worst dimensions.

It is possible to make the sloped section area calculation by means of Erone's formula. It is sufficient to know the length of the three sides of the *(Qe', Qs'. Qt')* triangle, called *a*, *b*, *c*, derived as the distance between two points in a 3D space:

$$\begin{cases} a = |Qe'Qs'| = \sqrt{(x_e - x_s)^2 + (y_e - y_s)^2 + (z_e - z_s)^2} = \sqrt{1 + e'^2 + s'^2 - e' - s' - e's'} \\ b = |\vec{Q}e'Qt'| = \sqrt{(x_e - x_t)^2 + (y_e - y_t)^2 + (z_e - z_t)^2} = \sqrt{1 + e'^2 + t'^2 - e' - t' - e't'} \\ c = |\vec{Q}s'Qt'| = \sqrt{(x_s - x_t)^2 + (y_s - y_t)^2 + (z_s - z_t)^2} = \sqrt{1 + s'^2 + t'^2 - s' - t' - s't'} \end{cases}$$

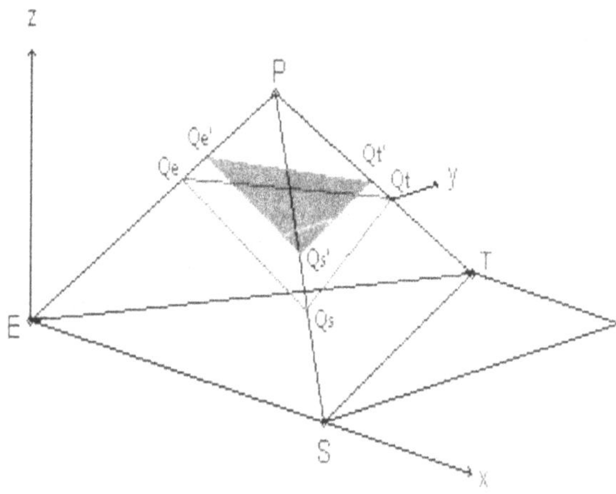

Figure 4: (Qe', Qs'. Qt') Area

The area can be obtained with the following formula:

$$A = \sqrt{sp(sp - a)(sp - b)(sp - c)}$$

where *sp* means the semiperimeter of the triangle. The *p* value is equal to:

$$p = 1 - \frac{A}{A_{max}}$$

where *Amax* is the maximum area value a triangle can have inside a regular tetrahedron, and corresponds to the area of the tetrahedron base, which is equal to $\sqrt{3}/4$ (see Figure 5). The smaller the area, the greater the *p* value. So, it is necessary to consider the ratio between the difference (*Amax* - *A*) on the *Amax* to arrive at an adequate value.

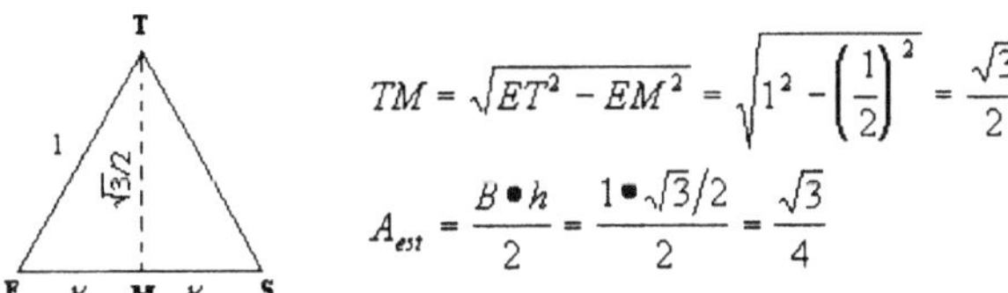

Figure 5: Tetrahedron Base Area

- the **volume** of the lower part of the truncated tetrahedron – the greater the volume, the higher the performance level.

The total volume of a regular tetrahedron is equal to: $V_{TOT} = \frac{l^3\sqrt{2}}{12}$ and, since in this case l=1, the total volume is: $V_{TOT} = \frac{\sqrt{2}}{12}$

It is possible to calculate the volume of the truncated tetrahedron as the difference between the total volume and the volume of the upper solid shape delimited by the sloped section.

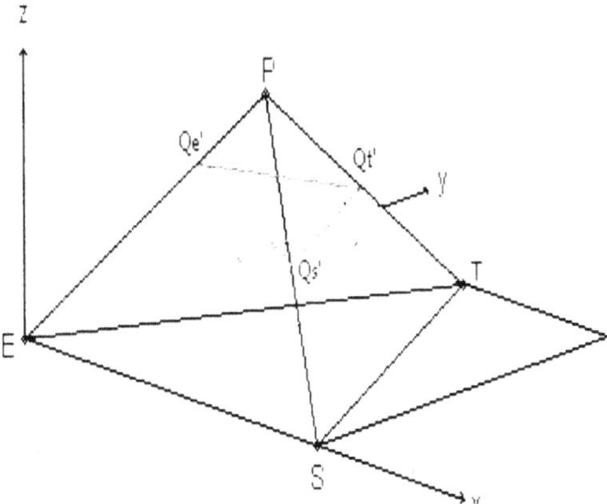

Figure 6: V Volume

It is possible to calculate this volume by determining the distance between the sloped section and the tetrahedron vertex. This distance can be considered to be the height of this oblique pyramid. Substituting the (a, b, c, d) coefficients of the sloped section equation in the following formula

$$h = \frac{|ax + by + cz + d|}{\sqrt{a^2 + b^2 + c^2}}$$

it is possible to obtain the volume from the well-known pyramid volume formula $\boxed{V = \frac{B \bullet h}{3}}$, where B means the sloped section area, calculated above.

So, the *p* value in this last case is equal to:

$$\boxed{p = 1 - \frac{V}{V_{TOT}}}$$

This third type of geometrical information of course carries more information than the previous two types, and it is the concept chosen for our model.

Exceptions. The above-cited formulas are not valid in a few particular cases, as described in the following table:

VALUES	GEOMETRICAL SHAPE EXPRESSED
[e'=1 | s'=1 | t'=1]	*(portion of the) face of the tetrahedron*
[e'=s'=1 | e'=t'=1 | s'=t'=1]	*segment*
e'=s'=t'=1	*point*

because it is no longer possible to determine the p value for all the three geometrical concepts (distance, area, volume) as discussed above[2].

4 Implementation of requirements

A procedure is presented now for the implementation of the QEST model. This procedure follows the **P**lan-**M**easure-**A**ssess-**I**mprove (**PMAI**) cycle, which conforms to the Shewhart and Deming PDCA cycle [9], as shown in Figure 7[3]:

[2] To make it possible to apply the formulas, it is sufficient to consider values very close to 1(using an automatic tool like a spreadsheet).

[3] The new figure is derived from the well-known PDCA representation, and is obtained through a 90° left rotation and by positioning the fourth phase on the vertex of the triangle. The reason for this is that it results in a better fit with the model concept.

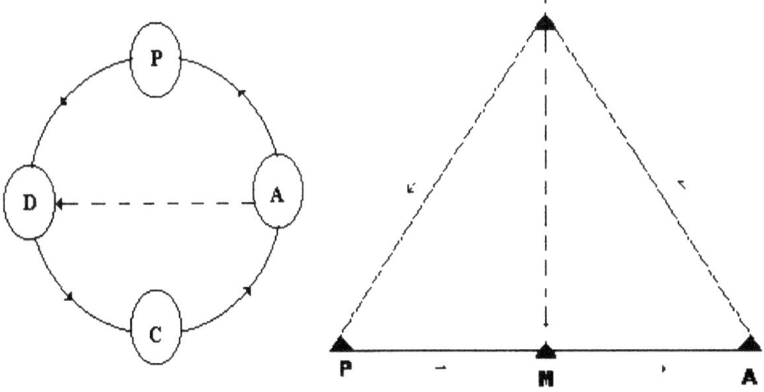

Figure 7: PDCA cycle (on the left) and PMAI cycle (on the right)

PLAN

1. Determination of measurement guidelines
2. Selection of representative measures for each dimension
3. Determination of relative importance between productivity and quality in the assessment of performance for a specific project, or set of projects
4. Determination of ratio weights
5. Establishment of acceptability threshold values

MEASURE

6. Data gathering
7. Application of numerical assignment rules
8. Normalization of the ratios
9. Calculation of QF, V and p

ASSESS

10. Presentation of measurement results
11. Analysis on the observed values

IMPROVE

12. Process Improvement

Various authors have proposed many distinct definitions of **quality**, but, for the purposes of this work, the definition of quality in [15] was selected: "the totality of features and characteristics of a product or service that bear on its ability to satisfy stated or implied needs." Referring to product quality, specifically that of software, it must be interpreted in light of the concept of

purpose of use, considering both internal attributes (product characteristics) and external ones (aim of use).

Therefore, software quality must also be viewed as the concurrent integration of the three different viewpoints previously mentioned:

- viewpoint of the **user**, for whom software quality is achieved by all the properties required to satisfy correctly and efficiently the present and future real needs of whoever buys and uses it;
- viewpoint of the **developer**, for whom software quality is achieved by "conformity to functional and performance requirements explicitly stated, to development standards explicitly documented and to implied characteristics supposed for every software developed in a professional way" [18];
- viewpoint of **management**, who are "interested in overall quality rather than in a specific quality characteristic [...] and the need to balance the quality improvement with management criteria" [16].

The relative mix of productivity and quality within a specific corporate model will be determined in each instantiation of the model by the corporate Software Measurement Working Group, which will determine the proper proportion between the two components for the project being assessed.

To facilitate ease of understanding and a greater applicability of the examples, *de facto* and *de jure* standards are recommended for the selection of the various measures within specific dimensions, such as:

- **ISO/IEC 9126** – the ISO list of software product quality characteristics and sub-characteristics – used in the Social dimension and the QF calculation;
- **Function Point Analysis**[4] – FPA measurement results can be used for both the Economic and Technical dimensions.

---

[4] The reason for the choice of Albrecht's Function Points Analysis [3, 4, 13, 14] can be summarized in the following points:

- **technology-independent**: an analysis based on external vision of product functionalities permits comparison of products written in different programming languages;
- **pre-development measurability**: Function Points Analysis (FPA) can be also used to estimate application size in the planning phase;
- ***de facto* standard**: Function Points Analysis is widely accepted in the international MIS community. FPA measurement rules are constantly being reviewed by the International Function Point Users Group (IFPUG).

The PMAI steps and sub-steps that represent implementation issues are described in greater detail in [2].

5 Summary

The QEST model addresses the need to obtain a richer multidimensional and integrated view of software performance which would take into account the many aspects - technical, economic and social - that exist concurrently in every organization, often not seen in a single view. Such a generic three-dimensional structure will allow organizations to choose the components of each dimension according to their own needs and will give them the ability to select relevant measures and to implement them. This type of model was referred to here as an *open multi-dimensional model of performance*.

References

[1] **Abran, A.**
Quality – The Intersection of Product and Process. The 6th IEEE International Software Engineering Standard Symposium, ISESS'95, Montréal, Québec, Canada, August 21-25 1995, IEEE Computer Society Press.

[2] **Abran, A. & Buglione, L.**
Implementation of a Three-Dimensional Software Performance Measurement Model. Technical Report, Université du Québec à Montréal, to be published, 1998.

[3] **Albrecht, A.J.**
Measuring Application Development Productivity. Proceedings of the IBM Applications Development Symposium, GUIDE/SHARE, Monterey, CA, 14-17/10/79, 83-92.

[4] **Albrecht, A.J.**
IBM CIS & A Guideline 313, *AD/M Productivity Measurement and Estimate Validation.* 01/11/84.

[5] **Basili, V.R. & Rombach, H.D.**
The TAME Project: Towards Improvement-Oriented Software Environment. IEEE Transactions on Software Engineering, IEEE Computer Society, Vol. 14, No. 6, June 1988, 758-773.

[6] **Borsuk, K.**
Multidimensional Analytic Geometry. PWN, Warsaw, 1969.

[7] **Buglione, L.**
Graphical User Interface (GUI): vantaggi tecnici, economici e sociali, Tesi di Laurea. Università "La Sapienza", Roma, 1995.

[8] **Cavallo, A. & Buglione, L.**
A 3D Software Productivity Measurement Model. in "Software Quality Engineering", Eds: C. Tasso, R.A. Adey & M. Pighin, 1st Software Quality Engineering Conference (SQE 97), May 5-7 1997, Udine, Italy, CMP, 1997, 191-200.

[9] **Deming, W.E.**
Out of the Crisis. MIT Press, 1986.

[10] **Donaldson, S.E. & Siegel, S.G.**
Cultivating Successful Software Development : A Practiotioner's View, Prentice Hall, 1997.

[11] **Gonzalez, R.R.**
A Unified Metric of Software Complexity : Measuring Productivity, Quality and Value. The Journal of Systems and Software, Elsevier Science North-Holland, Vol. 29, No. 1, April 1995, 17-37.

[12] **Hatfield, M.A.**
Managing to the Corner Tube : Three-Dimensional Management in a Three-Dimensional World. IEEE Engineering Management Review, IEEE Computer Society, Vol. 23, No. 3, Winter 1995, 63-68.

[13] **IFPUG**
Function Points as Assets: Reporting to Management. 1992.

[14] **IFPUG**
Function Points Counting Practices Manual (release 4.0) - Chairperson Robin Ragland, Atlanta, Georgia, January 1994.

[15] **ISO**
International Standard 8402: Quality – Vocabulary. 1986.

[16] **ISO/IEC**
International Standard 9126: Information Technology - Software product evaluation – Quality characteristics and guidelines for their use. 1991.

[17] **NASA/GSFC**
Software Measurement Guidebook, Revision 1. Software Engineering Laboratories Series, SEL-94-102, June 1995.

[18] **Pressman, R.**
Software Engineering: a beginner's guide. McGraw Hill, 1988.

[19] **Sernesi E.**
Geometria I. 1/e, Bollati Boringhieri, Torino, 1989.

A Pastry Cook's View on Software Measurement

Frank Niessink and Hans van Vliet, Vrije Universiteit of Amsterdam (The Netherlands)

Abstract

Many frameworks for implementing software measurement exist, ranging from collections of success factors to maturity growth models. One may ask to what extent these guidelines increase the chance of a successful measurement program. To aid in answering this question, we introduce a generic process model for measurement-based improvement. We use this model as a reference model to compare a number of existing software measurement implementation frameworks. From these assessments we conclude that the guidelines given by these frameworks provide a considerable amount of support for the basic activities needed to implement measurement programs. However, we also observe that the guidelines hardly provide any guidance to guarantee successful usage *of the measurement program.*

1 Introduction

Briand, Differding, and Rombach [3] state that `Despite significant progress in the last 15 years, implementing a successful measurement program for software development is still a challenging undertaking.' In this paper we take a closer look at different frameworks in the literature for implementing measurement programs. One may ask to what extent use of these frameworks increases the chance of a successful measurement program. Although this question is difficult to answer, we try to make a start by investigating to what extent these guidelines: (1) agree and disagree with each other, and; (2) cover different aspects of implementing software measurement.

The frameworks for implementing measurement programs we cover in this paper are quite different in nature and structure. This makes a straight comparison of the frameworks rather difficult. Therefore, we have developed an abstract representation of the measurement process, to be used as a reference model in the comparison of the different frameworks discussed in this paper.

This reference model is based on the assumption that measurement itself is never a goal, but is always a means to reach some organizational goal, or to help solve an organizational problem. Hence, we also assume that measurement activities are always performed in combination with other activities needed to solve the problem or to reach the goal; i.e. improvement activities.

These improvement activities change the organization, based on the results of the measurement activities. We call this combination of measurement and improvement activities 'measurement-based improvement'. The reference model presented in section 2 models these activities.

In section 3, we shortly describe five frameworks for implementing measurement programs from the literature. We show how each of these frameworks maps on the reference model. Section 4 then discusses the differences and similarities between the frameworks. Finally, section 5 presents our conclusions.

2 Modeling Measurement-based Improvement

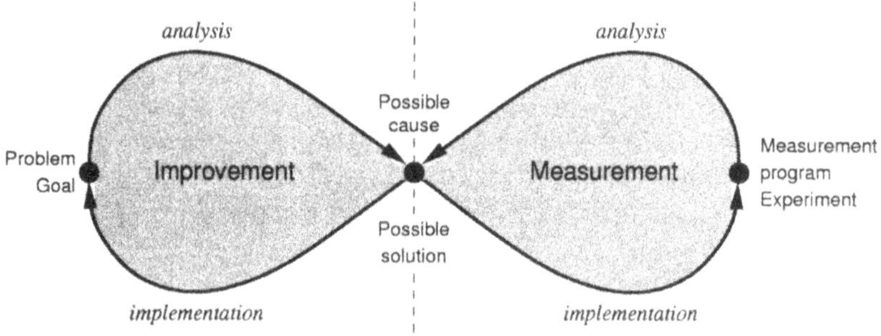

Figure 1: A generic process model for measurement-based improvement

Figure 1 displays a generic process model for measurement-based improvement. It more or less resembles a `pretzel', a loaf of bread in the form of a loose knot[1]. The pretzel consists of two parts--the two halves, three concepts--the black dots, and four steps--the four arrows.

The cycle starts with an organizational problem or goal (left black dot). We do not assume anything about the `size' of the problem or goal. A problem could only affect one developer or the whole organization, in both cases the same steps have to be passed through. The organization analyses the problem (upper left arrow), and arrives at one or more possible causes of the problem and/or possible solutions (middle dot). The analysis will generally be based on a combination of knowledge about the own organization, knowledge from literature (`theory'), and common sense. Next, the organization has to decide whether it has sufficient knowledge to establish the cause of the problem and

[1] Of course, from a mathematical point of view, the figure looks like a lemniscate of Bernoulli. That is, the locus of points P, such that distance(P,p_1) $\times$ distance(P,p_2) = (distance(p_1,p_2)/2)^2, where p_1, p_2 are fixed points called foci.

correct it, or to reach the stated goal. If this is the case, the organization need not traverse the right cycle. In most cases, however, the organization needs to find out which of the possible causes is the real cause of the problem, or which of the possible solutions is the best solution. Or, it may need extra information to implement the solution. To gather this information, the organization can design an experiment or set up a measurement program (lower right arrow). Executing the measurement program or experiment (right dot) results in the gathering of data, which is analyzed and related to the problem or solution at hand (upper right arrow). Finally, the organization solves the problem or reaches the goal by implementing the solutions found (lower left arrow).

Although both the preceding description and the arrows in figure 1 suggest a chronological sequence of steps, this is not necessarily the case. The arrows merely indicate causal relations. Hence, the model does not prescribe a single loop through the lemniscate. It is very well possible for an organization to iterate the right loop a number of times before implementing a solution. For example, it may be necessary to first implement an experiment to find the cause of a problem, and then implement another experiment to find a suitable solution. Moreover, organizations might also want to implement a solution and a measurement program in parallel, to monitor the implementation of the solution.

Let us illustrate the model by means of an example, see figure 2. Suppose a software maintenance organization has problems planning the implementation of change requests. Often, the implementation of specific change requests takes much more time than planned, and the organization fails to deliver the changed software in time. So, the problem this organization faces is the inaccurate planning of change requests (A). After analyzing the problem (*1*), the organization discovers that it does not know which factors influence the time needed to implement change requests (B). The organization decides to investigate this, and designs (*2*) a short-running measurement program (C) to investigate possible factors. After running this measurement program for a limited period of time, the gathered data are analyzed (*3*). We assume that a number of factors are found that influence the effort needed to implement change requests (D). Next, a planning procedure is developed and implemented (*4a*) in which the factors found are used to plan the change requests. An accompanying measurement program (E) is designed (*4b*) to gather the data needed for the new planning procedure and to monitor the accuracy of the planning (*5*).

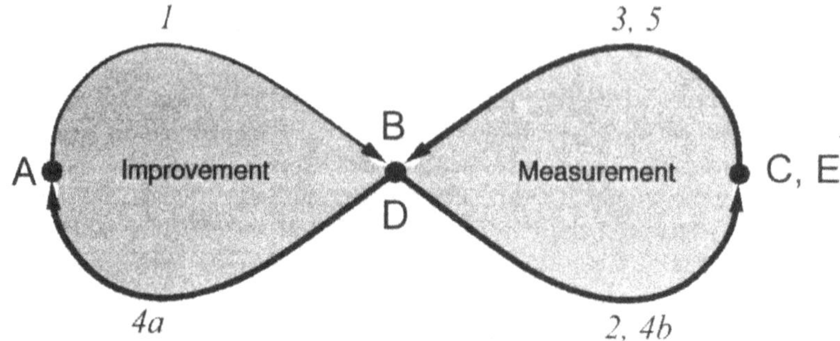

Figure 2: An example of measurement-based improvement

We conclude this section with a few remarks on the nature of the presented generic process model of measurement-based improvement.

First, one could wonder whether this model is prescriptive or descriptive. We assume that if software organizations want to improve their processes or products, and use measurement to support those improvements, they will perform the activities as we have described above. That means we use the model as a representation - though very abstract - of what goes on in reality; i.e. it is a descriptive model. One could argue that the model is also a prescriptive model; it tells us which activities to perform when conducting measurement-based improvement. However, because of the high level of abstraction, the model is probably unsuitable to directly support organizations in their measurement-based improvement efforts.

Second, the model resembles the Goal-Question-Metric paradigm [2]. One could be tempted to map the GQM goal on the left black dot, GQM questions on the middle dot, and the GQM metrics on the right dot. However, the goal of the GQM-paradigm and the goal of the process model are not the same: the goal in the pretzel is an organizational goal, whereas the goal in the GQM-paradigm is a measurement goal. Still, GQM can very well be used to support the design of the measurement program (lower right arrow), see paragraph 3.3.

Third, the distinction made in the model between improvement on the one hand, and measurement on the other hand, corresponds with the distinction made by Kitchenham, Pfleeger, and Fenton [9] between the empirical, real world and the formal, mathematical world. Their structural model of software measurement consists of two parts: an empirical world and a formal world. The empirical world contains entities that can have certain properties, called attributes. The formal world consists of values that measure the attributes of entities, expressed in certain units. Measurement now, is the mapping of a particular entity and attribute from the real world to a value in the formal world. The generic process model reflects the differences between these two worlds: measurement activities (the right half) are concerned with constructing a formal world based on the real world, whereas improvement activities (the left half) are concerned with changing the real world based on the formal world created by the measurement activities.

3 Assessing Measurement Frameworks and Guidelines

In this section we use the generic process model described in section 2 to compare different frameworks for measurement programs. In each subsection we indicate which activities and processes the respective frameworks prescribe, and position these activities and processes on the generic process model.

We discuss five different sources: the Measurement Technology Maturity Model described by Daskalantonakis, Yacobellis and Basili [5]; the Measurement Maturity Model presented by Comer and Chard [4]; the Goal-oriented Measurement Process described by Briand, Differding and Rombach [3]; the success factors for measurement programs by Hall and Fenton [8]; and the Measurement Capability Maturity Model proposed by ourselves in [10].

3.1 The Software Measurement Technology Maturity Framework

Daskalantonakis, Yacobellis and Basili [5] define a framework to be used to assess the measurement technology level of an organization. The article defines five levels of measurement technology maturity, divided into 10 themes, listed in table 1.

1	Formalization of the development process
2	Formalization of the measurement process
3	Scope of measurement
4	Implementation support
5	Measurement evolution
6	Measurement support for management control
7	Project improvement
8	Product improvement
9	Process improvement
10	Predictability

Table 1: The themes of the Software Measurement Technology Maturity Framework

The five levels of maturity are similar to the Software CMM; i.e. initial, repeatable, defined, managed and optimizing. However, the model does not prescribe any processes like the Software CMM does. Instead, the model gives characterizations of each of the ten themes on each maturity level. For example, the characterizations of the third theme, `scope of measurement', look as follows [5]:

Level 1. Done occasionally on projects with experienced people, or not at all.

Level 2. Done on projects with experienced people. Project estimation mechanisms exist. Project focus.

Level 3. Goal/Question/Metric package development and some use. Data collection and recording. Existence of specific automated tools. Product focus.

Level 4. Metric packages being applied and managed. Problem cause analysis. Existence of integrated automated tools. Process focus.

Level 5. Have learned and adapted metric packages. Problem prevention. Process optimization.

The major difference between the approach taken by Daskalantonakis *et al.* and the other approaches described in this paper is that the first uses a more declarative description of the different levels of measurement technology maturity. Instead of describing the activities organizations need to implement, the results of these activities are specified. Other approaches put much more emphasis on the activities and processes themselves that organizations need to implement; i.e. they follow an imperative approach. This declarative nature of the measurement technology maturity framework makes it difficult to map it onto our generic process model. We have to translate the declarative specification of the themes into corresponding activities. Figure 3 shows our approximation of how the ten themes could be placed in the model.

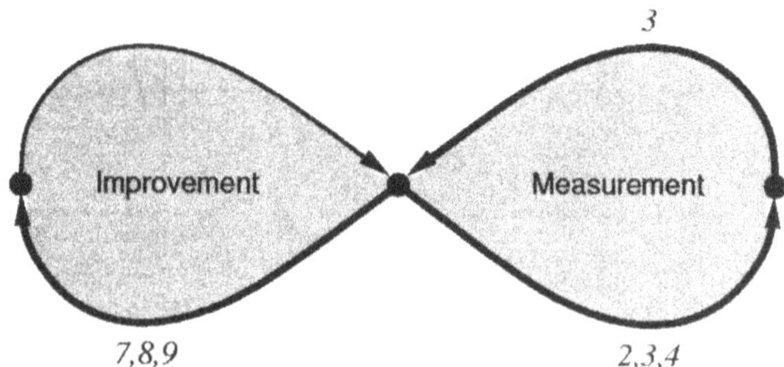

Figure 3: The Software Technology Maturity Framework mapped on the generic process model

Themes two, three, and four are concerned with the implementation of a measurement process. This measurement process includes automation of data collection, evaluation, and feedback. Themes seven, eight, and nine prescribe the usage of measurement data to improve projects, products, and processes, respectively. Unfortunately, the descriptions are more in terms of the results of the improvements than in terms of improvement activities to perform.

The other themes do not fit into the generic model. Theme one is concerned with the formalization of the development process, and essentially coincides with the Software CMM, and hence does not fit into the pretzel. We were not able to translate themes five, six, and ten into corresponding activities. Theme five, `measurement evolution', is concerned with the types of measures that are taken. Measuring different kinds of measures does not necessarily change the activities needed, so wc cannot place this theme in our process model. The same holds for the sixth theme, `measurement support for management control'. This theme is specified in terms of the type of support management receives from measurement. Different types of support do not necessarily require different activities. Theme ten, `predictability', describes how the predictability of measures increases as the maturity level of an organization increases. Again, this theme cannot directly be translated into measurement or improvement activities.

3.2 A Measurement Maturity Model

Comer and Chard [4] describe a process model of software measurement that can be used as a reference model for the assessment of software measurement process maturity. Unlike the maturity models described in sections 3.1 and 3.5, the measurement maturity model of Comer and Chard does not define different levels of maturity. The model consists of four key processes, derived from different sources:

a. **Process Definition** This process includes activities such as: specification of the products, processes, and resources in need of tracking or improvement; identifying goals of the organization and the development environment; derivation of metrics which satisfy the goals.

b. **Collection** Activities in the collection process include defining the collection mechanism, automation of the measurement gathering, implementing a measurement database, and data verification.

c. **Analysis** Data analysis.

d. **Exploitation** Exploitation of analyses to improve the software development process.

Unfortunately, Comer and Chard do not elaborate on the processes `analysis' and `exploitation', which makes it somewhat difficult to map them onto the generic process model. We assume the process `analysis' consists of analyzing the gathered data, and relating the data to measurement goals. The exact borders of the `exploitation' process are undefined. Especially the extent to which this process covers the actual activities needed to improve the software process remains unclear.

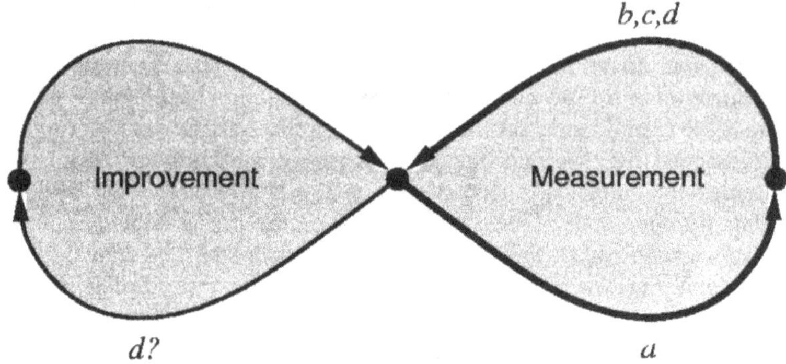

Figure 4: The Measurement Maturity Model mapped on the generic process model

Figure 4 shows how the four processes in our opinion map onto the generic process model. The process `exploitation' has been placed on the lower left arrow with a question mark, because the paper provides insufficient information to decide to what extent that process is meant to cover the implementation of solutions.

3.3 Goal-oriented Measurement

1	Characterize the environment
2	Identify measurement goals and develop measurement plans
3	Define data collection procedures
4	Collect, analyze, and interpret data
5	Perform post-mortem analysis and interpret data
6	Package experience

Table 2: Process for goal-oriented measurement

Briand, Differding and Rombach [3] present a number of lessons learned from experiences with goal-oriented measurement. Goal-oriented measurement is described as `the definition of a measurement program based on explicit and precisely defined goals that state how measurement will be used'. The process for goal-oriented measurement consists of six process steps, displayed in table 2.

During the first step the relevant characteristics of the organization and of its projects are identified. Typical questions to be posed are: What kind of product is being developed? What are the main problems encountered during projects? The characterization is intended to be mainly qualitative in nature. In the second step, measurement goals are defined, based on the characterization made during the first step. Measurement goals are defined according to Goal-Question-Metric templates [1,2], based on five aspects: object of study, purpose, quality focus, viewpoint, and context. Having defined the measurement goals by means of the GQM templates, data collection procedures are defined during step three. Step four is concerned with the actual collection, analysis, and interpretation of the gathered data. Step five puts the data in a broader perspective by e.g. comparing the gathered data of one project with the organization baseline. The final step consists of the packaging the data analysis results, documents, and lessons learned in a reusable form.

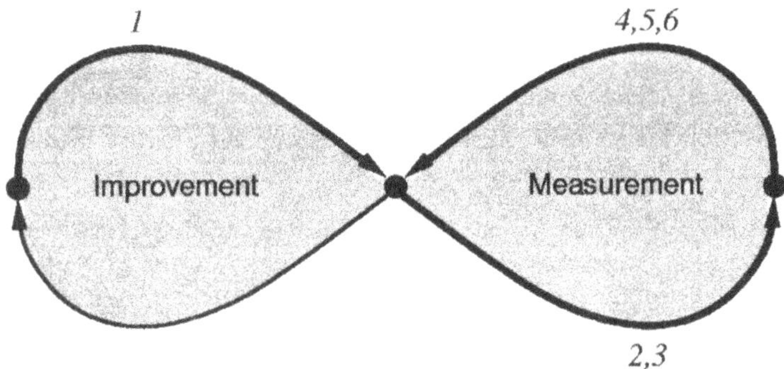

Figure 5: The goal-oriented measurement process mapped to the generic process model

Figure 5 shows how the six steps of goal-based measurement map onto the pretzel. Step one is concerned with the analysis of the organization and its problems and goals, and thus corresponds with the upper left arrow. Steps two and three deal with the translation of organizational goals into measurement goals and the design of the measurement program (lower right arrow). The last three steps consist of the collection, analysis, interpretation, and packaging of the measurement data, hence they belong to the upper right arrow.

3.4 Success Factors for Measurement Programs

1	Incremental implementation
2	Well-planned metrics framework
3	Use of existing metrics materials
4	Involvement of developers during implementation
5	Measurement process transparent to developers

6	Usefulness of metrics data
7	Feedback to developers
8	Ensure that data is seen to have integrity
9	Measurement data is used and seen to be used
10	Commitment from project managers secured
11	Use automated data collection tools
12	Constantly improving the measurement program
13	Internal metrics champions used to manage the program
14	Use of external metrics gurus
15	Provision of training for practitioners

Table 3: Consensus success factors

Fenton and Hall [8] identify a number of consensus success factors for the implementation of measurement programs. Table 3 shows these factors, that were identified after studying other literature, such as [7,11]. A closer look at the success factors shows that they are mainly targeted at reducing the risk of failure. For example, the motivation given by Hall and Fenton for factor six - usefulness of metrics data - is not that the measurement program should have added value for the organization, but rather that the usefulness should be obvious to the practitioners. From the 15 success factors, 10 are targeted at gaining the acceptance of the practitioners involved (4-9, 11, 13-15). The other five factors are concerned with reducing the risk of failure by advocating a gradual introduction and improvement of the program. The measurement program should be incrementally implemented, constantly improved, use existing materials, be supported by management, and a well-planned metrics framework should be used (1-3, 10, 12).

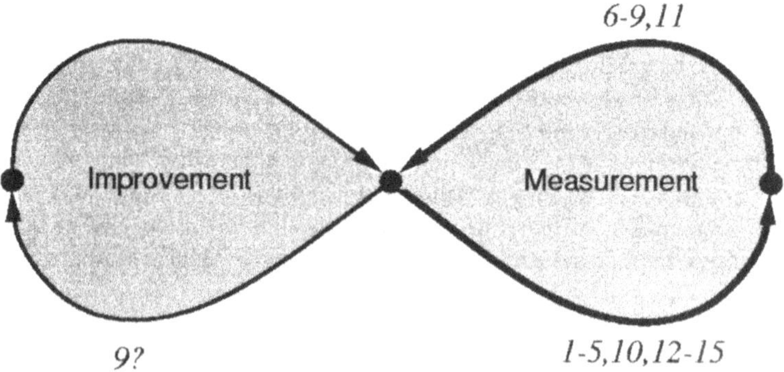

Figure 6: The success factors mapped to the generic process model

Figure 6 shows how the success factors can be mapped onto the generic process model. The majority of the success factors mentioned by Hall and Fenton refer to the implementation of measurement programs. Some are concerned with the collection and analysis part, and only one success factor is concerned with the usage of the measurement data (factor nine). That factor is marked with a question mark, because Hall and Fenton motivate it in terms of acceptance of the measurement program by the practitioners, rather than in terms of added value of the program to the company.

3.5 The Measurement Capability Maturity Model

In [10], we described a number of measurement program case studies. From these case studies we concluded that some organizations are better at software measurement than other organizations. Part of this difference can be explained by the fact that their *measurement capability* is higher; i.e. they are more mature with respect to software measurement. Measurement capability is defined as [10] `the extent to which an organization is able to take relevant measures of its products, processes and resources in a cost effective way, resulting in information needed to reach its business goals.'

Our Measurement CMM defines five different levels of organizational measurement capability, similar to the Software CMM:

1. **Initial:** The organization has no defined measurement processes, few measures are gathered, measurement that takes place is solely the result of actions of individuals.
2. **Repeatable:** Basic measurement processes are in place to establish measurement goals, specify measures and measurement protocols, collect and analyze the measures and provide feedback to software engineers and management. The necessary measurement discipline is present to consistently obtain measures.
3. **Defined:** The measurement process is documented, standardized, and integrated in the standard software process of the organization. All projects use a tailored version of the organization's standard measurement process.
4. **Managed:** The measurement process is quantitatively understood. The costs in terms of effort and money are known. Measurement processes are efficient.
5. **Optimizing:** Measurements are constantly monitored with respect to their effectiveness and changed where necessary. Measurement goals are set in anticipation of changes in the organization or the environment of the organization.

2a	Measurement Design
2b	Measure Collection
2c	Measure Analysis
2d	Measurement Feedback
3a	Organization Measurement Focus
3b	Organization Measurement Design
3c	Organization Measurement Database
3d	Training Program
4a	Measurement Cost Management
4b	Technology Selection
5a	Measurement Change Management

Table 4: M-CMM key process areas

Each of the maturity levels is defined by a number of key process areas that an organization needs to implement. When an organization has implemented all level-two key process areas, the organization is considered to be at level two of the M-CMM. When the organization implements both the level two and three key process areas, it is at level three, etc. The key process areas of the Measurement CMM are listed in table 4, numbered by maturity level.

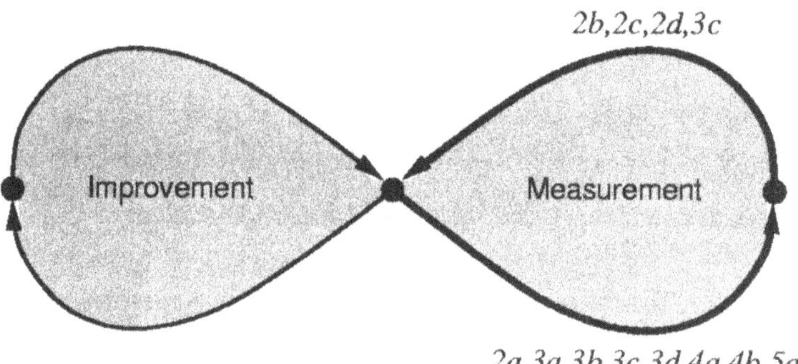

Figure 7: The M-CMM key process areas mapped to the generic process model

Figure 7 shows the M-CMM applied to the generic process model. It is not surprising that all of the key process areas map onto the right half of the 'pretzel'. After all, we made a clear choice in the development of the Measurement CMM to focus on the measurement capability of software organizations, thereby ignoring their capability with respect to improvement. Our argument in [10] was that the improvement capability is already covered by process improvement methods, such as the Software CMM. We assumed that the organizational goals are defined outside the scope of the M-CMM, so they are invariable from a measurement point of view. The measurement process then starts with the translation of business goals into measurement goals, and ends with the interpretation of the gathered data and feedback to the owner of the business goals.

4 Differences and Similarities

In the previous section, we have compared five different measurement program frameworks, using the generic process model for measurement-based improvement. There are a number of issues that deserve attention.

First, if we look at the intersection of the guidelines provided by the different approaches, we see that there is quite some consensus on what activities are needed to successfully design and implement measurement programs. Though the frameworks all stress different aspects of measurement programs, they agree on the basics of measurement programs, such as practitioner support, proper data analysis, feedback, etc.

Second, each of the approaches seems to offer guidelines that the other approaches do not offer. This probably is partly due to the different structure and nature of the frameworks. However, it does suggest that beyond the basic requirements for measurement programs, there are a number of issues on which consensus has not been reached yet. For example, only Briand *et al.* prescribes the packaging of measurement experiences in a reusable form. Of the five frameworks, Hall and Fenton are the only ones to advocate the use of external measurement guru's.

Third, if we look at each of the pretzels used in section 3 to show how the activities of the different approaches map onto the measurement-based improvement process, we see that none of the five frameworks covers the complete cycle. Either the frameworks only cover measurement activities, or they only partly cover the improvement activities. One could argue that this is not illogical, since these measurement program frameworks focus on the implementation of measurement programs, and not on improvement activities. However, failure factors for measurement programs suggest otherwise. Take for example the failure factors for measurement programs as suggested by Verdugo, reported in [6, p. 511]:

1. Management does not clearly define the purpose of the measurement program and later sees the program as irrelevant.
2. Systems professionals resist the program, perceiving it as a negative commentary on their performance.
3. Already burdened project staff are taxed by extensive data-collection requirements and cumbersome procedures.

4. Program reports fail to generate management action.
5. Management withdraws support for the program, perceiving it to be mired in problems and `no-win' situations.

From these failure factors we see that both support from practitioners for the measurement program, as well as management support, is important. A measurement program will fail if practitioners do not see the value of it, but it will also fail if management fails to take action based on the generated data. This means that a successful measurement program needs more than carefully designed metrics, accurate data analysis, measurement databases, etc. It needs to be used. Any measurement program that does not generate any action is to be considered a failed measurement program.

5 Conclusions

In this paper we have introduced a generic process model for measurement-based improvement. We have used this model as a reference model to assess five different measurement program frameworks. These frameworks have in common that they all provide guidelines on how to implement and improve measurement programs. From the assessments we conclude that:

- there is quite some consensus on the basic activities needed to successfully implement measurement programs; but,
- at the same time, different frameworks emphasize widely different aspects of measurement program implementation.

In addition, the assessment also reveals that:

- there is almost no consensus on, nor description of, activities needed to successfully *use* the results from measurement programs.

In a way, this is quite surprising. Usage of the results of measurement programs is probably the most important indicator of success: if the results are not used, the measurement program is doomed to fail. Still, the approaches to implementing and improving measurement programs described in this paper put little emphasis on the actual usage of the measurement results. They mostly concentrate on the implementation of the measurement programs themselves. They provide guidance on the derivation of metrics from goals, suggest a staged implementation, prescribe measurement protocols, etc. But, they do not tell us how to ensure that action will be taken, based on the measurement data.

We do not claim that this is necessarily a shortcoming of the presented frameworks. Most of them implicitly or explicitly focus on the activities needed to successfully implement measurement programs. Nevertheless, organizations implementing measurement programs need to be aware that the usage of measurement program outcomes to improve processes or products is at least as important as a `correct' implementation of the program. After all, like the proof of the pudding, or pretzel, is in the eating, the proof of software measurement is in its usage for improvement.

Acknowledgments

This research was partly supported by the Dutch Ministry of Economic Affairs, projects `Concrete Kit', nr. ITU94045, and `KWINTES', nr. ITU96024. Partners in these projects are Cap Gemini, Twijnstra Gudde, the Tax and Customs Computer and Software Centre of the Dutch Tax and Customs Administration, and the Technical Universities of Delft and Eindhoven.

References

[1] **Victor Basili, Lionel Briand, Steven Condon, Yong-Mi Kim, Walcélio L. Melo, and Jon D. Valett**
Understanding and Predicting the Process of Software Maintenance Releases. In Proceedings of the 18th International Conference on Software Engineering, pages 464-474, Berlin, Germany, May 25-29, 1996. IEEE Computer Society Press.

[2] **Victor R. Basili and H. Dieter Rombach**
The TAME Project: Towards Improvement-Oriented Software Environments. IEEE Transactions on Software Engineering, 14(6):758-773, June 1988.

[3] **Lionel C. Briand, Christiane M. Differding, and H. Dieter Rombach**
Practical Guidelines for Measurement-Based Process Improvement. Software Process - Improvement and Practice, 2(4):253-280, December 1996.

[4] **Peter Comer and Jonathan Chard**
A measurement maturity model. Software Quality Journal, 2(4):277-289, December 1993.

[5] **Michael K. Daskalantonakis, Robert H. Yacobellis, and Victor R. Basili**
A Method for Assessing Software Measurement Technology. Quality Engineering, 3:27-40, 1990-1991.

[6] **Norman E. Fenton and Shari Lawrence Pfleeger**
Software Metrics: A Rigorous and Practical Approach. Int. Thomson Computer Press, second edition, 1997.

[7] **Robert B. Grady**
Practical software metrics for project management and process improvement. Hewlett-Packard Professional Books. Prentice-Hall, Inc., 1992.

[8] **Tracy Hall and Norman Fenton**
Implementing Effective Software Metrics Programs. IEEE Software, 14(2):55-65, March/April 1997.

[9] **Barbara Kitchenham, Shari Lawrence Pfleeger, and Norman Fenton**
Towards a Framework for Software Measurement Validation. IEEE Transactions on Software Engineering, 21(12), December 1995.

[10] **Frank Niessink and Hans van Vliet**
Towards Mature Measurement Programs. In Paolo Nesi and Franz Lehner, editors, Proceedings of the Second Euromicro Conference on Software Maintenance and Reengineering, pages 82-88, Florence, Italy, March 8-11, 1998. IEEE Computer Society.

[11] **Shari Lawrence Pfleeger**
Lessons Learned in Building a Corporate Metrics Program. IEEE Software, 10(3):67-74, May 1993.

Metric for Effective Test Coverage

Vedha Kichenamourty, University of Marne la Vallée, France

Abstract

This paper highlights the concept of a software testing metric designed to improve the software testing effectiveness. The proposed metric ***Metric for Effective Test Coverage*** *is a* ***number of tests*** *metric which can be defined as a ratio between the number of test cases developed(****x****) and the number of test cases to be developed(****y****). The quantity* ***y*** *represents the actual test domain which gives full confidence in achieving the objectives of software testing. The metric focuses on a method to obtain a comparatively attractive value for* ***y****, a test pattern which will insure that all the pair wise combinations of a given set of selection have been exercised. The method builds on the concept of* ***Orthogonal Arrays(OA),*** *a mathematical tool developed by Dr. Genichi Taguichi, which helps to wisely determine the test cases from the large test suite.*

1 Introduction

The proposed metric is a simple and easily definable one which concentrates mainly on blackbox testing. Since functional testing, starts with the input specifications and the possible values for these specifications, the test domain to achieve full coverage is an exhaustive one which is naturally vast and increases the testing efforts. The metric attempts to check these problems by grouping the input specifications and their associated values based on input data partitioning and intelligently selecting the test cases with removed redundant tests. The article is divided into four sections, the first two presenting a theoretical study of various software testing techniques like functional testing, stress testing, robust testing etc., and the concept of software metrics. The third section concentrates on the design of the proposed metric and the last on the application of the proposed metric for functional testing.

2 Software Testing

Software testing is the process of systematic execution of a software under controlled circumstances to check if the software behaves as it is specified. These controlled circumstances include both normal and abnormal conditions. The risk involved with a software problem highly depends on the nature of the software. A computer system to control airplane landings or to direct substantial money transfers requires higher confidence in its proper functioning than does a game simulation program since the consequences of malfunction are severe.

The goal of software testing is to reduce the risk of an erroneous software to acceptable values without much testing efforts. It is more oriented to 'detection'. Among the various available software testing techniques functional tests, stress tests, robust tests are of interest and they are discussed below :

Functional tests

Software testing is functional when test data is developed from documents that specify a function's intended behaviour. These documents include the input specifications and the various possible values they are supposed to take. The goal is to test for each software feature of the specified behaviour, including the input domains, the output domains, categories of inputs that should receive equivalent processing and the processing functions themselves.

Stress tests

Stress testing helps to determine if the system can function when subject to large volumes - larger than would be normally expected. The areas that are stressed include input transactions, internal tables, disk space, output etc. If the application functions adequately under test, it can be assumed that it will function properly with normal volumes of work. The objective of the stress testing is to simulate an environment for determining normal or above-normal volumes of transactions can be processed within the expected time frame and available resources to meet the turnaround times.

Robust tests

Robust testing checks if the software is not prone to errors causing unexpected program crashes. Testing of robustness of the software indeed analyzes the behaviour of the software under plausible alternate assumptions. It attempts to examine the features for which the software is not designed to fit by checking its behaviour on improbable cases.

3 Software Metrics

Software Metrics can be defined as mathematical definitions, algorithms or functions used to obtain a quantitative assessment of the effectiveness of the software product or the process by which it is developed. This quantitative assessment helps to estimate/predict the software product costs and schedules and to measure its quality. Information gained from the metrics can then be used in the management and control of the development process leading to improved results.

An ideal metrics should be

- simple and precisely definable -definition and use of metric should be simple

- objective, to the greatest extent possible
- easily obtainable - the cost and effort to obtain the measure should be reasonable
- valid - it should measure what it is intended to measure
- robust - relatively insensitive to insignificant changes in the software.

Need for Software Metrics

The software development scene is characterized by

- scheduling and cost-estimation that are grossly inaccurate
- poor quality software and
- a productivity rate that is increasing more slowly than the demand for software.

This situation, commonly referred to as the software crisis can be addressed and resolved to the greatest extent possible, with the help of software metrics.

Software Testing Metrics

The main objective of measuring the effectiveness of the software testing process is that the evaluation results can be used to modify the test process. Identifying the ineffective aspects of testing identifies the major areas of improvement. Some of the software testing metrics can be:

(1) Number of tests ***(the number of test cases developed versus the number of test cases to be developed)***

Each and every test case in the test domain consumes information resources and has a greater impact on the test cost. The more conditions tested in a test, the more effective is the test. Moreover, care should be taken to see if the system is not under tested or over tested. Under testing may leaves defects in the software and over testing results in increased test cost efforts. This metric attempts to solve both the problems by determining a measure which gives the ratio between the number of test cases that are developed and to be developed. The strength of the metric lies in the fact that it overcomes the unavailability of a good measuring technique for blackbox testing and its weakness can be the need for a standardized test process to ensure the effectiveness of each test.

(2) User Participation ***(user participation test time divided by total test time)***

The metric attempts to measure user participation in testing on the basis that the more involved the user, the higher the probability that the installed software will meet the user objective. The personnel involved in testing can be end-users, project team personnels, etc. The strength of the metric is that it shows the user interest in ensuring that the software is adequately tested as expressed in terms of their participation in the test process while its weakness can be it is not sure that the user participation expressed in terms of hours of effort may express the extent of testing effort performed by the user.

(3) Test cost ***(test cost versus total system cost)***

Measuring the test cost helps to check if the goal of the testing process is reached with what level of test efforts. This metric identifies the amount of system resources used in the development or maintenance of the testing process. The strength of the metric is that it shows the amount of development effort allocated to testing and the extent of testing. The weakness of the metric can be it may fail to show a direct relationship between the effectiveness of the testing and the cost associated with each test.

(4) Paths tested ***(number of paths tested versus total number of paths)***

The validity of the system can be ensured by testing all the paths involved for their correctness. The metric attempts to demonstrate the extent of the logic paths that have been tested. The strength of the metric is it provides a high degree of assurance that the program will function properly if all the paths are identified and are in effect tested. The weakness of the metric is it does not detect the problems with the code or the requirement specifications. Moreover, it is restricted to white box testing.

4 The Proposed Metric

The proposed metric **"Metric for Effective Test Coverage"** is a *number of tests* metric and builds on the concept of *Orthogonal Arrays (OA),* a mathematical tool developed by Dr. Genichi Taguichi [2], and the Robust Testing^{TM} method [3].

The Orthogonal Approach

Orthogonal Arrays also called as Orthogonal latin squares are *nxn* arrays of the numbers 1, 2, 3,... n such that each number occurs exactly once in each row and in each column. This orthogonality concept is used here to select the test cases intelligently by choosing the minimal number of them that will be required to validate all the possible pair wise combinations in a large test coverage. An Orthogonal array for the above said purpose is a parameter - value table which can be constructed by assigning the parameter of the function to be tested to the columns of the table and their possible values form the integers in the table columns. The unassigned columns are deleted from the table.

Consider a function F(A,B,C) with three parameters A, B, C having two possible values each:

Parameters	**Value 1**	**Value 2**
A	a1	a2
B	b1	b2
C	c1	c2

Table 1: Parameter- value description of function F(A,B,C)

To test all the combinations of the above given set, requires almost eight discrete tests. The following table explains the eight tests required to exhaustively test each parameter value with all the combinations of every other parameter value

Test number	**parameter 1**	**parameter 2**	**parameter 3**
1	a1	b1	c1
2	a1	b2	c2
3**	a1	b1	c2
4**	a1	b2	c1
5**	a2	b1	c1
6**	a2	b2	c2
7	a2	b1	c2
8	a2	b2	c1

** -- tests that are redundant.

Table 2: Exhaustive test table for the function F(A,B,C)

Closely examining Table 2, the redundancy of the tests can be explained as follows:

Test 3 : (a1, b1) (b1, c2) ------ tested in test 1 and test 7 respectively
Test 4 : (a1, b2) (b2, c1) ------ tested in test 2 and test 8 respectively
Test 5 : (a2, b1) (b1, c1) ------ tested in test 7 and test 1 respectively
Test 6 : (a2, b2) (b2, c2) ------ tested in test 8 and test 2 respectively.

Thus the tests 3, 4, 5 and 6 are found to be redundant. Orthogonal arrays allow the use of much smaller subset of test conditions while providing a statistically valid means of testing all the individual components. It places the emphasis on the pair wise combination rather than on the entire one and hence the above exhaustive test table can be reduced as the OA table oa.4.3.2.

Test Number	**parameter 1**	**parameter 2**	**parameter 3**
1	a1	b1	c1
2	a1	b2	c2
3	a2	b1	c2
4	a2	b2	c1

Table 3: Orthogonal test table for the function F(A,B,C)

The OA selection procedure

Once the parameters and their respective values have been chosen, the task of finding a suitable orthogonal array is reduced to selecting the appropriate one from an already constructed list provided by N. J. A. Sloane[Sloane4]. The OA's are represented by the format **OA.k.s.t** with k parameters, s levels and strength t.

Table 1: read the number of functional parameters, K (K equals 3 in Table 1).

Table 2: read the maximum number of levels associated with the parameters, S. (S equals 2 in Table 1).

Table 3: In the standard list, look for an OA, with s and k greater than or equal to S and K respectively. (oa.4.3.2.2)

Table 4: If s and k are strictly equal to S and K respectively, choose OA.s.k.t as the required OA otherwise, choose OA.s.k.t with (k-K) columns removed and repeat important parameter levels of interest (s-S) times.

Application of the proposed metric for functional testing

In order to make the best possible use of *Orthogonal arrays* in obtaining a test pattern containing the smallest subset of test cases form the large test suite, the functional parameters are classified based on their values as parameters with

Table 1: valid values (e.g., valid stream) and

Table 2: invalid and unexpected values (e.g., invalid stream and request for a non existent device)

The parameters with invalid and unexpected values when included with others overrides the testing of other parameter values and in turn makes the test cases useless. Moreover, the test cases for the *unexpected conditions* indicate the tests for the robustness of the functions. For e.g., with fseek(), an unexpected condition like *a request was made of a non-existent device, or the request was outside the capabilities of the device (ENXIO),* are unpredictable ones and testing for such abnormal conditions infact tests for the robustness of the function. Hence these parameters are not considered, while constructing the OA.

Again, the parameters which takes single value are not considered since it helps to select an OA with comparatively lesser number of test runs. Hence a better approach to efficiently test the function is

Table 1: to construct an OA for the valid non single valued parameters

Table 2: include the valid single valued parameters with the resulting test cases and

Table 3: include separate test cases for the invalid conditions and abnormal conditions.

5 Implementation

The proposed metric "Metric for Effective Test Coverage" is applied on a list of functions. The list includes fseek, fread, fopen and fprintf for the various reasons explained below.

Table 1: to test the metric against functions having different number of parameters and values

Table 2: to test the metric with a function having comparatively a larger number of values. E.g., fprintf(). Here, for selecting the appropriate OA, the values for the *mode* parameter namely *escape sequences, conversion specifications* are grouped as parameters, based on input data partitioning since each of them in turn takes a set of possible values.

Table 3: to apply the metric on functions with single valued parameters. e.g., fread and fopen.

Name : **fseek ()**
Format : fseek (FILE *stream, long offset, int whence)

Parameter	value 1	value 2	value 3
file stream	valid		
Offset	positive	negative	zero
Whence	seek_set	seek_end	seek_cur

Table 4: Parameter and value description for fseek

The OA selection process:

Number of non single valued parameters = 2
Number of single valued parameters = 1
Maximum value = 3 (refer table4).

The orthogonal array which appropriately suits is oa.9.4.3.2, with nine test cases, four prearrangers, three levels and strength two. Since the number of non single valued parameters associated with fseek() is two, two columns are discarded from the OA table and the table is depicted below.

Test no.	Offset	Whence	column3**	column4**
1	positive	seek_set		
2	negative	seek_cur		
3	zero	seek_end		
4	positive	seek_cur		
5	negative	seek_end		
6	zero	seek_set		
7	positive	seek_end		
8	negative	seek_set		
9	zero	seek_cur		

** - empty column to be discarded.

Table 5: Orthogonal table for fseek()

Test 1: check for valid file stream with positive offset and seek_set as whence.
Test 2: check for valid stream with negative offset and seek_cur
Test 3: test for valid stream with zero offset and seek_end
Test 4: test for valid stream with positive offset and seek_cur
Test 5: test for valid stream with negative offset and seek_end
Test 6: check for valid stream with zero offset and seek_set
Test 7: check for valid stream with positive offset and seek_end
Test 8: check for valid stream with negative offset and seek_set
Test 9: check for valid stream with zero offset and seek_cur.

and two test case for invalid conditions

Test 10: test for OVERFLOW condition - offset value is beyond the maximum limit.
Test 11: test for INVALID condition - invalid whence argument
Test 12: test for INVALID condition - invalid file stream.

Name : **fprintf ( )**
Format : fprintf (FILE *strm, const char * format, /*args*/)

Parameters	**1**	**2**	**3**	**4**	**5**
file stream	valid				
plain characters	valid				
escape sequences	\a	\b	\n	\t	\v
integer	d	i	o	u	X
real & character	f	e	g	c	s
flags	+	-	space	#	0

Table 6: Parameter and value descriptions for fprintf()

The OA selection process

Number of non single valued parameters = 4
Number of single valued parameters = 2
Maximum value = 5 (refer table8).

The orthogonal array which appropriately suits is oa.25.6.5.2 with 25 test cases, six parameters, five levels and strength two. Since the number of non single valued parameters associated with fprint() is four, two columns are discarded from the OA table and the table is depicted below:

Test-number	escape sequences	integer	real & character	flags	column5**	column 6**
1	\a	d	f	+		
2	\b	o	c	0		
3	\n	u	s	-		
4	\t	X	e	space		
5	\v	i	g	#		
6	\b	i	e	-		
7	\n	X	f	#		
8	\v	d	c	space		
9	\a	u	g	0		
10	\t	o	s	+		
11	\n	o	g	space		
12	\t	u	e	+		
13	\b	i	f	0		
14	\a	d	s	#		
15	\v	X	c	-		
16	\t	u	c	#		
17	\a	i	s	space		
18	\b	X	g	+		
19	\v	o	f	-		
20	\n	d	e	0		
21	\v	X	s	0		
22	\v	d	g	-		
23	\a	o	e	#		
24	\a	i	c	+		
25	\b	u	f	space		

** - empty column to be discarded.

Table 7: Orthogonal test table for fprintf()

Name : **fread**
Format : fread (void *ptr, size_t size. size_t nitems, FILE *stream)

parameter	value 1	value 2	value 3	value 4	value 5
ptr	valid	ptr_to_woa	ptr_to_roa	null	dangling
size	positive				
nitems	positive				
stream	valid				

Table 8: Parameter and value descriptions for fread

The OA selection process:

Number of non single valued parameters = 1
Number of single valued parameters = 3
Maximum value = 5(refer table10).

The orthogonal array which appropriately suits is oa.25.6.5.2 with 25 test cases, six parameters, five levels and strength two. Since the number of non single valued parameters associated with fread() is only one, five columns are discarded from the OA table and will result in the following five test cases.

Test 1: test for valid pointer, positive size, positive no. of items and valid stream.
Test 2: test for null pointer, positive size, positive no. of items and valid stream.
Test 3: test for pointer to read-only area, positive size, positive no. of items and valid stream.
Test 4: test for pointer to wittingly area, positive size, positive no. of items and valid stream.
Test 5: test for dangling pointer with positive size, positive no. of items and valid stream.

The test cases for invalid parameters and unexpected conditions are to be added with the above given set of test cases.

Again, for fopen the use of Orthogonal arrays can be replaced by directly selecting test cases for each parameter value.

6 Conclusion

The application of the proposed metric **"Metric for Effective Test Coverage"** results in the following ***y*** values for fseek, fread, fopen and fprintf.

Sl.no	**Function**	**Traditional Factorial approach *y***	**Orthogonal approach *y***
1	fseek	2*3*3 = 18	9+3 = 12
2	fread	4*3*3*2 = 72	5+5 = 10
3	fopen	2*6 = 12	6+1 = 7
4	fprintf	2*2*5*5*5*5 =2500	25+2 = 27

Table 9: Table depicting the results of Orthogonal method

The interesting feature of the Orthogonal approach is that the higher the number of parameter values the more attractive is the value for y, that is the number of test cases to be developed. Though the metric is applied only for functional testing, it can be enhanced in the future to suit other software testing techniques like robust testing, stress testing etc.

References

[1] **William Perry**
Effective Methods for Software Testing.

[2] **Taguchi, Genichi**
Introduction to Quality Engineering: Designing Quality into Products and Processes. Asian Productivity Organization, Tokyo, 1986. American distribution by UNIPUB/Kraus International Publications, New York.

[3] **Phadke, Madhav S.**
Quality Engineering Using Robust Design. Prentice Hall, Englewood Cliffs, N.J., 1989.

[4] **Sloane, N.J.A.**
A Library of Orthogonal Arrays. http://www.research.att.com/~njas/oadir/index.html

[5] **Borris Beizer**
Software Testing Techniques.

[6] **Tatsumi, Keizo**
Test Case Design Support System. Proceedings of ICQC, Tokyo, 1987.

[7] **Mantle, Robert**
Orthogonal Latin Squares: An Application of Experiment Design to Compiler Testing. Communications of the ACM, Vol. 128, No. 10, October 1985, pp. 1054-1058.

APPENDIX

Some Sample Orthogonal Arrays

oa.4.3.2.2

0	0	0
0	1	1
1	0	1
1	1	0

oa.9.4.3.2

0	0	0	0
0	1	1	2
0	2	2	1
1	0	1	1
1	1	2	0
1	2	0	2
2	0	2	2
2	1	0	1
2	2	1	0

III. Software Measurement Applications

Measuring Legacy Database Structures

Harry M. Sneed and Oliver Foshag, Software-Engineering Service, Ottobrunn/Munich (Germany)

Abstract

Metrics for databases have been neglected in the metric community. On the other hand, there is a great need to measure the size, complexity and quality of legacy data bases, in particular in regard to conversion and reuse. This paper presents a set of metrics for doing this. These metrics have been build into a tool for measuring database structures and have been applied to assess user applications in accordance with the ISO Standard 9126 for product evaluation.

1 Motivation for this Research

Most all of the measurement work done so far has concentrated on measuring programs. In the leading metric text books there is hardly any reference to database metrics.[1] The same applies to reusability research. There too, all of the attention has been directed toward the reusability of programs.[2] Work has been done on the reverse and reengineering of databases. Aiken has published a book on the subject.[3] However, in this work, little use has been made of database metrics. Thus, there is a need in the measurement community to fill this gap and to find means of measuring databases, in particular, in regard to their structural design.

In software migration, one can choose between rewriting, converting or wrapping programs, but there is no such choice when it comes to data. Data has to be reused in one form or the other, either by converting or encapsulating. The decision which alternative to choose is driven by the characteristics of the data itself. If the data structure is amiable for reuse, i.e. it is adaptable to the target data structure, then it is converted. If not, it has to be wrapped.[4]

There is, therefore, a definite need to measure database structures in order to support the decision making process. The questions are

- when should data be converted,
- when should it be wrapped,
- when should it be left alone.

To answer these questions one needs to measure the size, complexity and quality of the database and to sort out those measures which influence convertability. This is the motivation for the research reported on in this paper. (See Figure 1)

2 Quantitative Factors in Database

Programs have quantitative measures such as

- Lines of code,
- Statements,
- Branches
- Decisions,
- Operators and
- Operands.[5]

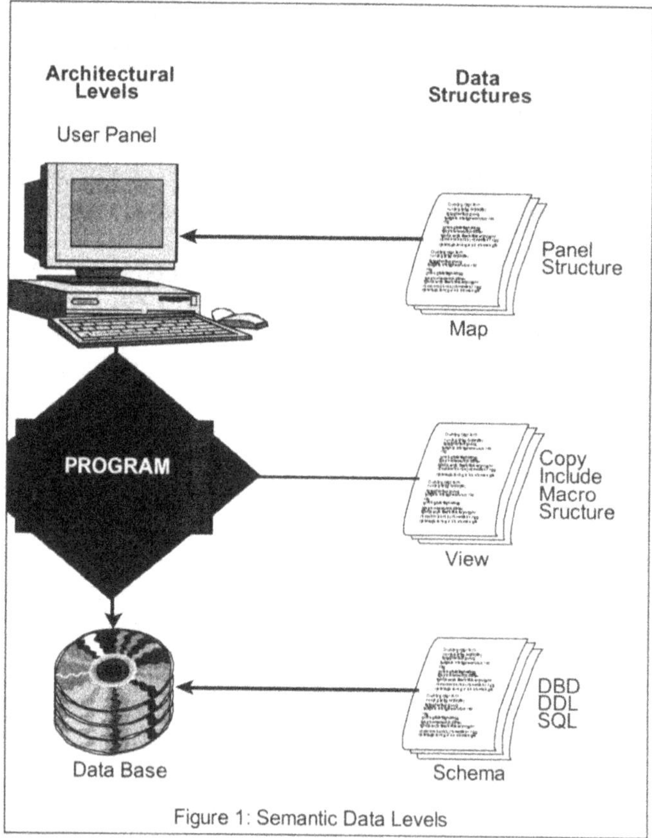

Figure 1: Semantic Data Levels

Databases have other quantitative measures. The primary ones are as follows:

- the number of entity types
- the number of entity occurrences
- the number of entity attributes
- the number of entity keys

- the number of entity relationships
- the number of storage bytes per entity
- the number of indexes per entity
- the number of views per entity
- the number of rules per entity [6] (See Figure 2)

The entity-types are in the hierarchical database system IMS from IBM the segments. In CODASYL databases such as IDMS and IDS they are the record types. In relational databases such as ORACLE and DB-2 entity-types are represented by tables.

Entities or entity-occurrences are in hierarchical databases the segment occurrences. In CODASYL databases, they are the record occurrences. In relational databases, they are the rows of an SQL table.

The attributes are in hierarchical databases fields which are defined in the database segment description. Attributes in network databases are the elementary data items of the database schema. In relational databases, attributes are equivalent to columns in the SQL table.

Keys are common to all database types. They are the attributes through which the entities are accessed. In hierarchical and network databases the entities are accessed by either primary or secondary keys. In relational databases one distinguishes between primary and foreign keys. Primary keys are used to access rows in the target table. Foreign keys connect the target table to other tables.

Relations are connections between different entity types. In hierarchical databases parent segments are related to child segments per definition. In addition there are logical child relations between a parent in one database and a child in another. In network databases relations are depicted by sets. A set connects an owner record with a member record. As opposed to hierarchical databases where a child can have only one parent, member records can have one or more owner. Relations in relational databases are relations between tables and or implemented through foreign keys.

Indexes are also common to all database types. They are additional attributes of the entities which can be used to access them. These secondary keys are maintained in a separate index table for accessing the database indirectly.

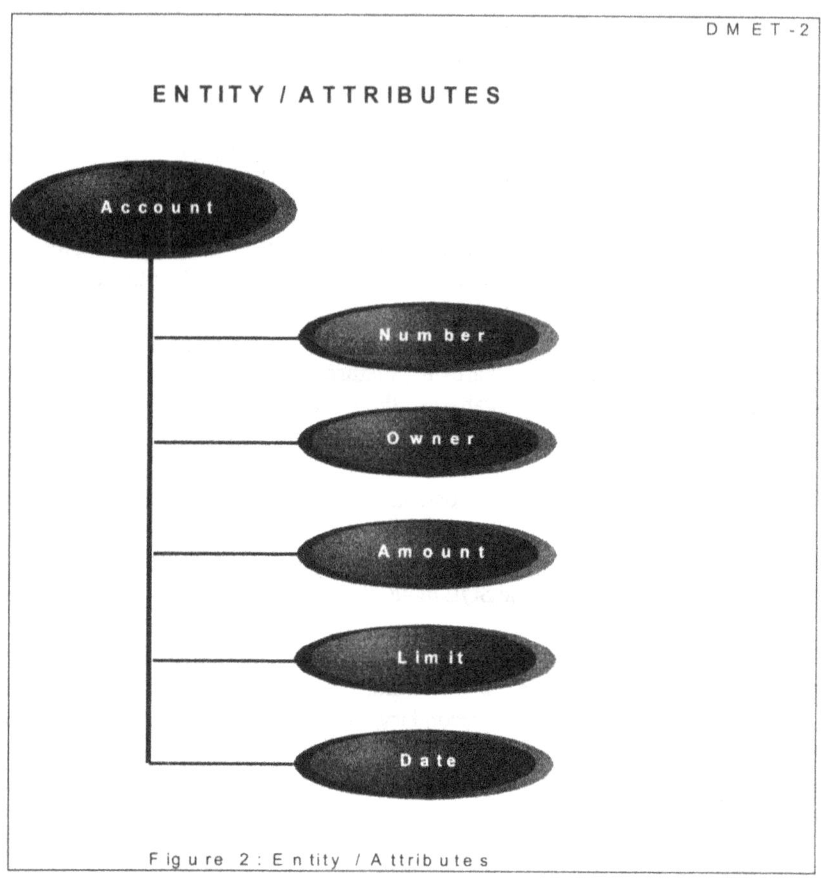

Figure 2: Entity / Attributes

Views are as the name implies how a program perceives the data. The program perception can be a pure subset of a single database or a union of several databases. Views in IMS are logical databases. They are depicted in Program Specification Blocks. Views in CODASYL databases are subschemas or fragments of database descriptions. In relational databases, views can be either subsets of tables or joins of attributes of several tables. They can be either part of the database description or part of the program.

Rules are, finally, integrity rules which define invariant relationships between different entity types. They are to be found in CODASYL data base schemas as well as in SQL database definitions. Rules in SQL databases can be supported by stored procedures.

The first step in measuring database structures is to parse the database description - the IMS-DBD, the CODASYL Schema, or the relational table definitions - to count the number of primary quantities upon which the other metrics are based. This parsing can be done one database at a time and the counts accumulated in an aggregate table. After the parsing of the database descriptions, this table contains

- the number of lines of code
- the number of comment lines
- the number of database description lines
- the number of databases
- the number of database entity types
- the number of planned database entity occurrences
- the number of database entity attributes
- the number of database keys
- the number of relationships between database entities
- the number of database indexes
- the number of database views
- the number of attributes in each data view
- the number of database rules
- the number of stored procedures
- the number of storage bytes per entity (See Figure 3)

3 Complexity Factors in Database Structures

Programs have quantitative measures such as

- Lines of code,
- Statements,
- Branches
- Decisions,
- Operators and
- Operands.[5]

The size of a database structure is determined by the number of elements

- entities
- attributes and
- views

In the Data-Point method for sizing data models entities are weighted by 8 and views by 4, attributes are weighted by 1 and relationships by 2 to compute the raw data point count.[7]

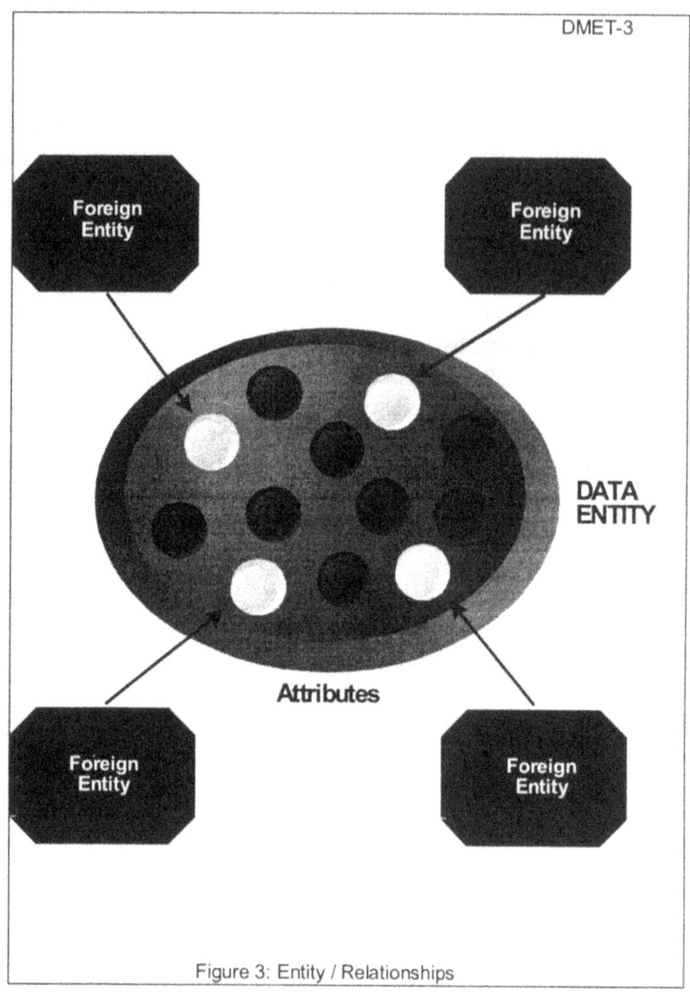

Figure 3: Entity / Relationships

The complexity of a database structure is determined by the number of relationships between those database elements. These relationships are expressed as coefficients such as

$$\frac{\text{Entities}}{\text{Attributes}} \qquad \frac{\text{Keys}}{\text{Attributes}}$$

$$\frac{\text{Entities}}{\text{Relationships}} \qquad \frac{\text{Keys}}{\text{Entities}}$$

$$\frac{\text{Entities}}{\text{Indexes + Pointers}} \qquad \frac{\text{Views}}{\text{Entities}}$$

It is clear that the more keys an entity has, the greater is its access complexity since the same entity can be accessed via many paths. The same relation holds for indexes and pointers. The more indexes and pointers there are, the more ways there are to access database entities. This is equivalent to the fan-in/fan-out metric for programs.[8]

It is also obvious that the greater the number of attributes pro entity the greater the entity complexity. This is similar to the number of statements per module in a program. Relationship complexity is a question of the number of relationships per database entity. Relationships between entities correspond to the coupling of modules. The more there are, the higher the degree of coupling. Finally, the greater the number of views upon an entity, the greater the usage complexity since each view depicts another usage.

The average database structure complexity can be expressed as the arithmetic mean of

- Access complexity
- Entity complexity
- Relationship complexity and
- View complexity (See Figure 4)

4 Quality Factors in Database Structures

Databases can be judged by their content and their structure. The quality of the content is relevant to the data usage. The quality of the structure is relevant to maintenance and reuse.

Measuring Data Content Quality

Data content is measured in terms of accuracy and integrity. Data accuracy, or correctness, has been dealt with in depth in the database literature. A recent issue of the ACM Communications was devoted to this subject.[9] In one article Ken Orr describes data accuracy from the viewpoint of a feedback control system. According to this model, data is a reflection of the reality it is describing. However, as the real world changes, which it does so at an ever increasing rate, the data must change with it. If it does not, it becomes increasingly inaccurate. The only way to prevent this aging is by frequent usage.

The more frequently data is used, the more frequently it will be updated. Data which is seldom used will be neglected. From Orr's observation one can conclude that data accuracy is a relational measure

$$\frac{\text{update interval}}{\text{time}}$$

whereby 1 would denote continual update as is the case with hard real time systems.[10]

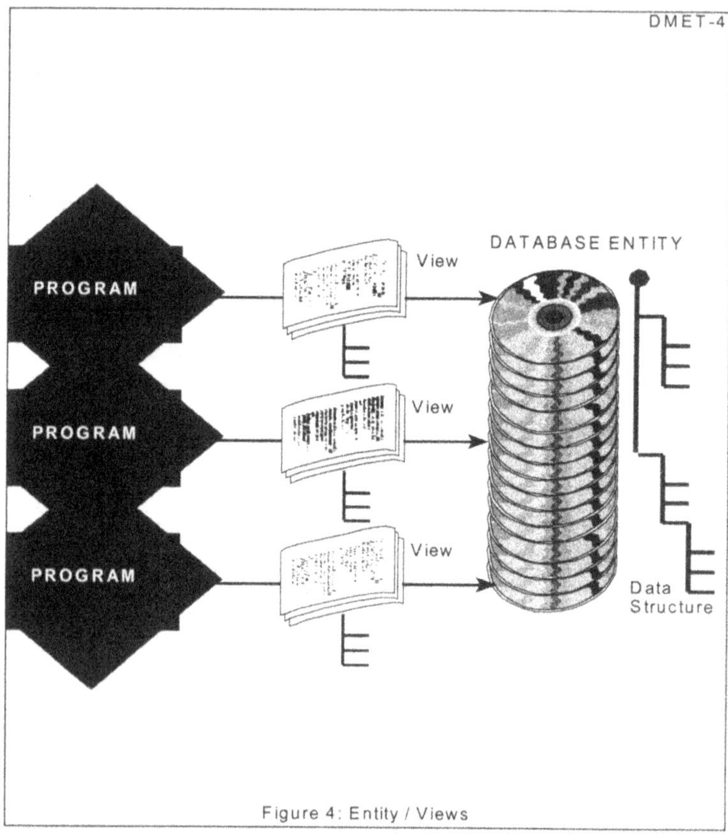

Figure 4: Entity / Views

Data integrity is a question of consistency. To measure integrity one must deal with the semantics of the data. For instance, there should be no incorrect or inconsistent data values. A person who is less than 16 years old could never be employed if the minimum employment age is 16. This would be a violation of an integrity rule. In recent database systems integrity rules are stored along with the data in the form of stored procedures which are activated upon request.

Kaplan, Krishnan, Padman and Peters describe how the integrity of data is checked in accounting information systems.[11] The data integrity is controlled by professional assessors known as auditors using both formal and judgment based methods. The formal methods are supported by tools which scan the data and check the contents against specified integrity rules. Any entities which appear to violate the rules are listed out. It is then up to the judgement of the auditors to decide whether the data is incorrect or not. For that they have a model of error classes to refer to.

Richard Wang has developed a total data quality management methodology (TDQM) which is used to assess and control both the accuracy and the integrity of data. The key to this data measurement are the IQ metrics.

IQ metrics are

- accuracy
- timeliness
- completeness
- consistency.

Consistency is measured as the number of records that violate referential integrity relative to the total number of records.

$$\frac{\text{Inconsistent Entities}}{\text{Total Entities}}$$

Completeness is measured as the number of missing data items or fields, relative to the total number of data items.

$$\frac{\text{Missing data items}}{\text{Total data items}}$$

Timeliness is measured as the difference between time stamps on the data relative to a required update interval

$$\frac{\text{Last Time Stamp - Proceeding Time Stamp}}{\text{Required Update Interval}}$$

Accuracy is measured as the number of records with an erroneous content relative to the total of records in that file or database.

$$\frac{\text{Records containing errors}}{\text{Total Records}}$$

Wang points out that these IQ metrics can be enhanced by business rules and weighted in accordance with their contribution to total information quality.[12] Inaccurate and inconsistent records can be identified by various file comparison techniques derived from testing technology. Data is either compared against specified and generated data or against previous data which is known to be correct.

Measuring Data Structure Quality

Data Structure measurement is the primary focus of the research reported on in this paper. The assumption is that a well structured database is easier to access, to adapt and to reuse as well as to convert. The question is how well is the data structured to accommodate these intrinsic design goals. In addition, a well structured database will require less storage for more information. Thus, there are at least five quality characteristics which can be associated with data structure. These are:

- accessability,
- storage efficiency,
- adaptability,
- convertability and
- reusability

Accessability is the degree to which the same data can be accessed via different access paths. The number of access paths is determined by the number of keys - primary and secondary - which an entity has, as well as the number of pointers pointing to it from a previous, subsequent, parent or child entity as denoted by the operations

Select by key
Fetch next
Fetch previous
Fetch member
Fetch owner

These access paths should be seen in relation to the number of attributes the entities have. This gives the quality coefficient

$$\frac{\text{Keys + Pointers}}{\text{Entities + Attributes}}$$

The greater the number of keys and pointers relative to the number of entities and attributes, the better the accessability.

Storage Efficiency is the degree of information stored relative to the physical storage space. The more information is packed into the least space, the better the storage efficiency. This can be expressed by the coefficient

$$\frac{\text{Number of Attributes of an Entity}}{\text{Entity Storage Space in Bytes}}$$

Adaptability is the degree to which a database entity can be changed or enhanced without affecting the other entity types. This is the case when fields are added or deleted and when new access paths are defined. Such storage mutations should be possible with a minimum of effort. The key to adaptability is modularity. Each entity should have a minimum number of attributes and a maximum number of relationships. The coefficient for measuring adaptability is then

$$\frac{\text{Entity + Relationships}}{\text{Total Attributes}}$$

Convertability is the degree to which a database can be easily migrated from one form to another. In effect, this is a question of compatibility. The question is how compatible is the current data structure with the potential target structures. It is known that relational databases do not accommodate redefinitions and repeating groups. Therefore, if these structural characteristics exist in a hierarchical or networked database, they present a problem when converting to a relational database. Such incompatibilities increase the costs of a database conversion. They are measured by the coefficient

$$\frac{\text{Incompatible Definitions}}{\text{Definitions}}$$

Reusability is finally the degree to which an existing database can be reused in a new context, for instance as a server database in a client/server network or as a media for storing persistent objects. This has to do with the data independence from the current applications. The greater the degree of data independence, the greater is the degree of reusability. Reusability is measured as a relationship between program dependent access paths and program independent access paths. It is expressed in the coefficient.

$$\frac{\text{Program dependent access paths}}{\text{access paths}}$$

The median value of the five coefficients for measuring data structure quality is a good indicator of the overall data structure quality. It can be used together with the median value of the IQ metrics proposed by Wang to assess the quality of a database in its entirety.

5 Application of Database Metrics

The author has developed a tool named DATAUDIT for parsing the following types of database descriptions

- IMS DBDs,

- CODASYL Schemas,
- ADABAS DDMs, and
- SQL, DDLs

From these source texts counts are made of the various database characteristics e.g. entities, attributes, keys, pointers, indexes, relationships, bytes, etc. The counts are collected in a table with a row per entity and a column per count. The columns are then aggregated by database and used to express the size of the database. The same aggregated counts are also used as arguments to compute the database complexity in terms of the relationships, keys, indexes, pointers and views. Finally, the counts are used as arguments in the coefficients for measuring data structure quality. (See Figure 5)

The report produced by DATAUDIT provides all the information necessary for assessing the size, complexity and quality of existing database structures. This again is an important part of an overall software product assessment, since the data architecture is equally as important as the program architecture and the configuration of the user interfaces. Together these measurements add up to a total assessment of the application system under investigation in accordance with the ISO Standard 9126.[13]

SQL DATA BASE AUDITOR REPORT
DATE: 21.11.97 PAGE: 01
SYSTEM: sqlaudit
****

DB-NAME	NR TABS	NR LINES	NR FIELDS	DATA TYPES	PRIM KEYS	FOR KEYS	NR RELS	NR INDEX	ROW SIZE	DAT PTS	FCT PTS	NR DEFI
TBDA0100	01	041	34	34	02	00	00	00	207	50	07	02
TBGK0020	01	051	41	28	01	01	01	00	282	57	07	02
TBGK0030	01	046	36	31	01	01	01	00	228	52	07	02
TBGK0040	01	068	58	49	01	01	01	00	774	74	10	03
TBGK0200	01	062	51	34	02	01	01	00	2643	71	10	03
TBGK0220	01	060	49	33	02	01	01	00	2642	69	07	03
TBGK2980	01	051	46	17	00	00	00	00	457	54	07	02
TBIS0000	01	090	84	44	01	00	00	00	389	96	10	02
TBIS0100	01	027	20	14	02	00	00	00	791	36	07	02
TBIS0110	01	022	12	10	00	02	01	00	046	24	07	01
TBZD0100	01	030	21	14	03	00	00	00	099	41	07	02
TBZD2000	01	060	46	30	01	02	02	00	644	66	10	03
TBZD2010	01	065	59	40	01	00	00	00	771	71	10	03

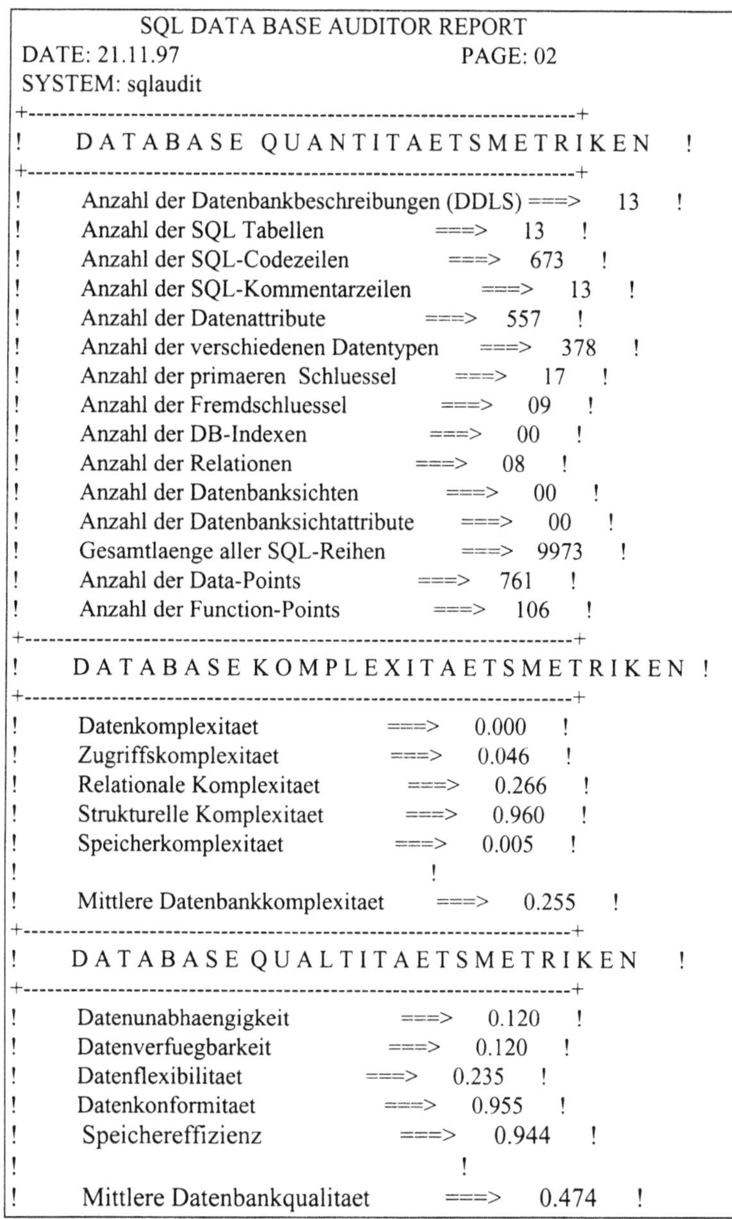

```
SQL DATA BASE AUDITOR REPORT
DATE: 21.11.97                                  PAGE: 02
SYSTEM: sqlaudit
+-------------------------------------------------------------------+
!   D A T A B A S E   Q U A N T I T A E T S M E T R I K E N   !
+-------------------------------------------------------------------+
!    Anzahl der Datenbankbeschreibungen (DDLS) ===>    13    !
!    Anzahl der SQL Tabellen                 ===>    13    !
!    Anzahl der SQL-Codezeilen               ===>   673    !
!    Anzahl der SQL-Kommentarzeilen          ===>    13    !
!    Anzahl der Datenattribute               ===>   557    !
!    Anzahl der verschiedenen Datentypen     ===>   378    !
!    Anzahl der primaeren Schluessel         ===>    17    !
!    Anzahl der Fremdschluessel              ===>    09    !
!    Anzahl der DB-Indexen                   ===>    00    !
!    Anzahl der Relationen                   ===>    08    !
!    Anzahl der Datenbanksichten             ===>    00    !
!    Anzahl der Datenbanksichtattribute      ===>    00    !
!    Gesamtlaenge aller SQL-Reihen           ===>  9973    !
!    Anzahl der Data-Points                  ===>   761    !
!    Anzahl der Function-Points              ===>   106    !
+-------------------------------------------------------------------+
!   D A T A B A S E   K O M P L E X I T A E T S M E T R I K E N !
+-------------------------------------------------------------------+
!    Datenkomplexitaet                       ===>  0.000   !
!    Zugriffskomplexitaet                    ===>  0.046   !
!    Relationale Komplexitaet                ===>  0.266   !
!    Strukturelle Komplexitaet               ===>  0.960   !
!    Speicherkomplexitaet                    ===>  0.005   !
!                                                          !
!    Mittlere Datenbankkomplexitaet          ===>  0.255   !
+-------------------------------------------------------------------+
!   D A T A B A S E   Q U A L T I T A E T S M E T R I K E N   !
+-------------------------------------------------------------------+
!    Datenunabhaengigkeit                    ===>  0.120   !
!    Datenverfuegbarkeit                     ===>  0.120   !
!    Datenflexibilitaet                      ===>  0.235   !
!    Datenkonformitaet                       ===>  0.955   !
!    Speichereffizienz                       ===>  0.944   !
!                                                          !
!    Mittlere Datenbankqualitaet             ===>  0.474   !
```

Figure 5: DATAUDIT Report from 13 SQL Databases

6 Conclusion

The data structure metrics defined in this paper have been applied to assess user application systems for banks, insurance companies and telecommunication prouders. In all cases they enabled the user to quantify the size, complexity and quality of his existing database structures. They also contributed to the overall assessment of product quality. It is clear that these metrics can be refined and improved on. However, in lack of other metrics for measuring data structure they serve a purpose in getting database designers to think about the quality of their designs in numeric terms and also in giving managers the possibility of comparing database designs on a numeric scale. As Lord Kelvin put it, one only begins to understand something, when one can measure it.[14] It is time that this principle be applied to database design as well as program design.

References

[1] **Fenton, N.**
Software Metrics - A Rigorous Approach. Chapman & Hall, London, 1991.

[2] **Abran, A./Desharnais, J.-M.**
Measurement of Functional Reuse in Maintenance. in Journal of Software Maintenance, Vol. 7, No. 4, July 1995.

[3] **Aiken, P.**
Data Reverse Engineering. McGraw Hill, New York, 1996.

[4] **Sneed, H.**
Encapsulating Legacy Software for Use in Client/Server Systems. in Proc. of WCRE-96, IEEE Computer Society, Monterey, Cal., Nov. 1996.

[5] **Jones, C.**
Applied Software Measurement. McGraw Hill, New York, 1991.

[6] **Shlaer, S./Mellor, S.**
Object-oriented Analysis - Modelling the World in Data. Yourdon Press, Englewood Cliffs, 1988.

[7] **Sneed, H.**
Die Data-Point Methode. in Online, ZfD, Rudolf Müller, Köln, Mai 5/1990.

[8] **Henry, S./Kafura, D.**
Software Structure Metrics based on Information Flow Analysis. in IEEE Trans. on S.E., Vol. 7, No. 5, 1981.

[9] **Tayi, G./Ballou, D.**
Examining Data Quality. in Comm. of ACM, Vol. 41, No. 2, Feb. 1998.

[10] **Orr, K.**
Data Quality and System Theory. in Comm. of ACM, Vol. 41, No. 2, Feb. 1998.

[11] **Kaplan, D./Krishnan, R./Padman, R./Peters, J.**
Assessing Data Quality in Accounting Information Systems. in Comm. of ACM, Vol. 41, No. 2, Feb. 1998.

[12] **Wang, R.**
Total Data Quality Management. in Comm. of ACM, Vol. 41, No. 2, Feb. 1998.

[13] **ISO/IEC**
Software Product Evaluation - Quality Characteristics and Guidelines for their Use. ISO/IEC Standard ISO-9126, Geneva, 1994.

[14] **Kelvin, N.**
Theory of Measurement. Cambridge University Press, Cambridge, 1954.

REST - A tool to Measure the Ripple Effect of C and C++ Programs

Sue Black, South Bank University London (UK)

Abstract

This paper describes the reformulation and subsequent implementation of the ripple effect measure first proposed by Yau and Collofello [10]. Ripple effect traces the paths of variables through a program, providing a compound measurement of the effect that one module has upon the other modules. It may be used during software development to compare the stability of subsequent versions of a program, or during software maintenance to decide which modules within a program may need reengineering. The implementation of this reformulated measure REST (Ripple Effect and Stability Tool) gives ripple effect measurements for each individual module within a program and an overall stability measure: the reciprocal of the summed ripple effect for the program. During the reformulation of this measure using matrix algebra it was noticed that the computation algorithm for a certain matrix, D, which describes definition / use pairings, could be approximated, eliminating the need to use control-flow information. The simplified version of matrix D requires less memory and less time to compute. A previous implementation of the ripple effect measure [13] suffered from slow computation times. REST has been tested on two versions of a mutation testing software tool and the approximate results compared with the ripple effect measure produced using the original matrix D. Initial results show that the simplified matrix D is a valid alternative to the original matrix D and as such the reformulation gives an acceptable approximation to the original measure.

1 Introduction

This research has been carried out in the general area of software measurement but is also connected with software maintenance. More specifically our research has been carried out in the area of impact analysis which determines the impact of a change to the source code of one module on the other modules within a system and provides a measure of its complexity. Ripple effect analysis is a type of impact analysis, it describes the way in which a change to one variable in a line of code may affect the code within that module and then propagate through other modules across a whole system. Logical stability uses a measure of the ripple effect to predict the stability of a module in a program, the resistance to the ripple effect that a program would have if modified.

2 Relation to prior work

The term ripple effect was first used in a paper by Haney [2] to describe the way that a change in one module would necessitate a change in any other module. He used a technique called `module connection analysis' which applied matrix algebra to estimate the total number of changes needed to stabilise a system. Myers [6] used matrices to quantify matrix independence. A complete dependence matrix was formulated describing dependencies between modules within a system and then used to predict the stability of the system. Soong [8] used the joint probability of connection of all elements within a system to produce a program stability measure. All of the aforementioned methods use matrices to measure the probability of a change to a variable or module affecting another variable or module.

When Yau and Collofello first proposed their ripple effect analysis technique in 1978 [10] they saw it as a complexity measure which could be used during software maintenance to evaluate and compare various program modifications to source code. Computation of ripple effect involved using error flow analysis where all program variable definitions involved in an initial modification represented primary error sources from which inconsistency could propagate to other program areas. Identification of affected areas could then be made by internally tracking each primary error source and its respective secondary error sources within the module to a point of exit. At each point of exit a determination was made as to which error sources propagated across module boundaries. Those that did became primary error sources within the relevant modules. Propagation continued until no new error sources were created.

In [11] a software maintenance process is identified which includes accounting for the ripple effect as one of its phases (see Fig.1). A logical stability measure is proposed which uses a measure of the ripple effect in a module to predict the *stability* of a module or program: the resistance to the potential ripple effect that a program would have if modified. If additional information is available concerning the type of maintenance to be performed and therefore the modules most likely to be modified, the probabilities of each module being used can be taken into account and the measures adjusted accordingly. Taken on its own the logical stability measure could be misleading: a large program with only one module will have no ripple effect between modules but maintainability will probably be poor. Used in conjunction with other measures the logical stability measure can be used to compare alternate versions of a program or to locate modules with poor stability perhaps with a view to reengineering. In general, the smaller the ripple effect or greater the logical stability measure the more stable the program.

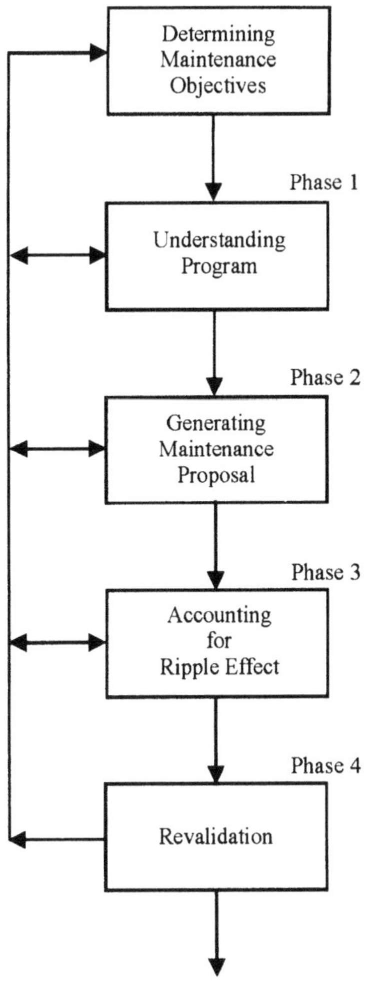

Figure 1: A methodology for software maintenance (from [11]).

An algorithm for computing *design* stability was presented in [12] which facilitated computation of stability based solely on design information. It was proposed that a design stability measure would be more useful than previous stability measures because it could be used at a much earlier stage in the software lifecycle, before any code was produced, thus potentially saving time and money. Some of the detailed algorithms used in the computation of logical ripple effect analysis throughout the software lifecycle are given in [15].

The software maintenance process is further developed in [14] which gives a methodology for software maintenance using graph rewriting rules. In [1] a method is proposed that identifies the side-effects which can be introduced to modules from system modification. The authors classify the relationships existing between components into both potential and actual relationships, the latter being a subset of the former.

Computing the ripple effect for a small program manually is possible if tedious, but for large programs it is completely infeasible. It is therefore desirable to automate this process to some extent. Even when automated, computation of ripple effect can be time consuming. Yau and Chang [13] give an example of a two thousand line Pascal program's stability measure taking thirteen hours of CPU time to compute. They also present an algorithm which can compute ripple effect faster than this but which treats modules as black boxes, thus not taking information from inside modules of code into account. We have taken Yau and Collofello's algorithm and reformulated it using matrix algebra. Our aim is to exploit the clarity imparted by this mathematical formulation. In particular, it highlights opportunities for approximation which may significantly simplify the computation.

This paper is structured as follows: section two has given background information on the ripple effect and logical stability including a review of papers published in this area. Section three is an overview of the REST software. Section four gives a precise definition of Yau and Collofello's calculation of ripple effect and logical stability measures. Intramodule and intermodule change propagation are introduced and the new matrix formulation of Yau and Collofello's algorithm is explained. Using this formulation it is shown how matrix Z_m a fundamental component in the computation of ripple effect and logical stability can be automatically derived from source code.

Section five gives details of the software used to test REST, and section six gives concluding remarks and suggestions for further work.

3 An overview of REST

REST is comprised of four separate software modules as detailed in figure 2. The parser written in PCCTS [7] with embedded C, uses preprocessed C or C++ code to produce output files containing data on each variable within each module. This is used by LISTFUNS to produce function list information and matrix C. The output from LISTFUNS is then used alongside the parser output by FUNMAT to produce the matrices V, A, D and X for each module, the matrices are then manipulated by RIPPLE to compute ripple effect and logical stability measures for each module within the program and for the program as a whole.

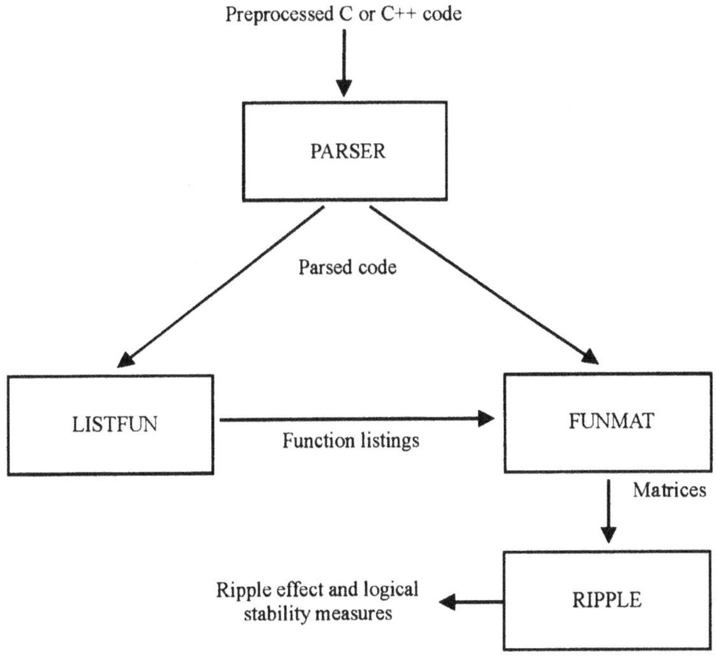

Figure 2: Components of the REST software.

4 Ripple Effect and Logical Stability

This section is an explanation of the recasting of Yau and Collofello's ripple effect metric as a matrix problem. Their original formulation is at times difficult to understand, its recasting as a matrix problem has clarified the actual operations involved, thus making automation more straightforward. Joiner and Tsai [3] found ripple effect analysis to be a semi-automatic process and in fact used program slicing to compute the ripple effect.

```
(1)    a := b;
(2)    c := d + b;
(3)    d := a * 2;
(4)    return (d);
```

Figure 3: Sample code.

4.1 Intramodule Change Propagation

The computation of ripple effect is based on the effect that a change to a single variable will have on the rest of a program. Matrices V_m, A_m and D_m are concerned with representing *intramodule change propagation*, that is, propagation from one variable to another within a module. Given the piece of code in Fig. 3, a change to the value of *b* in (1) will affect the value of *a* in (1), which will subsequently propagate to line (3). There will be no propagation of change from line (2) as *c* is not used in lines (3) or (4). In line (3) *a* will affect *d* which will then propagate to *d* in line (4).

Matrix V_m represents the starting points for intramodule change propagation through a module. These starting points are called 'definitions' by Yau and Collofello and can be any of the following:

1. a global variable on the right-hand-side of an assignment (a *use*);
2. an output parameter in the invocation of a function;
3. an input parameter;
4. the reading of an input;
5. a variable on the left-hand-side of an assignment (a *definition*);

In matrix V_m variable occurrences which satisfy any of the above conditions are denoted by '1' and those which do not by '0'. Matrix V_m for the code in our example (where a and c are global) is therefore:

$$V_m = \begin{pmatrix} a_1^d & b_1^u & c_2^d & d_2^u & b_2^u & d_3^d & a_3^u & d_4^u \\ 1 & 0 & 1 & 0 & 0 & 1 & 1 & 0 \end{pmatrix}$$

the notation x_i^d (respectively, x_i^u) denotes a *definition* (respectively, *use*) of variable *x* at line *i*. For example, a_1^d means variable *a* is *defined* in line *1* and b_2^u means variable *b* is *used* in line *2*. Note that a_3^u is considered a definition because it is global.

A 0-1 matrix Z_m can be produced to show which variables' values will propagate to other variables within module *m*. The rows and columns of Z_m represent each individual occurrence of a variable. Thus for the above code we get the following matrix:

$$
Z_m = \begin{array}{c} a_1^d \\ b_1^u \\ c_2^d \\ d_2^u \\ b_2^u \\ d_3^d \\ a_3^u \\ d_4^u \end{array}
\overset{\begin{array}{cccccccc} a_1^d & b_1^u & c_2^d & d_2^u & b_2^u & d_3^d & a_3^u & d_4^u \end{array}}{\begin{pmatrix}
1 & 0 & 0 & 0 & 0 & 1 & 1 & 1 \\
1 & 1 & 0 & 0 & 0 & 1 & 1 & 1 \\
0 & 0 & 1 & 0 & 0 & 0 & 0 & 0 \\
0 & 0 & 1 & 1 & 0 & 0 & 0 & 0 \\
0 & 0 & 1 & 0 & 1 & 0 & 0 & 0 \\
0 & 0 & 0 & 0 & 0 & 1 & 0 & 1 \\
0 & 0 & 0 & 0 & 0 & 1 & 1 & 1 \\
0 & 0 & 0 & 0 & 0 & 0 & 0 & 1
\end{pmatrix}}
$$

For example the '1' in the 6th position in row 2 reflects the fact that the use of b in defining a in line 1 b_1^u propagates to the definition of d in line 3 d_3^d. We observe that Z_m is reflexive and transitive; that is, every variable occurrence is assumed to propagate to itself, and if v_1 propagates to v_2 and v_2 propagates to v_3 then v_1 also propagates to v_3. In graph theory terms we conclude that Z_m represents the reachability matrix of some graph, an idea which we now pursue in some detail.

4.2 Constructing matrix Z_m automatically

Matrix Z_m representing intramodule change propagation can be constructed automatically as the reachability matrix of a graph whose adjacency matrix is B_m. B_m representing direct intramodule change is obtained as the sum of two matrices: a definition/use association matrix D_m and an assignment matrix A_m.

In the sample code (Fig. 3) a takes its value from b in line 1, thus b, a is an assignment pair. The assignment matrix A_m is an $n \times n$ matrix:

$$
A_m = \begin{array}{c} a_1^d \\ b_1^u \\ c_2^d \\ d_2^u \\ b_2^u \\ d_3^d \\ a_3^u \\ d_4^u \end{array}
\overset{\begin{array}{cccccccc} a_1^d & b_1^u & c_2^d & d_2^u & b_2^u & d_3^d & a_3^u & d_4^u \end{array}}{\begin{pmatrix}
0 & 0 & 0 & 0 & 0 & 0 & 0 & 0 \\
1 & 0 & 0 & 0 & 0 & 0 & 0 & 0 \\
0 & 0 & 0 & 0 & 0 & 0 & 0 & 0 \\
0 & 0 & 1 & 0 & 0 & 0 & 0 & 0 \\
0 & 0 & 1 & 0 & 0 & 0 & 0 & 0 \\
0 & 0 & 0 & 0 & 0 & 0 & 0 & 0 \\
0 & 0 & 0 & 0 & 0 & 1 & 0 & 0 \\
0 & 0 & 0 & 0 & 0 & 0 & 0 & 0
\end{pmatrix}}
$$

which shows that a_1 is assigned the value of b_1, c_2 is assigned the value of d_2 and b_2, and d_3 is assigned the value of a_3.

The definition of a in line 1 is used by a in line 3. This is a definition/use association. The definition/use association matrix D_m is an $n \times n$ matrix:

$$
D_m = \begin{array}{c} a_1^d \\ b_1^u \\ c_2^d \\ d_2^u \\ b_2^u \\ d_3^d \\ a_3^u \\ d_4^u \end{array}
\overset{\begin{array}{cccccccc} a_1^d & b_1^u & c_2^d & d_2^u & b_2^u & d_3^d & a_3^u & d_4^u \end{array}}{\begin{pmatrix}
0 & 0 & 0 & 0 & 0 & 0 & 1 & 0 \\
0 & 0 & 0 & 0 & 0 & 0 & 0 & 0 \\
0 & 0 & 0 & 0 & 0 & 0 & 0 & 0 \\
0 & 0 & 0 & 0 & 0 & 0 & 0 & 0 \\
0 & 0 & 0 & 0 & 0 & 0 & 0 & 0 \\
0 & 0 & 0 & 0 & 0 & 0 & 0 & 1 \\
0 & 0 & 0 & 0 & 0 & 0 & 0 & 0 \\
0 & 0 & 0 & 0 & 0 & 0 & 0 & 0
\end{pmatrix}}
$$

this shows that a_1 is associated with a_3, and d_3 is associated with d_4. Replacing this matrix with a matrix of all *possible* definition/use pairs greatly simplifies the computation, since to produce a completely accurate version of matrix D_m control-flow information has to be taken into account. Using the code in Fig. 3 again, if we include all possible definition/use pairs matrix D_m will become:

$$
D_m^0 = \begin{array}{c} a_1^d \\ b_1^u \\ c_2^d \\ d_2^u \\ b_2^u \\ d_3^d \\ a_3^u \\ d_4^u \end{array}
\overset{\begin{array}{cccccccc} a_1^d & b_1^u & c_2^d & d_2^u & b_2^u & d_3^d & a_3^u & d_4^u \end{array}}{\begin{pmatrix}
0 & 0 & 0 & 0 & 0 & 0 & 1 & 0 \\
0 & 0 & 0 & 0 & 0 & 0 & 0 & 0 \\
0 & 0 & 0 & 0 & 0 & 0 & 0 & 0 \\
0 & 0 & 0 & 0 & 0 & 0 & 0 & 0 \\
0 & 0 & 0 & 0 & 0 & 0 & 0 & 0 \\
0 & 0 & 0 & 1 & 0 & 0 & 0 & 1 \\
0 & 0 & 0 & 0 & 0 & 0 & 0 & 0 \\
0 & 0 & 0 & 0 & 0 & 0 & 0 & 0
\end{pmatrix}}
$$

There is an extra invalid entry in this version of matrix D_m : d_3 is paired with d_2. We will use the simplified version of matrix D_m for the computation of ripple effect.

When added together these matrices give us the matrix B_m representing direct intramodule change propagation:

$$
B_m = \begin{array}{c} \\ a_1^d \\ b_1^u \\ c_2^d \\ d_2^u \\ b_2^u \\ d_3^d \\ a_3^u \\ d_4^u \end{array}
\begin{array}{c} \begin{array}{cccccccc} a_1^d & b_1^u & c_2^d & d_2^u & b_2^u & d_3^d & a_3^u & d_4^u \end{array} \\
\left(\begin{array}{cccccccc}
0 & 0 & 0 & 0 & 0 & 0 & 1 & 0 \\
1 & 0 & 0 & 0 & 0 & 0 & 0 & 0 \\
0 & 0 & 0 & 0 & 0 & 0 & 0 & 0 \\
0 & 0 & 1 & 0 & 0 & 0 & 0 & 0 \\
0 & 0 & 1 & 0 & 0 & 0 & 0 & 0 \\
0 & 0 & 0 & 1 & 0 & 0 & 0 & 1 \\
0 & 0 & 0 & 0 & 0 & 1 & 0 & 0 \\
0 & 0 & 0 & 0 & 0 & 0 & 0 & 0
\end{array} \right) \end{array}
$$

We can now find the reachability matrix for B_m, namely Z_m using:

$Z_m = \mathrm{I} + \mathrm{B} + \mathrm{B}^2 + \ldots + \mathrm{B}^n$
n = number of variables, in this case eight.

Which gives us:

$$
Z_m = \begin{array}{c} \\ a_1^d \\ b_1^u \\ c_2^d \\ d_2^u \\ b_2^u \\ d_3^d \\ a_3^u \\ d_4^u \end{array}
\begin{array}{c} \begin{array}{cccccccc} a_1^d & b_1^u & c_2^d & d_2^u & b_2^u & d_3^d & a_3^u & d_4^u \end{array} \\
\left(\begin{array}{cccccccc}
1 & 0 & 1 & 1 & 0 & 1 & 1 & 1 \\
1 & 1 & 1 & 1 & 0 & 1 & 1 & 1 \\
0 & 0 & 1 & 0 & 0 & 0 & 0 & 0 \\
0 & 0 & 1 & 1 & 0 & 0 & 0 & 0 \\
0 & 0 & 1 & 0 & 1 & 0 & 0 & 0 \\
0 & 0 & 1 & 1 & 0 & 1 & 0 & 1 \\
0 & 0 & 1 & 1 & 0 & 1 & 1 & 1 \\
0 & 0 & 0 & 0 & 0 & 0 & 0 & 1
\end{array} \right) \end{array}
$$

4.3 Intermodule Change Propagation

Propagation from one module to another is called *intermodule change propagation*. A change to a variable can propagate to other modules if the variable occurrence is:

1. a global variable appearing on the left-hand-side of an assignment.
2. an output parameter.
3. an input parameter to a called module.

If the above code is part of module m then d clearly propagates to any module calling m. If a and c are global then their occurrences on the left-hand-side of the assignments in lines (1) and (2) will cause propagation to any modules using these variables. Even if it were global, b cannot propagate since it is not changed in the above code. Suppose that the above code constituting module m is called by a module m_1, that a and c are global and module m_1 uses a and that a further module m_2 uses a and c. We can represent the propagation of these variables using an $n \times 3$ matrix X_m:

$$X_m = \begin{array}{c} \\ a_1^d \\ b_1^u \\ c_2^d \\ d_2^u \\ b_2^u \\ d_3^d \\ a_3^u \\ d_4^u \end{array} \begin{array}{c} \begin{array}{ccc} m & m_1 & m_2 \end{array} \\ \begin{pmatrix} 0 & 1 & 1 \\ 0 & 0 & 0 \\ 0 & 0 & 1 \\ 0 & 0 & 0 \\ 0 & 0 & 0 \\ 0 & 0 & 0 \\ 0 & 0 & 0 \\ 0 & 1 & 0 \end{pmatrix} \end{array}$$

We now observe that the intermodule change propagation of all variable occurrences in m can be found by multiplying Z_m and X_m giving:

$$ZX_m = \begin{pmatrix} 1 & 0 & 1 & 1 & 0 & 1 & 1 & 1 \\ 1 & 1 & 1 & 1 & 0 & 1 & 1 & 1 \\ 0 & 0 & 1 & 0 & 0 & 0 & 0 & 0 \\ 0 & 0 & 1 & 1 & 0 & 0 & 0 & 0 \\ 0 & 0 & 1 & 0 & 1 & 0 & 0 & 0 \\ 0 & 0 & 1 & 1 & 0 & 1 & 0 & 1 \\ 0 & 0 & 1 & 1 & 0 & 1 & 1 & 1 \\ 0 & 0 & 0 & 0 & 0 & 0 & 0 & 1 \end{pmatrix} \begin{pmatrix} 0 & 1 & 1 \\ 0 & 0 & 0 \\ 0 & 0 & 1 \\ 0 & 0 & 0 \\ 0 & 0 & 0 \\ 0 & 0 & 0 \\ 0 & 0 & 0 \\ 0 & 1 & 0 \end{pmatrix} = \begin{pmatrix} 0 & 2 & 1 \\ 0 & 2 & 2 \\ 0 & 0 & 1 \\ 0 & 0 & 1 \\ 0 & 0 & 1 \\ 0 & 1 & 1 \\ 0 & 1 & 1 \\ 0 & 1 & 0 \end{pmatrix}$$

The occurrences of '2' in the matrix above denote two intermodule change propagation paths, for example the '2' in row 1 column 2 denotes propagation from a_1^d in module m through variable a_1^d (a is global) and d_4^u to a^u in module $m1$.

Now the product of V_m and ZX_m shows how many variable definitions may propagate to each module from module *m*:

$$\begin{pmatrix} 1 & 0 & 1 & 0 & 0 & 1 & 1 & 0 \end{pmatrix} \begin{pmatrix} 0 & 2 & 1 \\ 0 & 2 & 2 \\ 0 & 0 & 1 \\ 0 & 0 & 1 \\ 0 & 0 & 1 \\ 0 & 1 & 1 \\ 0 & 1 & 1 \\ 0 & 1 & 0 \end{pmatrix} = \begin{pmatrix} 0 & 4 & 4 \end{pmatrix}$$

In this instance we can see from matrix VZX_m there are 0 propagations to module *m*, 4 to module m_1 and 4 to m_2.

4.4 Complexity and Logical Stability

A complexity measure is factored into the computation by Yau and Collofello so that the complexity of modification of a variable definition is taken into account. Matrix C, a 1 * *m* matrix represents McCabe's cyclomatic complexity [5] for the modules in our code (the values for m_1 and m_2 have been chosen at random):

$$C = \begin{matrix} m \\ m_1 \\ m_2 \end{matrix} \begin{pmatrix} 1 \\ 2 \\ 1 \end{pmatrix}$$

The product of VZX_m and C is:

Version	Logical Stability using approximated matrix D	Logical Stability using approximated matrix D
1	0.025	0.060
2	0.024	0.041

Figure 4: REST results.

$$\begin{pmatrix} 0 & 4 & 4 \end{pmatrix} \begin{pmatrix} 1 \\ 2 \\ 1 \end{pmatrix} = 12$$

This number represents the complexity-weighted total variable definition propagation for module *m*. If we now multiply this by the reciprocal of the number of variable definitions in module *m* i.e. $(jV_mj)^{-1}$ we get the mean complexity-weighted variable definition propagation per variable definition in module *m*. In our example $|V_m| = 4$, and the logical ripple effect for module *m* is defined to be 12/4. The logical stability measure for module *m* is defined to be is reciprocal, i.e. 4/12 .

5 Case study

REST has been tested using two of four versions of a mutation testing software tool written between November 1997 and July 1998 using the C programming language. The size of the tool ranges from 20 modules, 864 lines of code for the first version to 44 modules, 1636 lines of code for the final version.

Ripple effect measures have been calculated for two versions of the tool, firstly using the simplified version of matrix D and subsequently the original version. As the original matrix D contains less entries than the approximated version it was only necessary to check through the programs for definition/use pairs and change any extra 1s for zeros, then compute the final ripple effect calculations. The results (see Fig. 4) show the difference between the approximate and correct matrix D's logical stability. Further experimentation is now being undertaken to check that the error factor of approximately 1/2 has sufficiently low variance to be used with confidence.

6 Conclusions and further work

This paper has described the reformulation of the ripple effect algorithm using matrix algebra and the approximation of matrix D, a definition/use matrix used in the computation of ripple effect. The reformulated algorithm has been implemented in a tool - REST which has been tested using C code from a mutation testing software tool. Initial test results show that logical stability measures produced by REST give an acceptable approximation to the original measure. Further work will include extensive testing of REST on code of varied size and content to discover whether these results hold true for a larger subset of C and C++ code.

Acknowledgements

The author would like to thank BT Laboratories, Martlesham Heath who partly funded this research. Thanks also to Robin Whitty and David Wigg from the Centre for Systems and Software Engineering at South Bank University for their help in producing this paper.

References

[1] **Canfora, G., Di Lucca, G.A. and Tortorella, M. (1996)**
Controlling side- effects in maintenance. Proceedings of the 3rd International Conference on Acheiving Quality in Software , Chapman and Hall, London. pp. 89-102.

[2] **Haney, F.M. (1972)**
Module connection analysis-a tool for scheduling software debugging activities. Proceedings of the 1972 Fall Joint Computer Conference, December, pp. 173-179.

[3] **Joiner, J.K. and Tsai, W.T. (1993)**
Ripple effect analysis, program slicing and dependence analysis. TR 93-84, University of Minnesota technical report, Minneapolis, MN 55455.

[4] **Kafura, D. and Reddy, G.R. (1987)**
The use of software complexity metrics in software maintenance. IEEE Transactions on Software Engineering, 13(3): 335-343.

[5] **McCabe, T. J. (1976)**
A complexity measure. IEEE Transactions on Soft- ware Engineering, 2(4): 308-320.

[6] **Myers, G. J. (1975)**
Reliable software through composite design. Van Nos- trand Reinhold Company, 135 West 50th Street, New York, NY 10020.

[7] **Parr, T. J. (1996)**
Language translation using PCCTS and C++. Automata Publishing Company, San Jose, CA 95129, USA.

[8] **Soong, N.L. (1977)**
A program stability measure. Proceedings 1977 Annual ACM Conference, pp. 163-173.

[9] **Turver, R.J. and Munro, M. (1994)**
An early impact analysis technique for software maintenance. Software Maintenance: Research and Practice, vol. 6, 35-52.

[10] **Yau, S.S. , Collofello, J.S. and MacGregor, T.M. (1978)**
Ripple effect analysis of software maintenance. Proc. COMPSAC '78, pp. 60-65.

[11] **Yau, S.S. and Collofello, J.S. (1980)**
Some stability measures for software maintenance. IEEE Transactions on Software Engineering, Vol. SE-6, No. 6, pp. 545-552, November.

[12] **Yau, S.S. and Collofello, J.S. (1985)**
Design stability measures for software maintenance. IEEE Transactions on Software Engineering, Vol. SE-11, No. 9, pp. 849-856, September.

[13] **Yau, S.S. and Chang, S. C. (1984)**
Estimating logical stability in software maintenance. Proc. COMPSAC '84, pp. 109-119.

[14] **Yau, S.S. Nicholl, R.A., Tsai, J.J.P. and Liu, S. (1988)**
An integrated lifecycle model for software maintenance. IEEE Transactions on Software Engineering, Vol. 14, No. 8, pp. 1128-1144, August.

[15] **Yau, S.S. and Liu, S. (1988)**
Some approaches to logical ripple effect analysis. Software Engineering Research Centre technical report SERC-TR-24-F, University of Florida, Gainesville, FL 32611.

Y2K from a Metrics Point of View

Reiner R. Dumke and Achim S. Winkler, University of Magdeburg, Government Financial Computer Center Magdeburg (Germany)

Abstract

The year 2000 problem (Y2K) is "not just a technical problem, it is a worldwide business problem affecting people and organizations everywhere" [11]. The complexity of this problem and its solution can be resolved succesfully only on a measurement-based software development or maintenance environment.

In this paper we analyse the "measurement situation" on the Y2K area and consider the possibilities of the application of the existing results on the field of software measurement. In order to present the measurement aspects in a systematic manner, we use our measurement framework that leeds to a persistent metrics program in a given software development or application environent.

1 Introduction

Plenty of industrial metrics program approaches, measurement frameworks and metrics applications exist to support the management of the quality of the software processes, products and resources [9]. However, many open problems are to be solved for a real measured software development process. The current situation is described the figure 1.

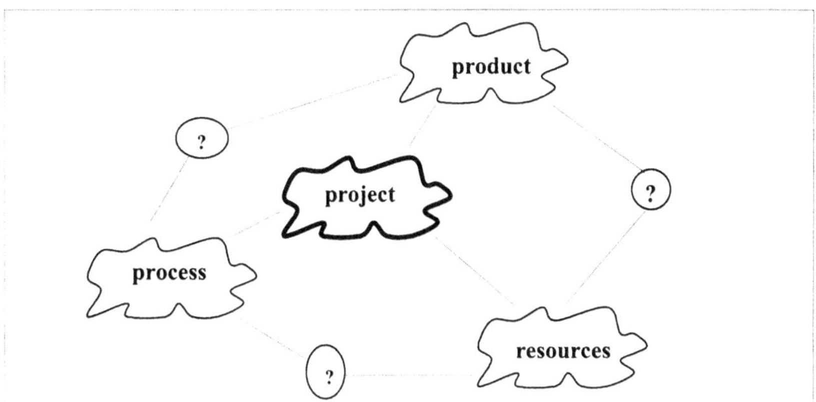

Figure 1: Current situation in quantification of the software development

Some of the existing benefits of metric applications can be characterized in short as

- Clarification of measured/analyzed software components
- Essential results of validated measured aspects for component evaluation
- Applicability of software metrics for the comparison and improvement of components.

But, the main goal of the application of software metrics can be shown in a simplified manner in figure 2 ([10], [25]). We want to manage the software development and maintenance processes by sustaining or achieving a measured quality of the software product based on the appropriate use of the resources. This level is well known as Capability Maturity Model level "four".

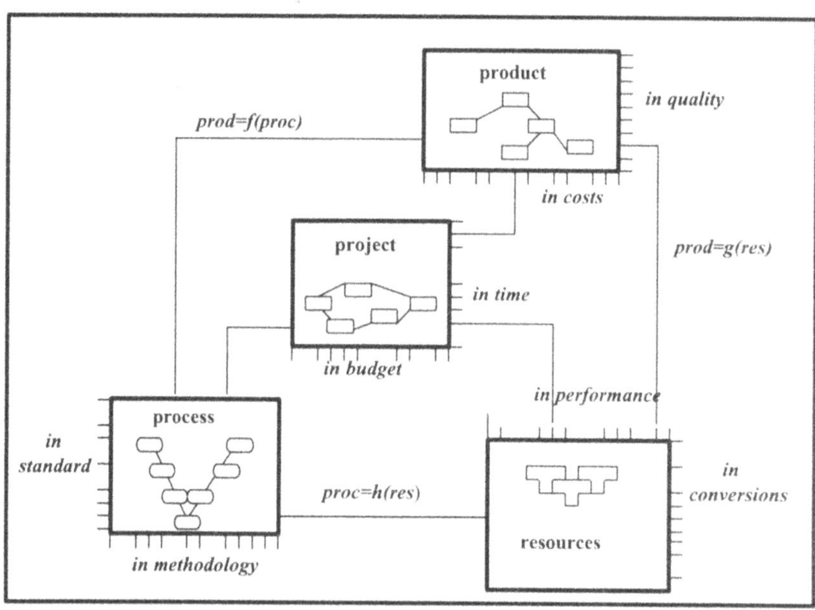

Figure 2: Future situation of software development based on software measurement

Software metrics used to quantify the software development are one main aspect of a real software ***engineering.***

The general process of the (industrial) metrics application as ***metrication*** includes the mapping of the counting or quantifying of software components to an appropriate empirical evaluation of the environment (see figure 3).

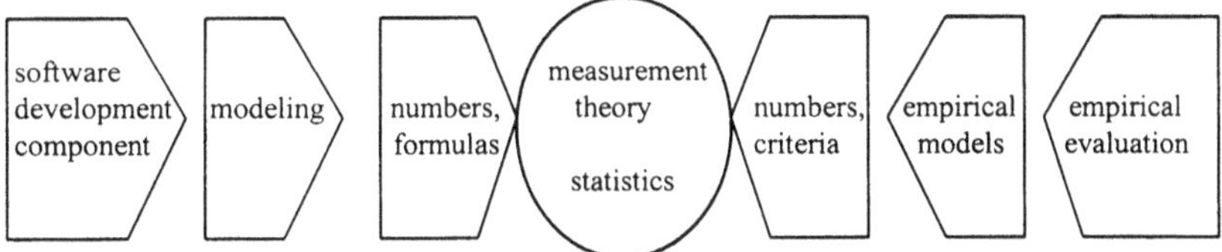

Figure 3: The metrication process in the software development

The metrication process helps us to explain empirically evaluated software aspects such as cost of an implemented C++ class, effort of one kilo lines of code etc. Note, only these empirical-based metrics we can be used as ***measures.*** Nowadays, measures are defined for a concrete software development environment or product. In this manner, we must consider the Y2K area with their existing metrics for both cost estimation and Y2K problem solution.

2 Year 2000 Characteristics

A convincing description of the year 2000 (Y2K) charcteristics is given in [18] (see also [1], [15], [26] and [32]) as

1. *Thousands of software applications are affected simultaneously*
2. *Not only software but physical devices and data bases must be repaired*
3. *Unusual activities such as "triage" must be estimated*
4. *Possible damages and litigation expenses must be estimated*
5. *Hundreds of programming languages are involved in the problem*
6. *Both in-house and outsource work can take place simultaneously*
7. *Year 2000 search and repair technologies are new and uncertain*
8. *Multiple forms of year 2000 repairs are occuring simultaneously*
9. *For some applications, the source code is missing or uncompilable.*

Some of the typical aspects and ingredients of the Y2K problems and solutions are described by the following citations.

- *"The impact of the year 2000 problem is not appreciated by computer experts and business leaders. The problem is easy to understand, and this is probably what leads most to be naive and assume that the solution is just as easy to implement."* [22]
- *"It's going to take a long, difficult, miserable unpleasant scramble to get it done."* [33]
- *"Had adaptive maintenance been properly funded over the past 30 years, we would have no Y2K problem."* [30]

An impressive description of the Y2K impacts in the whole (world wide) society described by Jones in [18] is given in the following two tables (see also [2], [3], [7] and [29]).

National Government ***(Citizen record hazards)***	**Public Utilities** ***(Safety hazards)***	**Telecommunication** ***(Service disruption hazards)***
• *Tax records in error* • *Annuities and entitle-ments miscalculated* • *Pensions miscalculated* • *Disbursements mis-calculated* • *Retirements benefits miscalcu-lated*	• *Electric meters malfunction* • *Gas meters malfunction* • *Distribution of electric power disrupted* • *Billing record in error* • *Nuclear power plants malfunction*	• *Intercontinental switching disrupted* • *Domestic call switching disrupted* • *Billing records in error*
Airlines ***(Safety hazards)***	**Defense** ***(Security hazards)***	
• *Air traffic malfunctions* • *Fligh schedule confusion* • *Navigation equipment failures* • *Maintenance schedule disruption*	• *Base security compromised* • *Computer security compromised* • *Encryption compromised* • *Strategic weapons mal-function* • *Command and communication network problems*	• *Aircraft maintenance records disrupted* • *Logistics and supply systems disrupted* • *Satellite malfunction*

Table 1: Y2K problems

Finance *(Financial transaction hazards)*	**Health Care** *(Safety hazards)*	**Insurance** *(Liability and benefits hazards)*
• *Interest calculations in error* • *Account balances in error* • *Credit card charges in error* • *Funds tranfer disrupted* • *Mortgage/loan interest payment in error* • *Lease record in error*	• *Patient monitoring devices malfunction* • *Operation room supports system disrupted* • *Medical instruments malfunction* • *Patient billing records in error* • *Medical insurance billing in error*	• *Policy due dates in error* • *Benefits and interest calculations in error* • *Annuities miscalculated* • *Payment records in error* • *Year 2000 damages under-estimated*
Local Government *(Local economic hazards)*		**Manufacturing** *(Operational hazards)*
• *Property sales misdated* • *Jury records in error* • *Real estate transactions misdated* • *Divorce records misdated* • *Marriage records misdated* • *Birth records misdated*	• *Death records misdated* • *Traffic ticket dates incorrect in computer* • *Traffic light synchronization disrupted* • *Court dates in error*	• *Subcontract part delivery* • *Just-in-time arrivals disrupted* • *Assembly line shut down* • *Aging of accounts receivable and cash flow* • *Aging of accounts payable and cash flow* • *Pension payment miscalculated*

Table 2: Y2K problems (cont.)

3 Examples of Y2K Metrics

The following list gives an overview and an impression of the quantifications and estimations used as "metrics" in the Y2K area (methods, components, solutions). We also include nominal and ordered evaluations of Y2K aspects.

Y2K Project Steps [12]:

- Awareness 1%
- Inventory 1%
- Project Scoping 4%
- Examination, Analysis and Solution Design 20%
- Modification 20%

- Unit Test 10%
- Integration Test 10%
- Systems/User Acceptance Test 25%
- Implementation, Disaster Recovery, Documentation 9%
- Project Management 25% (+ overall cost of project)

Mainly used Programming Languages [17]:

80 % (COBOL, BASIC, FORTRAN, C)

Current Solution Level (0: no activities, I,..., V: full Y2K compliance) [12]:

- USA, Canada, Australia, Belgium, Sweden, Holland: I – IV
- England, Switzerland, Japan: 0 – III
- Germany, Italy, Russia: 0 - II

Used Y2K Methods [11]:

- Field Expansion: 40 %
- Bridging: 23 %
- Sliding Window: 16 %
- Data Store Duplex: 9 %
- Other: 6 %

(Y2K) Consultants [17]:

- Planning Consultants
- Testing Consultants
- Contract Service Consultants
- Legal Consultants
- Business Consultants
- Recovery Consultants
- Consultants via Internet.

Kinds of Y2K Problems [22]:

- Wrong day of the week calculations
- Applications with a built-in destruction date
- Errors in reports
- Future demands on the system
- Complexity of the modification
- Computer date is not compliant
- Incorrect date comparison and calculation
- Leap year miscalculation
- Missing source code
- Cost for replacing the system
- A vendor who decides not to make the system year 2000 compliant
- Legal entanglements that hinder fixing Y2K problems.

Y2K Impact Categories [6]:

of Dates:	of Files:	of Programs:	of User Interfaces:
C1:Y2K insensitive *C2: self-defining century* *C3: require explicite century specification*	*C1F: no C1 or C3* *C2F: no C3* *C3F: contain C3*	*C1P: no C2,C2F, C3 or C3F* *C2P: C2 and/or C2F* *C3P: C3 and/or C3F*	*C1U & C2U: no C3i* *C3U: C3 being used*

Applications vs. Y2K Project Costs [11]:

1 – 5 Mio $: 35 %

5 – 10 Mio $: 21 %
10 – 20 Mio $: 19 %
20 – 100 Mio $: 18 %

General Y2K Project Costs [18]:

- $2000 per working person in the USA
- 30% of the current IT costs

Team Effort for Large Systems [17]:

Application development representatives:	5
Operation representatives :	2
Technical programming representatives:	1
Database administration:	1
Production planners:	2
Forms development:	1
Facility enigineer:	1
Purchasing:	1
Security:	1
Legal:	1
Audit:	1
Vendors:	3
TOTAL:	**20**
(minimum: 7)	

Project Efort (USA 100%) [18]:

Japan	47%	Brazil	20%	India	14 %	Turkey	9%
Russia	34%	France	19,6%	Mexico	11,4%	Australia	5,4%
Germany	28%	China	19%	Spain	11%		
UK	20%	Italy	18,5%	Canada	9,2%		

Y2K Costs per LOC [33]:

$1.5 per LOC
+ repair or replacement of PC or client/server systems
+ upgrading of COTS
+ business problem costs (related to Y2K)
+ staff time (such as invoicing)
+ special Y2K insurance
+ Y2K litigation

LOC Impacted in Programs [11]:

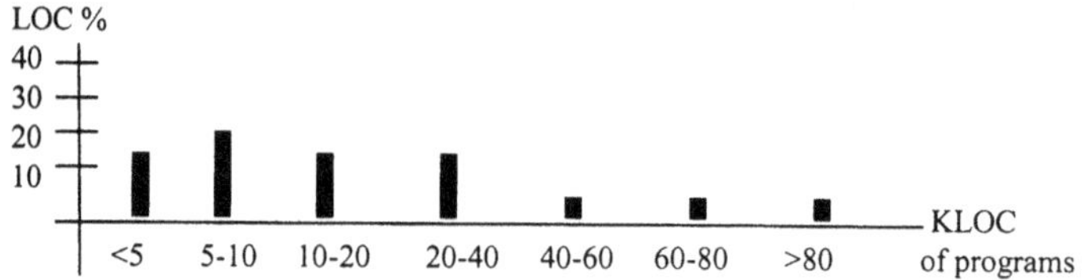

Effort of Y2K per LOC [19]:

1 Month for 1500 LOC.

How can or should we use the software measurement for the Y2K problems, solutions and aspects? In general, we can establish three main aspects

1. Analysis existing Y2K metrics
   - through validation of these metrics
   - by scale transformation (from nominal to ordinal or from ordinal to ratio scale),
2. Looking for new kinds of metrics
   - Y2K as a new kind of complexity
   - new granularities of measurement or estimation,
3. Application of existing metrics for the Y2K problem solution
   - Y2K is mainly a data flow problem
   - the Y2K problem could have been avoided or minimized by the CMM level "four".

In the following section we will give a basic idea for using the main software measurement intentions and application approaches.

4 A General Software Measurement Framework

The application of a software measurement approach must be embedded in a business strategy as described in the following figure [8].

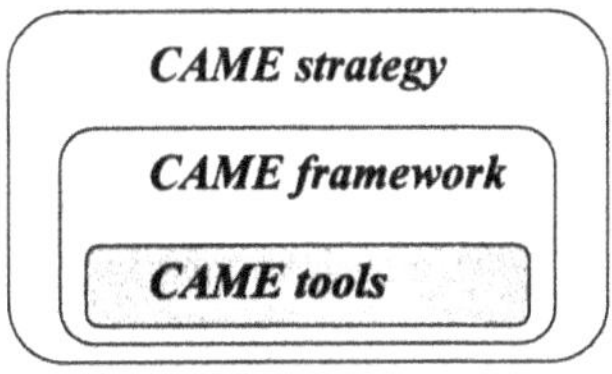

Figure 4: The general software measurement principles

The CAME strategy stands for

- ***Community***: the necessity of a group or a team that is motivated and qualified to initiate software metrics application
- ***Acceptance***: the agreement of the (top) management to install a metrics program in the (IT) business area
- ***Motivation***: the production of measurement and evaluation results in a first metrics application which demonstrate the convincing benefits of the metrics
- ***Engagement***: the willingness to implement the software measurement as a persistent metrics system.

We define our (CAME) software measurement framework with the following four phases:

- Measurement views as ***choice*** of the kind of measurement and the related metrics/ measures
- The ***adjustment*** of the metrics for the application field
- The ***migration*** of the metrics along the whole life cycle and along the system structure (as behaviour of the metrics)
- The ***efficiency*** as construction of a tool-based measurement.

In the following we will describe these four steps of the software measurement and evaluation framework.

Measurement Choice

This step includes the choice of the software metrics and measures from the general ***metrics hierarchy*** (derived from an analysis of the SQA literature and IEEE or ISO standards), that can be transformed into a ***class hierarchy***. This hierarchy (see figure 5) includes three model-based metrics (***size, structure*** and ***complexity***) and one empirical metric related to the ***quality.***

The choice of metrics includes the definition of an object-oriented software metric as ***class/object*** with the ***attributes:*** the metrics value characteristics, and ***services***: the metrics application algorithms.

Software Metrics

Process:		***Quality:***	- functionality
Size:	- number of components		- reliability
	- size of components		- efficiency
	- volume of product line		- usability
Structure:	- life cycle model		- maintainability
	- management areas		- portability
	- organizational strcuture	**Resources:**	
Complexity:	- dimensions of components	***Size:***	- number of platforms, teams etc.
	- granularity of components		- size of standard software
	- integrity of components		- volume of COTS
Quality:	- maturity	***Structure:***	- team structure
	- certification		- computer network structure
	- management (risks) level		- system software structure
Product:		***Complexity:***	- kinds of dev. cultures
Size:	- number of elements		- parameters of platforms
	- size of product components		- dimensions of COTS
	- volume of versions	***Quality:***	- personnel experience
Structure:	- design structure		- product quality of COTS
	- implementation structure		- hardware reliability
	- architecture		
Complexity:	- psychological complexity		
	- computational complexity		

Figure 5: Software metrics (class) hierarchy

Measurement Adjustment

The adjustment is related to the experience (expressed in values) of the measured attributes for the evaluation. Hence, the adjustment includes the metrics validation and the determination of the metrics algorithm based on the measurement strategy. The steps of the measurement adjustment are

- The determination of the ***scale type*** and (if possible) the *unit*
- The determination of the ***favourable values*** (***thresholds***) for the evaluation of the measurement component including their calibrating
- The ***tuning*** of the thresholds during software development or maintenance
- The ***calibration*** of the scale depending on the improvement of the knowledge in the problem domain.

Measurement Migration

The migration step is addressed to the definition of the ***behaviour*** of a metric class such as the ***metrics tracing*** along the life cycle and ***metrics refinement*** along the software application. These aspects keep the dynamic characteristics that are necessary for the persistent installation of metrics applications and require a ***metrics data base*** or other kinds of repositions to store background informations related to the metrics values.

Measurement Efficiency

This step includes the ***instrumentation*** or the automatization of the measurement process by tools. It requires to analyze the algorithmic character of the software measurement and the possibility of the integration of tool-based ''control cycles'' in the software development process. The tools supporting our framework are ***CAME*** (Computer Assisted software Measurement and Evaluation) ***tools.*** In order to use CAME tools efficiently, some rules should be kept in mind [10]:

- The (combined) tool(s) must cover all measurement phases
- The tool(s) must consider the whole software life cycle
- CAME tools should keep the (ISO 9126) quality aspects themselves.

The given class icon in figure 6 describes the general contents of a metrics class based on our CAME framework.

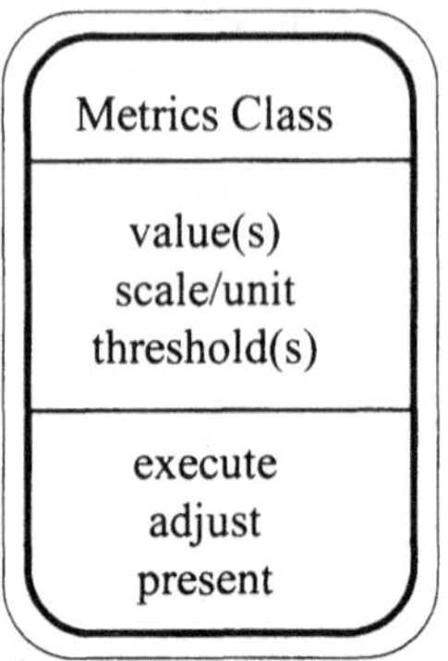

Figure 6: An abstract software metrics class

The term "execute" in the figure above stands for execution, counting, estimation or evaluation. The application of the CAME tools with the background of a metrics data base is the first phase of measurement efficiency, and the ***metrics class library*** the final OO framework installation.

5 Y2K vs. Measurement Strategy and Framework

The following citations should demonstrate the appropriation of the Y2K community to our CAME strategy.

- ***Community:***
  "Highly capable, skilled, motivated poeple to drive the project within the organization" [33]
  "The team must have full responsibility for reassigning and aquiring the resources that are necessary to address the problem." [22]
- ***Acceptance:***
  "Gain senior management's acknowledgment of Y2K impacts" [27]
  "Absolute commitment from top-level management" [33]
- ***Motivation:***
  "The impact prioritization list is developed by the business..." [12]
  "A set of programs and related files must now be chosen for the purpose of executing a pilot conversion." [24]
- ***Engagement:***
  "It's going to take a long, difficult, miserable unpleasant scramble to get it done." [33]

We can establish a general agreement of the current Y2K community with our CAME strategy from a world-wide perspective.

Y2K Measurement Choice

In this step, we will map our general metrics hierarchy with the Y2K metrics considered in the literature (see 2], [16], [20], [23], [28] and [31]). The table 3 gives an overview about the current situation.

Software Metrics			Y2K
Process:	***Size:***	- number of components	**Y2K Effort estimation**
		- size of components	**Y2K Cost estimation**
		- volume of product line	**Impacted LOC per industry**
	Structure:	- life cycle model	**Gartner level 0 to V**
		- management areas	**Y2K litigations**
		- organizational structure	**Y2K portfolios**
	Complexity:	- dimensions of components	**Kinds of Y2K solutions**
		- granularity of components	
		- integrity of components	**Y2K project complexity**
	Quality:	- maturity	**Y2K compliance**
		- certification	**Y2K certification**
		- management (risks) level	**Y2K damages**
Product:	***Size:***	- number of elements	**Impacted LOC, FP estimations**
		- size of product components	**Y2K C classification**
		- volume of versions	
	Structure:	- design structure	
		- implementation structure	**Y2K sensitiveness**
		- architecture	
	Complexity:	- psychological complexity	
		- computational complexity	
	Quality:	- functionality	
		- reliability	
		- efficiency	**Decreasing by Y2K**
		- usability	
		- maintainability	**Increasing by Y2K**
		- portability	
Resources:	***Size:***	- number of platforms, teams etc.	**Y2K team**
		- size of standard software	**Y2K effort per language**
		- volume of COTS	
	Structure:	- team structure	**Y2K team structure**
		- computer network structure	
		- system software structure	**Y2K system problems**
	Complexity:	- kinds of development cultures	
		- parameters of platforms	**Y2K vs. platform**
		- dimensions of COTS	
	Quality:	- personnel experience	**COBOL experience**
		- product quality of COTS	**Y2K vendor classification**
		- hardware reliability	**Y2K problems**

Table 3: Kinds of software metrics and the appropriate Y2K quantifications

Note, the missing part of quality (functionality, reliability and usability) metrics is due to the fact that the Y2K problem is a sole maintanance problem. We will discuss the ''complexity'' area in the next section.

Y2K Measuremenet Adjustment

In th e following, we will evaluate the Y2K metrics situation by examples of this area. Figure 7 shows the open problems of chosen Y2K quantifications.

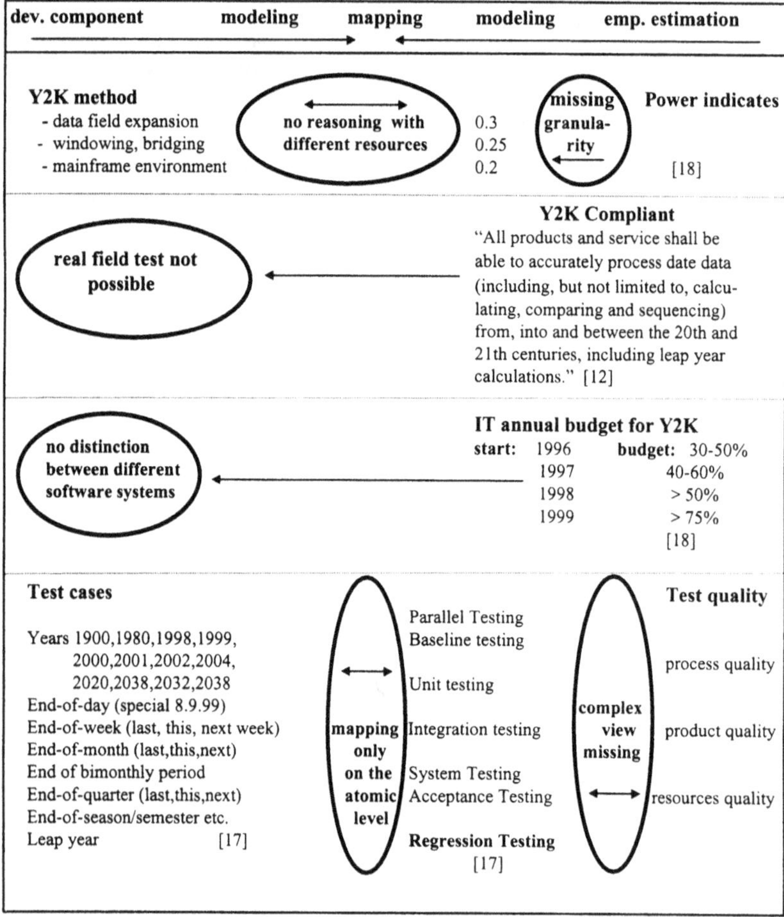

Figure 7: Problem areas in the Y2K metrics field

This demonstrates that the estimation methods and metrics are very rough and mostly not comprehendable. However, we can observe this situation in the software estimation field also. Note, that the complexity of the Y2K problem is the highest one in the history of computing.

The figure 8 demonstrates the distribution of responsibilities and different classes of software and hardware components involved.

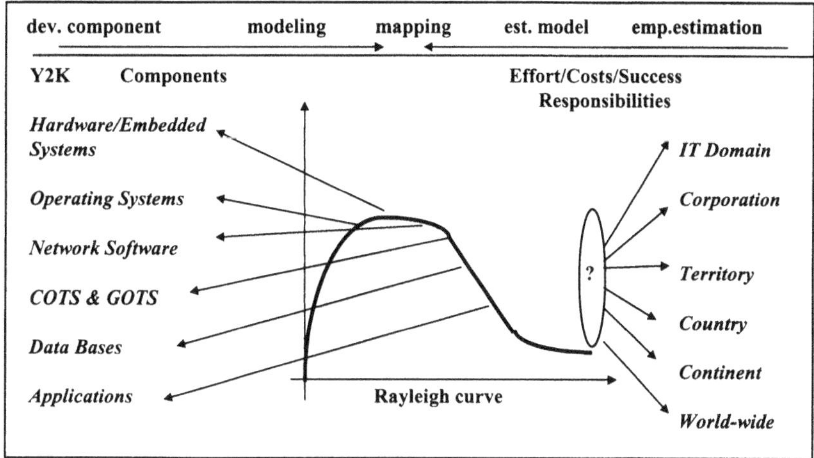

Figure 8: Different involved aspects

The idea of figure 8 is to demonstrate that the effort estimation on the basis of the Rayleigh curve leads to a partitioning relating the different components involved to the different responsibilities. We can establish a "world-wide"-based Rayleigh curve that demonstrate the need of a meaningful phase-based solution of the Y2K problem which is not visible today.

On the other hand, the complexity of the Y2K is the main problem. The "kernel complexity" is given by the date algorithm. It is interesting to assess the compexity of the date algorithm themselves that must be handled during a Y2K solution process. The table 4 describes such an examples. The date algorithm are described in a pseudocode form cited from [24].

Algorithm	LOPC	McCabe	Comment rate	#variables
leap year	14	7	**0**	2
date proof	27	9	0.3	10
date format proof	30	11	0.3	9
date difference	**53**	12	0.26	15
date interval difference	**111**	**24**	0.2	**27**
date transformation	13	5	**0**	9
week day	18	5	**0**	11
date conversion	**56**	**22**	0.3	10
eastern	**52**	10	0.35	13

Table 4: Evaluation of date handling algorithm based on complexity metrics

Y2K Measurement Migration

We will use the Y2K solution steps by [33] to demostrate the metrication level on this area described in figure 9.

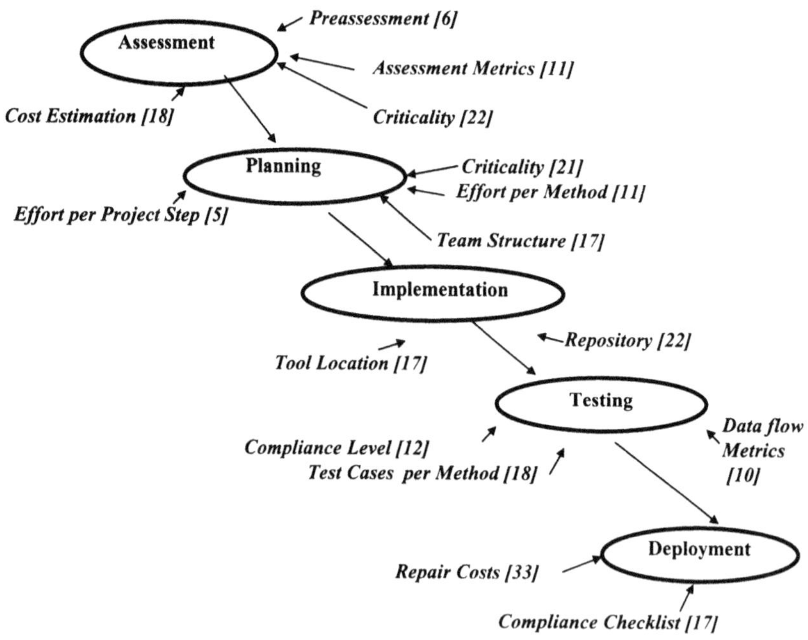

Figure 9: Y2K solution phases and related metrics

A real "migration" is given in the case of causing from the metrics in the first phases to the last one, e.g. *criticality* → *tool location* → *data flows* → *compliance,* etc.

Y2K Measurement Efficiency

The Y2K tool application should based on a meaningful concept, e. g. by [17]:

> "We discuss building a process using methodologies first, since methodologies provide the rational for the use of all other tools."
> "We have seen other organizations spend a year looking at tools and conducting pilots with no appreciable movement toward getting the change process started."

Y2K solutions should use the existing maintenance tools extended by the nessecary Y2K tools only. Table 5 gives an overview about the tools for the different Y2K phases by [34]:

Assessment		*Planning*	*Implementation*		*Testing*
Project Estimation	Data Modeling	Data (Check) Simulator	Rule-Based Change Tools	Migration Tools	Interactive Debugger
Inventory Analysis	Scanner & Parser	Time Simu-lators	Code (Static) Analyzer	Date Libraries	Data Base Conv. Tools

Table 5: Y2K phase related tools

Examples of Y2K projects relating tools to the Zetlin [33] phases are given in figure 10.

It is necessary to keep appropriate coverage of the Y2K project phases by tool supporting. Y2K includes CASE, CARE and CAME tools (especially analysis (CARE/CAME) tools) and should consider the following tool application criteria by [4] as

- Identification
- Criteria (Vendor, Experience of vendor, Availability)
- Method description
- Integration aspects.

Note, that the tool location and ist application should be in accordance with the existing platforms in the IT area.

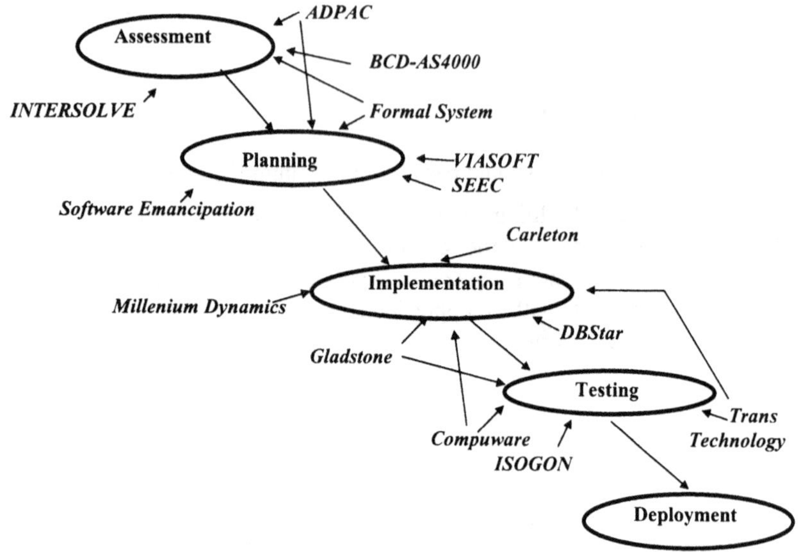

Figure 10: Y2K Tools per Project Step by [Gruhn 97]

6 Conclusions

We have investigate the area of Y2K solutions based on a review of related literature and some experience in Y2K analysis in practice. Our intension was to demonstrate some of the requirements in order to keep the CMM level ''four'' during the Y2K solution. This is the chance to deal with the ''unpleasant'' and high complex world-wide Y2K maintenance problem. An actual description of our Y2K solution service is located at **http://ivs.cs.uni-magdeburg.de/sw-eng/us/.**

References

[1] **Aebi, D.**
Zeitsprung 2000. Carl Hanser Publ., 1998.

[2] **Bartsch, M.**
Software und das Jahr 2000 - Haftung und Versicherungsschutz für ein technisches Großproblem. Nomos Publ., Germany, 1998.

[3] *Leitfaden zum Jahr-2000-Problem (J2K) in der Bürokommunikation.* Bundesministerium des Innern, December 1997.

[4] **Blazey, U.**
Comparison and Evaluation of Y2K solutions (German), Study, University of Magdeburg, April 1998.

[5] **Bohner,S.A.**
Evolving Software Practice for Year 2000 and Beyond. Proc. of the 6th Reengineering Forum, Florence, March 1998, pp. 1-1 to 1-21.

[6] **Chapman, R.B.**
Practical Methods for Your Year 2000 Problem. Manning Publ., 1998.

[7] **Compartner**
Jahr 2000: Ein Datum verändert die Welt. Düsseldorf, 1998.

[8] **Dumke, R.**
An Object-Oriented Software Measurement and Evaluation Framework and ist Application in an Industrial Environment. Proc. of the CONQUEST 2, Nuernberg, 28/29 September 1998, pp. 52-61.

[9] **Dumke, R.**
Really Object-Oriented Software Metrics. in Lehner et al.: Software Metrics, DUV Publ., 1997, pp. 28-58.

[10] **Dumke/Foltin/Koeppe/Winkler**
Softwarequalität durch Meßtools. Vieweg Publ., 1996.

[11] **Feiler, J.; Butler, B.**
Finding and Fixing Your Year 2000 Problem. Academic Press, 1998.

[12] **Gartner Group**
Deadline 2000 - Your Next Steps. Internal Report, April 1998.

[13] **Grimmer, J.**
Der Euro - Das Jahr 200 - Herausforderung für Ihre DV, Interest Publ., 1997.

[14] **Gruhn, V.; Chavan, S.**
Das Jahr-2000-Problem. Addison Wesley Publ., 1997.

[15] **Haase, P.**
Das Jahr 2000 in der EDV. Oldenbourg Publ., 1998.

[16] **Hildebrand, K.**
Das Jahr 2000: Vorgehensweise für die Konvertierung zweiziffriger Jahresdarstellungen in betrieblichen Informationssystemen. in: Oberweis/Sneed: Software-Management'97, Teubner Publ., 1997, pp. 120-133.

[17] **Jager, P. de; Bergeon, R.**
Managing 00 - Surviving the Year 2000 Computing Crisis. John Wiley & Sons Publ., 1997.

[18] **Jones, C.**
The Year 2000 Software Problem. Addison Wesley Publ., 1998.

[19] **Jones, C.**
Rules of Thumb for Year 2000 and EURO-Currency Software Repairs. Metrics News, 3(1998)1, pp. 13-22.

[20] **Kappelman, L.A.; Fent, D.; Keeling, K.B.; Prybutok, V.**
Calculating the Cost of Year-2000 Compliance. CACM, 41(1998)2, pp. 30-39.

[21] **Knolmayer, G.F.**
Determining Work Units in Year 2000 Maintenance Projects. in: Oberweis/Sneed: Software-Management'97, Teubner Publ., 1997, pp. 11-32.

[22] **Koegh, J.**
Solving The Year 2000 Problem. Academic Press, 1997.

[23] **Lefkon, D.**
Year 2000 - Best Practices for Y2K Millenium Computing. AIT Publ., 1998.

[24] **Murray, J.T.; Murray, M.J.**
The Year 2000 Computing Crisis. McGraw Hill, 1996.

[25] **Pfleeger, S.L.**
The Nature of System Change. IEEE Software, May/June 1998, pp. 87-90.

[26] **Sanders, J.**
Y2K: Don't Play it Again, Sam. IEEE Software, May/June 1998, pp. 100-102.

[27] **Schultz, J.E.**
Managing a Y2K Project-Starting Now. IEEE Software, May/June 1998, pp. 63-71.

[28] **Sims et al.**
Die Jahr-2000-Lösung. Thomson Publ., 1998.

[29] **Thaller, G.E.**
Die Doppel-Null - Das Jahr-2000-Problem. bhv Publ., 1998.

[30] **Thomsett, R.**
The Year 2000 Bug: A Forgotten Lesson. IEEE Software, July/August 1998, pp. 91-93, 95.

[31] see the large link List related to the Y2K in ***http://ivs.cs.uni-magdeburg.de/sw-eng/us***

[32] **Yourdon, E.**
A Tale of two Futures.IEEE Software, Jan./Febr. 1998, pp. 23-29.

[33] **Zetlin, M.**
The Computer Time Bomb. AMA Publ., 1997.

[34] **Zvegintzov, N.**
A Resource Guide to Year 2000 Tools. IEEE Computer, March 1997, pp. 58-63.

Software Metrics for Multimedia Languages

Stephen H. Edwards, Sallie M. Henry, and Roger P. Bodnar, Jr.,
Virginia Tech, Blacksburg (USA)

Abstract

Software engineering researchers have attempted to improve the software development process for over two decades. A primary thrust in this process lies in the arena of measurement. "You can't control what you can't measure" [5]. This research applies software metric techniques to the development of multimedia products. Problem areas such as education, instruction, training, and information systems can all benefit from more controlled approaches to development with multimedia tools. As an example, we focus on one multimedia language for creating multimedia products: Macromedia's Authorware. This paper describes the measurement of various distinguishing properties of this language, together with an evaluation of the measurement process. The evaluation gives insight into the next step in establishing the goal of control, through measurement, of the multimedia software development process.

1 Introduction

Software maintenance, a stage in the software development lifecycle, requires up to 60% of the total software budget [4]. Over the years, many techniques for reducing the effort and cost involved in this stage of a product's life cycle have been implemented and practiced. One such technique is the use of software metrics. Several types of software metrics exist that measure different properties of a product. This research focuses on software metrics for code complexity.

Software metrics exist for the procedural and object-oriented paradigms. These established metrics have demonstrated the ability to indicate error prone source code in a given module. As fourth generation language (4GL) techniques have been applied to task-specific purposes, however, new *problem-oriented languages* have arisen. Such languages are aimed at developers who are not experts in programming or software engineering, and this class of languages does not belong to either the procedural or the object-oriented paradigm. At present, there are no known software metrics available for this class of languages.

In this paper, we describe the creation and validation of a suite of software metrics for problem-oriented languages aimed at multimedia programming tasks. Specifically, these metrics have been applied to software projects developed using Authorware, a Macromedia product. The approach to metrics described in this paper is easily extended to other multimedia languages, and suggests possibilities for developing metrics for problem-oriented languages focused on other problem areas.

2 Background

2.1 Multimedia Languages

Multimedia languages are a new class of languages that have arisen in the past decade. The term "multimedia" refers to "a presentation or display that involves more than one method or medium of presentation" [10]. Such media may include audio, video, still images, and animations that accompany the standard text display. Therefore, a multimedia application is one that uses and includes more than one of these media in a cohesive manner. A multimedia language "is a set of software tools for creating multimedia applications" [10]. All multimedia languages present the developer with a set of software tools to aid in the development process. Although they all aid in manipulating similar presentation media, the functionality of these software tools may vary greatly from language to language. As of yet, no standard development environment exists.

Software development for a multimedia language typically takes place in an interactive development environment (IDE) that hides from the developer the underlying low level programming required to handle multimedia objects. To be concrete, our research has focused on one multimedia language: Macromedia's Authorware. Authorware provides an IDE where software development takes place on a graphic flow line. The IDE presents the developer with thirteen different types of development icons. These icons are divided into three classes: icons that manipulate multimedia objects, icons that manipulate the flow of control within the application, and one icon that allows scripting. Creating software in Authorware requires the developer to choose which icon is needed, drag the icon from the palette, and place it on the flow line. Once placed, the icon's properties can be edited to customize its settings. Flow of control icons allow the developer to add branches to the flow line and affect the path(s) taken by the end user. For sophisticated applications, the flow line can be partitioned into "modules" that can call each other and that can be nested. Flow of control and scripting are described in problem-oriented terms and controlled by direct manipulation, so that the developer does not need any formal programming experience.

2.2 Maintenance

Software maintenance is that phase of the development life cycle devoted to the elimination of post-delivery errors and the enhancement or extension of the product to cover new or changing requirements. The amount of effort that software companies spend on maintenance is large: typically 40-60%, and sometimes as much as 90%, of the total life cycle budget for a product [6].

As a result, to significantly reduce the cost of a software project, reducing the effort devoted to maintenance is a necessity. A large portion of maintenance effort is devoted to the elimination of post-delivery errors [8], and the earlier in the development process such errors are detected and corrected, the less costly they are to fix. As a result, identifying potential "problem areas" in source code during development for the purposes of reducing the number of defects that survive product delivery is one method of controlling maintenance cost. Identifying "problem areas" also helps to reduce the cost of enhancement and extension activities during maintenance, since tricky source code is also likely to be more difficult to modify and more expensive to retest. Software metrics are one tool for identifying problem areas in source code so that the goal of reduced maintenance cost can be achieved.

2.3 Software Metrics

Software metrics measure code complexity based on a set of properties of a development language. Such measures provide a relative, quantitative evaluation of source code for this development language [4]. Research has shown that a strong correlation exists between the problem areas pointed out by software metrics and the main areas where maintenance efforts have been concentrated. Several different types of software metrics exist for both the procedural and object-oriented paradigms.

The three standard categories of software complexity metrics for procedural languages are: code metrics, structure metrics, and hybrid metrics. Code metrics measure properties of the source code by tallying its syntactic entities to give quantitative results. Some typical examples include: lines of code [4], Halstead's software science indicators [7], and McCabe's cyclomatic complexity [11].

Unlike code metrics, structure metrics attempt to measure the interconnectivity between the logical parts of the product being analyzed. Examples include: Henry and Kafura's information flow metric [8], McClure's invocation complexity metric [12], and Belady's cluster metric [1].

Hybrid metrics combine code and structure metrics to capture some information about the syntactic structure of the source code in addition to capturing overall information on the product. Examples include: Woodfield's review complexity [Woodfield] and the weighted form of Henry and Kafura's information flow metric [8].

Unfortunately, object-oriented languages contain many properties that do not exist in procedural languages, and as a result, procedural metrics do not effectively capture all the sources of complexity in OO programs. As a result, a new collection of software metrics have been developed for gauging complexity in OO software. Such metrics include: weighted methods per class, depth of the inheritance tree, number of children, coupling between classes, response for a class, and lack of cohesion in methods [3][9].

Just as metrics for procedural languages do not effectively capture the properties of object-oriented programs, neither procedural nor OO metrics capture the properties of multimedia languages. New metrics that measure properties ranging from the number of icons on the flow line to the maximum depth of a module are needed.

3 Metrics for Multimedia Languages

The classic software metrics, including code, structure, and hybrid metrics, were designed to analyze programming languages whose source code exists in text files. These programming languages all have a similar structure to their source code—i.e., user-defined procedures or functions, looping structures, and so on. Authorware's source code exists in the development environment as a graphical flow line. The IDE stores this code at the raw file level in a binary format that is not human readable. Further, there are major differences between text-based program source code and the graphical representation of Authorware's source code. As a result, a new suite of software metrics was developed specifically for use with multimedia languages.

To generate the new metrics, first a taxonomy of programming paradigms and the key classes of program properties characterizing each was created [2]. By mapping existing software metrics to classes of language properties, it is possible to see which metrics can be appropriately applied to which paradigms. Second, a group of four expert Authorware developers were interviewed to uncover software properties that answer the following two questions [2]:

- What properties of Authorware can potentially be measured?
- What makes some Authorware source code modules better than others?

The goal was to reveal the measurable properties of Authorware software projects that are good indicators of complex, error prone sections of code.

The suite of metrics for multimedia languages consists of six new software metrics. Four of the six are adaptations of existing software metrics, reinterpreted in a new context. The new metrics are: Number of Icons,

Audio/Video Icons, Variable Passing, Depth of Module, Flow of Control, and Variables on Display Icons.

3.1 Number of Icons (NOI)

The Number of Icons metric (NOI) is based on the traditional lines of code metric. Lines of code measures how many source lines of code are in each function or module in the program being analyzed. As the number of lines increases, so does the likelihood that the particular function or module contains an error [4]. A threshold can be used to flag units deemed overly complex by this metric.

NOI measures the number of icons in a module. As the number of icons increases, so does the complexity of the code. Keeping the number of icons low reduces code complexity and improves readability. Table 1 gives a representative threshold for flagging modules with too many icons. The thresholds in Table 1 were determined by developer experience and assessed by the Authorware experts, but they are by no means meant to convey an exact threshold for all developers. These numbers may vary from company to company or development approach to development approach, and require fine tuning by each organization.

3.2 Audio/Video Icons (AVI1 and AVI2)

In Authorware, the use of audio and video icons present an opportunity for reusability. Such icons can be placed in libraries so that the actual icons placed on the flow line are links to the original in the library. This allows audio and video clips to be replaced or modified in the library, affecting all linked occurrences. Further, from the library, the developer can locate all references to a given clip without having to scour the code.

The pair of Audio/Video Icon metrics are based on Halstead's software science indicators, which count the number of unique operators and the total number of occurrences of operators. For multimedia languages, the counts represent the total number of occurrences of linked audio and video icons in the source code (AVI1) and the number of unique audio and video icons in the libraries (AVI2). Threshold values for AVI1 and AVI2 appear in Table 1.

3.3 Variable Passing (VP)

The Variable Passing metric originated from Henry and Kafura's information flow metric [8], which measures the complexity of source code as the amount of information flowing into and out of procedures or functions. It is defined as:

$$C_p = (\textit{fan-in} \times \textit{fan-out})^2 \times \textit{LOC}$$

Where

C_p = the complexity measure for procedure p.
fan-in = the number of local flows into p plus the number of global data structures from which p retrieves information.
fan-out = the number of local flows out of p plus the number of global data structures that p updates.
LOC = then number of lines of code in p.

The information flow metric was developed for languages that support user-defined procedures and functions. Authorware does not support this functionality, but Authorware does have a "module" construct that allows a single flow line to be "called" from one or more points in other flow lines. As a result, the information flow metric can be extrapolated to Authorware modules. The number of variables being passed into or out of a module is counted and used in this modified definition:

$C_m = (\textit{fan-in} \times \textit{fan-out})$

Where

C_m = the complexity measure for module m.
fan-in = the number of local flows into m from which the module retrieves information.
fan-out = the number of local flows out of m that the module updates.

As the value of C_m becomes larger, the complexity of the module increases. A threshold value for VP appears in Table 1.

3.4 Depth of Module (DOM)

The Depth of Module metric measures how deep the levels of nesting are for the current module. This metric is based on the object-oriented Depth of Inheritance Tree metric that reports the maximum depth of a given class in the class hierarchy [3]. In Authorware, map and framework icons provide the ability for one flow line to "call" other modules. Thus, every time a map or a framework icon is added to the flow line, another level of nesting is added to the source code. The belief is that as the DOM becomes large, the source code becomes more complex. Table 1 indicates threshold values for the DOM metric.

3.5 Flow of Control (FOC)

Authorware provides the ability to unconditionally branch from one point to another in an application's flow line through a navigation icon and through a *Goto* function. Counting the number of uses of these two features gives an indication of additional complexity in the application's flow of control. The acceptable threshold value for this metric is shown in Table 1. Note that this threshold is slightly higher than one might expect, because the framework icon—used for calling nested modules—requires the use of navigation icons to perform certain tasks. The threshold shown in Table 1 is inflated to take this into account.

Metric	Acceptable	Too Great/ Raise Warning
NOI	< 500	≥ 500
AVI1	< 300	≥ 300
AVI2	< 300	≥ 300
VP	< 10	≥ 10
DOM	< 6	≥ 6
FOC	< 30	≥ 30
VDI1	< 20	≥ 20
VDI2	< 20	≥ 20

Table 1: Warning Thresholds for the Multimedia Metrics Suite

3.6 Variables on Display Icons (VDI1 and VDI2)

Display icons allow the content of variables to be displayed on the screen during the application's execution. These icons allow simple equations to be embedded in the visual display as well. All dynamic output to the screen in Authorware applications, other than predefined graphics, text, audio, or video, is handled through display icons.

Display icons must be used with care, since it is difficult to determine whether or not variables are embedded in the display during development. In particular when a variable is initialized as a null string and is embedded in the display, nothing will appear in its place. An uninitialized variable, on the other hand, will appear as a zero. This functionality invites errors. In addition, the developer can choose to display either the variable value at the current point in the application's execution, or to display a continuously updated representation of the variable's value. The Authorware experts considered variables on display icons to be likely sources of some kinds of errors.

The two pieces of data measured for this pair of metrics are the total number of variables in display icons (VDI1) and the total number of display icons with variables on them (VDI2). Table 1 shows acceptable threshold values for these two metrics.

Module	NOI	AVI1	AVI2	VP	DOM	FOC	VDI 1	VDI2	# Exceeded	Error s
A-1	21	1	1	0	2	0	0	0	0	6
A-2	26	1	1	1	4	0	0	0	0	0
A-3	162	5	5	1	4	18	0	0	0	1
A-4	143	15	14	1	4	3	0	0	0	1
A-5	28	1	1	1	4	0	0	0	0	1
A-6	593	35	35	1	6	29	21	12	3	11
A-7	302	39	29	1	4	29	14	7	0	12
A-8	398	47	38	1	6	46	9	9	2	8
A-9	957	37	36	1	6	75	39	20	5	14
B-1	77	7	7	12	4	8	1	1	1	0
B-2	205	3	3	0	7	39	3	1	2	1
B-3	373	20	20	0	6	52	2	2	2	2
B-4	4752	479	370	12	10	552	4	3	6	61

Table 2: Metric and Error Data for Products A and B (Gray Cells Indicate Over-Threshold Values)

4 Evaluating the Metrics

4.1 Data Collection

To evaluate the six multimedia language metrics, data were collected on two commercial software products created using Authorware, Product "A" and Product "B". These products were both created by a small, privately owned, commercial software company that develops multimedia applications for education, training, and information systems that are targeted at a diverse clientele. Both products are interactive training applications that incorporate audio, video, text, and graphics; both products were considered to be small products by their developers.

Data were collected one product at a time. Product A consisted of nine modules and Product B consisted of four modules. All metrics from Section 3 were collected on a per module basis. Because Authorware's binary file format is not human-readable, all measures were taken manually for this evaluation, although it is possible to create measurement software to analyze stored Authorware code directly.

The NOI metric measures the total number of icons for an entire module. The Authorware IDE provides a *File Setup* command that returns information on the current module, including the total number of icons in the module.

Collecting data for the AVI metric is a process that gathers two pieces of information at the same time. The first piece of information sought (AVI1) is the number of audio/video icons in the source code that are links to a library. To find this information a depth first search of the source code was performed, counting all audio and video icons linked to a library in the process. The second piece of information sought (AVI2) is the number of audio/video icons that exist in the libraries. This number may be obtained by inspecting the libraries themselves.

The information that the VP metric requires is easily obtainable, although all of the information is not available until every module for a product is inspected. There are two ways of calling another module, using the *Jumpfile* function and using the *Jumpfilereturn* function. While viewing the source code for the current module in the Authorware IDE, the references to these two built-in functions can be viewed using the *Show Functions* command on the *Data* menu. Using this command, all calls out of the module were inspected to calculate the fan-out for the module. Calculating the fan-in requires an inspection of the fan-outs of all the other modules in the product.

In order to compute the DOM metric, the level of the deepest branch of the module is recorded. Authorware source code can be represented by a binary tree, so computing the DOM metric is as simple as finding the longest branch in the tree.

The fifth metric, FOC, requires a count of the number of references to the *Goto* function and a count of the number of uses of the navigation icon. Gathering the information on the *Goto* function can be done using the *Show Functions* command on the *Data* menu. Gathering the number of uses of the navigation icon required a depth first search of the module during which a running total of the number of navigation icons found in the source code was accumulated.

The last measurement is for the VDI metric. There are two pieces of information to gather here: first, the number of variables that are on display icons (VDI1), and second, the number of display icons that have variables on them (VDI2). To find this data, a depth first search for all display icons was performed and every display icon was inspected to tally both measures.

All six metrics were collected for both Products A and B, along with the number of errors discovered in each module during development. Table 2 summarizes this data.

4.2 Data Analysis

In analyzing the data collected from Products A and B, the collected data were compared against the threshold values shown in Table 1. These results were then subjectively validated by interviewing the application programmers responsible for these two products.

Table 1 shows threshold values for the metrics presented in Section 3. A measured value that exceeds the threshold indicates a greater likelihood that the given module contains errors. These values may need fine tuning by each organization that employs them.

After the data for Products A and B were collected, a comparison against the threshold values in Table 1 was conducted and the results are shown in Table 2. The data cells that are highlighted with a gray background in Table 2 exceed the threshold value for the corresponding metric. As noted in Table 2, module A-6, A-9, and B-4 all exceed the threshold for the NOI metric. For AVI1 and AVI2, B-4 was the only module exceeding the suggested threshold. B-1 and B-4 both exceeded the threshold for the VP metric. The DOM metric flagged modules A-6, A-8, A-9, B-2, B-3, and B-4 as having exceeded the threshold value. For the FOC metric, modules A-8, A-9, B-2, B-3, and B-4 all exceeded the threshold. Both A-6 and A-9 exceeded the VDI1 threshold, and A-9 also exceeded the VDI2 threshold. Modules exceeding the thresholds were then presented to the product developers for review.

For Product A, modules A-1, A-2, and A-5 are small, lack any major functionality, and violate none of the proposed thresholds. The programmers agreed that due to the simplistic nature of these three modules they would not expect them to exceed any proposed thresholds. Modules A-3, A-4, and A-7 also did not exceed any threshold values. The programmers stated that although these modules are larger than A-1, A-2, and A-5, they still perform simple tasks. Module A-6 exceeded three of the proposed thresholds: NOI, DOM, and VDI1. The programmers stated this module was more complex and therefore more errors were encountered than in other modules. The programmers went on to say that the modules A-6, A-8, and A-9 all contain similar source code. Also, the basic concepts used to develop these modules were the same. The programmers were not surprised to learn that A-8 exceeded the DOM and FOC metric thresholds. Further, module A-9 exceeded thresholds for five metrics: NOI, DOM, FOC, VDI1, and VDI2. The programmers agreed that module A-9 was the most complex and error prone of the modules in Product A, and that it also took longer to test and debug than the others.

All four modules for Product B exceeded at least one of the proposed thresholds. Module B-1 exceeded the VP metric. This puzzled the programmers, since to them B-1 was a relatively simple module. After explaining the VP metric, they believe that it is not measuring the full picture for module B1. Therefore, the threshold value for VP may be too low. The programmers continued by saying that since the variables in Authorware are string based, they commonly concatenated several variables together into one variable, which was then passed in an array format between modules. Because of this practice, it was their opinion that unless the VP metric was adjusted to take these points into account, this metric would not accurately report anything about the source code.

Both modules B-2 and B-3 exceeded two of the threshold values for DOM and FOC. The programmers stated that these modules contained more complex functionality. The last module, B-4, exceeded six of the thresholds: NOI, AVI1, AVI2, VP, DOM, and FOC. These results matched the programmers' expectations, since B-4 is extremely complex; it was created by combining two modules into one. The programmers stated that this module was difficult to debug due to the interaction between the various parts of the module. However, the programmers expressed their concern over the threshold values for the AVI1 and AVI2 metrics. They believe that these metrics require further study to determine more accurate threshold values, since module B-4 was the only module with properties approaching the suggested thresholds.

Comparing the metric data collected for Products A and B against the number of errors found in each module suggests that this suite of metrics does indicate modules that are likely to contain errors. Further, the subjective validation of these results by the application programmers that developed the two products indicates that these metrics are on the right course.

5 Conclusions

In this paper, a suite of new software metrics for multimedia languages was presented. Each metric in this suite measures different properties of source code in such a language. Four of these metrics are adaptations of proven software metrics and the other two are completely new.

The new software metrics were applied in the context of a specific multimedia language, Authorware. They were computed on two commercially produced software products and data were collected. The software metrics were designed to indicate source code that has a greater likelihood of containing errors before the product under development is delivered to the client. Analyzing the collected metric data from the two products studied revealed that a number of modules in both products exceeded suggested thresholds for some of the metrics, and that these modules were ones that contained greater numbers of errors. These results were shared with the application programmers who developed the two products, and the programmers provided subjective validation that the metrics were indeed indicating modules that were likely to contain greater numbers of errors. Together, these two indicators suggest that this research is on the right track toward measuring properties of Authorware source code that indicate error proneness.

The strengths and weaknesses of this research can be summarized as follows:

Strengths:

1. A suite of software metrics were proposed for multimedia languages and applied to specific products written in Authorware.

2. The suite of software metrics was evaluated. Even though the sample products were relatively small, the suite of metrics was effective in indicating modules that were more likely to contain errors. This establishes an effective basis for a more complete set of multimedia metrics.

Weaknesses:

1. Additional Authorware products need to be evaluated to fine tune the suite of proposed metrics.

2. Another multimedia language and associated products must be evaluated to establish and further validate the suite of metrics.

3. While the subjective validation provided by this study has given promising results, larger products are also needed to perform additional statistical validation of regression models.

This work also opens several avenues for future research in the area of software metrics. Within the context of multimedia languages, addressing the weaknesses delineated above is a prime goal. In particular, applying these metrics to larger products, and to products developed using other multimedia languages, are important steps in refining this metric suite.

Further, the programming paradigm taxonomy developed by Bodnar [2] suggests that similar metrics can be designed for problem-oriented languages in other domains. Future research in metrics for other classes of problem-oriented languages shows promise.

Finally, no suite of metrics will ever be accepted by industry until an automated tool is provided to gather the metric values and the necessary data to perform a validation. Developing a automated method of collecting metric values for this suite is important, both for promoting industrial use of such metrics and for pursuing the weaknesses mentioned above as part of future research.

In the end, however, it is clear that graphically oriented languages designed for a non-programming audience are still amenable to metric analysis. Metrics for such languages can identify potentially troublesome spots in source code, and hold the promise for allowing one to reduce maintenance costs by focusing resources on the portions of the code most likely to contain errors.

References

[1] **L.A. Belady and C.J. Evangelisti**
System Partitioning and Its Measure. Journal of Systems and Software, Vol. 2: 23-29, 1981.

[2] **R.P. Bodnar, Jr.**
A Methodology, Based on a Language's Properties, for the Selection and Validation of a Suite of Software Metrics. MS Thesis, Virginia Tech, 1997.

[3] **S.R. Chidamber and C.F. Kemerer**
A Metrics Suite for Object-Oriented Design. IEEE Transactions on Software Engineering, 20 (6): 476-493, June, 1994.

[4] **S.D. Conte, H.E. Dunsmore, and V.Y. Shen**
Software Engineering Metrics and Models. Reading, MA: Bejamin/Cummings, 1986.

[5] **T. DeMarco**
Controlling Software Projects: Management, Measurement, and Estimation. New York: Yourdon Press, 1982.

[6] **R.E. Fairley**
Software Engineering Concepts. New York: McGraw-Hill, 1985.

[7] **M.H. Halstead**
Elements of Software Science. New York: Elsevier, 1977.

[8] **S. Henry and D. Kafura**
Software Structure Metrics Based on Information Flow. IEEE Transactions on Software Engineering, SE-7 (5): 510-518, September, 1981.

[9] **W. Li and S.M. Henry**
Object-Oriented Metrics which Predict Maintainability. Journal of Systems and Software, 23(2): 111-122, November, 1993.

[10] **A.C. Luther**
Authoring Interactive Multimedia. New York: AP Professional, 1994.

[11] **T.J. McCabe**
A Complexity Measure. IEEE Transactions on Software Engineering, SE-2 (4): 308-320, December, 1976.

[12] **C. McClure**
A Model for Program Complexity Analysis. Proceedings of the 3rd International Conference on Software Engineering, Atlanta, GA: May 1978, pp. 149-157.

Improving Reliability of Large Software Systems

Christof Ebert, Thomas Liedtke, Ekkehard Baisch,
Alcatel Telecom, Antwerp (Belgium) / Stuttgart (Germany)

Abstract
Improving field performance of telecommunication systems is one of the most relevant targets of both telecom suppliers and operators, as an increasing amount of business critical systems worldwide are relying on dependable telecommunication. Finding defects earlier of course should improve field performance in terms of reduced field failure rates and reduced intrinsic downtime. This paper describes an integrated approach to improve early defect detection and thus field reliability of telecommunication switching systems. The assumptions at the start of the projects discussed in this paper are: Wide application of code inspections and thorough module testing must lead to a lower fault detection density in following test phases. At the same time criteria for selecting the right modules for code reviews, code inspections and module test have to be improved in order to optimize efficiency. Experiences from projects of Alcatel Telecom's Switching System Division are included to show practical impacts.

1 Introduction

Quality improvement such as increased reliability and maintainability are of utmost importance in software development. In this field, which was previously ad hoc and unpredictable rather than customer oriented, increasing competition and decreasing customer satisfaction have motivated management to put more emphasis on quality. Failures in telecommunication systems, such as a nationwide switching circuit failure in 1992, recently showed that low software quality in such a sensible field has much more effect than defects in many other applications. Compared to other products with high software complexity (e.g. scientific computing, real-time systems) telecommunication systems provide manifold risks (based on the product of probability and effect) due to high coupling, which lets failures being distributed rapidly nationwide. To make it even worse, numerous other applications dependent on correct functionality of real-time information exchange.

This paper provides insight in techniques for criticality prediction as they are applied within the development of *Alcatel 1000 S12* switching software. Modules identified as overly complex are undertaken additional inspection or test effort. Release time prediction and field performance prediction are both based on tailored and superposed ENHPP (exponential non-homogeneous Poisson process) reliability models. For the complete approach of criticality and reliability prediction recent data from the development of a switching system with more than 2.5 MStmt is provided. The switching system is currently in operational use, thus allowing for validation and tuning of the prediction models.

The paper is organized as follows. The introductory chapter 2 presents an overview of the environment in which the development takes place. System features and organizational dimensions are provided in this section to facilitate benchmarking. Chapter 3 briefly introduces techniques for reliability engineering to provide the entire context from which these experiences described here were taken. Definitely the three relevant techniques for effectively improving reliability are

- defect prevention during development;
- early defect detection during design;
- fault tolerance of the entire system and its components.

Ch. 4 digs into techniques for early defect detection. Finally, chapter 5 summarizes the results and provides an outlook on further goals.

2 The Environment

The *Alcatel 1000 S12* is a digital switching system that is currently used in over 40 countries world-wide with over 130 million installed lines. It provides a wide range of functionality (small local exchanges, transit exchanges, international exchanges, network service centers, or intelligent networks) and scalability (from small remote exchanges to large local exchanges). Its typical size is over 2.5 MStmt of which a big portion is customized for local network operators. The code used for *S12* is realized in Assembler, C and CHILL. Recently object-oriented paradigms supported by C++ and Java are increasingly used for new components. In terms of functionality, *S12* covers almost all areas of software and computer engineering. This includes operating systems, database management and distributed real-time software.

The organization responsible for development and integration is registered to the ISO 9001 standard. Typically total effort for development, testing, integration, and field delivery of such a system reaches several hundred person years and provides one or even more local functional releases for different customers per year. Development staff at Alcatel (not responsible for integration and field delivery) is distributed over several sites worldwide. In terms of effort or cost, the share of software is increasing continuously and is currently in the range of 80 %.

For this study we are providing data gathered during development and field operation of several releases of the *Alcatel 1000 S12* switching system. For average values and evolution over time, over 30 comparable projects were taken from our history database. At the beginning of our approach to improve reliability the focus was on two objectives closely related to Alcatel's business goals:

- improving the customer-perceived quality;
- reducing the total cost of non-quality.

3 Techniques for Reliability Improvement

3.1 Effective Defect Prevention

Defect prevention surely is the single best approach to avoid costly defect detection in later development phases. Many constructive approaches are available to reduce the amount of defects inserted in the software

- application of formal methods and cleanroom engineering;
- application of common design principles to ensure high quality designs (e.g. modularity, understandability, low complexity, no Assembler language and direct access to databases);
- redundancy of software components;
- distributed functions;
- impact analysis of faults in order to avoid that corrections are incomplete;
- root cause analysis of known faults in order to detect similar occasions and reasons for faults.

Especially root cause analysis combined with defect prevention to our experience is a good instrument for reducing software faults. We therefore introduced root cause analysis for all reported field failures and for a sample of internally detected faults. Root causes are clustered, prioritized and then carefully considered in the development processes to remove them or at least reduce their impact. Defect preventive actions have been embedded within the overall defect prevention process to avoid artificial checks that would not be applied in the daily project environment as their trade-off would not be immediately visible to the project team. A selection of few defect preventive checks for different design phases is provided in table 1. The checks have been extracted from the overall applicability database and show different objectives. They are based on an analysis of defects over some time and are continuously updated, priories and weighted to support decision making during the project. This is why cost and risk are not filled in. they would be checked as part of upfront risk analysis when the most appropriate actions are determined. After being selected the status is filled out, first to see which activities are applicable and later to track the implementation.

3.2 Defect Detection, Quality Gates and Reporting

Since defects can never be entirely avoided, several techniques have been suggested for detecting defects early in the development life cycle:

- design reviews;
- code inspections with checklists based on typical fault situations or critical areas in the software;
- enforced reviews and testing of critical areas (in terms of complexity, former failures, expected fault density, individual change history, customer's risk and occurrence probability);
- tracking the effort spent for analyses, reviews, and inspections and separating according to requirements to find out areas not sufficiently covered;
- test coverage metrics (e.g. C0 and C1);
- dynamic execution already applied during integration test;
- application of protocol testing machines to increase level of automatic testing;
- application of operational profiles / usage specifications from start of system test.

We will further focus on several selected approaches that are applied for improved defect detection before starting with integration and system test.

One important tool for effectively reducing defects and improving reliability is to track all faults that are detected independent in which development process. Counting faults is one of the most widely applied and accepted methods used to determine software quality. Typically development views quality on the basis of faults, while it is failures that reflect the customer's satisfaction with a product. Counting faults during the complete project helps to estimate the end of distinct phases (e.g. module test or subsystem test) and improves the underlying processes. Failure prediction is used to manage release time of software. This ensures that neither too much time or money are spent on unnecessary testing that could possibly result in late delivery, nor that early release occurs which might jeopardize customer satisfaction due to undetected faults. More advanced techniques in failure prediction focus on typical user operations and therefore avoid wasting time and effort on wrong test strategies. Failures reported during system test or field application must be traced back to their primary causes and specific faults in the design (e.g. design decisions or lack of design reviews).

An example of good reporting is when a customer provides adequate data and is interested in detecting as many faults as possible in order to get them corrected. Based on fault reports since module test, predictive models have been developed on the basis of complexity metrics and on the basis of reliability prediction models [8]. As a result, it was possible to determine defective modules already during design and field failure rates during test!

Fig. 1 shows that in organizations with rather low maturity (i.e. ranked according to the capability maturity model) faults are often detected at the end of the development process despite the fact that they had been present since the design phase. Late fault detection results in costly and time consuming correction efforts, especially when the requirements were misunderstood or a design flaw occurred. Organizations with higher maturity obviously move defect detection towards the phases where they have been introduced.

3.3 Fault Tolerance

Defects cannot be entirely avoided and not even completely be removed before the product is shipped to the customer. This is the sad reality in most commercial software systems, although tremendous effort is spent to improve this situation. Only high reliability systems can spend the lead time and additional efforts necessary to apply rigorous formal methods that can prove that code performs according to requirements. It is for these reasons that commercial systems in high reliability environments must also prevent faults from causing harmful failures.

Constructive fault-tolerance starts with system design and architecture (e.g. design diversity, global fault tolerance functions, and redundancy). Often plain redundancy on the system level is for economic reasons not feasible, thus asking for means to introduce diversity or redundancy within the software. Necessary diversity on the software level for example can be specified precisely with design languages and methods, test strategies and algorithms. Distributed functionality and replicated processes and databases of course also facilitate redundancy on the software level. Top-level design reviews already allow for checking what architectural means could contribute to fault tolerance.

During subsystem design algorithms for fault detection and fault recovery procedures during runtime can be implemented depending on specific functionality and design constraints, while design fault removal is more of analytic relevance.

After detailed design, reviews include models, experiments, and simulation to identify potential fault reasons and to evaluate or validate fault detection and recovery procedures. Knowing about typical (external) reasons or triggers for failures suggests another efficient technique closely related to defect prevention, namely addressing and removing reasons for running into such critical situations, for instance by means of changing physical (environmental) or human interfaces.

This means that for telecommunication systems the primary goal is to achieve system availability without overhead in terms of systems being installed. Practical instruments include mechanisms for overload detection and effective traffic management combined with a distributed architecture both for the processes and for the databases. Internal fault detection mechanisms associated with and supervising each running process help in detecting critical runtime modes and bring the software back to stable modes without loosing calls. Examples include supervision of running processes and resource allocation based on timers or the check of data and messages that are distributed on their completeness and consistency.

4 Early Defect Detection

4.1 Reducing Cost of Non-Quality

Reducing total cost of non-quality is driven by the fault detection distribution (see fig. 1 again). Assuming a distinct cost for fault detection and repair (which includes regression testing, production, etc.) per detection activity, allows to calculate the total cost of non-quality for a distinct project. Obviously the activities of fault detection are taken into consideration and not necessarily the achieved milestone. Milestones in today's incremental development might completely mislead the picture because a distinct milestone could be achieved early, while major portions of the software are still in an earlier development phase. Cost of non-quality in terms of average cost per fault is then calculated based on the respective detection activity. This also supports using a fixed value per fault and activity in a distinct timeframe, because finding a fault with module test including the correction takes a rather stable effort, as well as for instance the detection, correction, regression test, production and delivery during system test.

Obviously both in ch. 2 mentioned improvement objectives challenged that faults are often detected too late in the development process. For that reason both were approached simultaneously when we started the driving software process improvement program. Our approach to achieve these goals was as follows:

1. Since the effects of defect prevention would clearly take longer to achieve measurable improvements, focus was on defect detection. Although we started at the same time a defect prevention program (achieving a 10% reduction of code defects per year) and also improved the upfront design process (i.e. TLD and DD), most short-term impact was expected in detecting code faults as early as feasible.

2. As a consequence several "root causes" of late fault detection were investigated. We ended up with three areas which would allow earlier fault detection: code inspections, module test, and improved integration test.

3. For each of these three areas we started a distinct improvement activity with the target to define the underlying process, pilot and provide tools support, train the people involved with these activities and institutionalize the processes.

4. Both module test and code inspection showed up with rather coherent approaches, namely a target value of faults per new/changed statement to be detected. Finding more faults per statement would directly impact the overall design fault detection effectiveness which then should have measurable impact on fault cost.

5. To facilitate achieving these fault per statement objectives, both working groups came up with more pragmatic process targets, such as limits for reading speed, preparation time, C0 coverage, etc. Piloting and institutionalization showed big improvements in terms of design defect detection effectiveness which was continuously improved in the described three year timeframe (fig. 2). While reading speed indeed was a perfectly suitable input parameter for driving the inspection process, a distinct coverage objective during module test was not feasible due to a very heterogeneous testing approach. Module test thus only took the faults found per new or changed statement as the input parameter. New and changed statements were taken because the stable legacy code was not validated during design.

6. To avoid the well-known trap of any improvement initiative, namely to ask for unachievable goals, we combined the results of inspections and module test working groups with planning and estimation changes. Inspections for instance needed a high peak load of designers during the short inspection timeframe, while module test required improved tools in line with training and set up of test environments. All this additional effort and sometimes lead time

had to be committed by respective middle management and team leaders to facilitate the changes.

While module test and code inspections could be triggered with almost cook-book style approaches, the situation in integration was less obvious. It became even worse with finding more faults upfront, because the effectiveness of test decreased and still many faults could only be detected in the subsystem or even within the entire switch due to the many data-driven interactions with other components. Fig. 3 shows the early effects of increasing design defect detection effectiveness at the cost of reduced test case effectiveness. More test cases had to be run to detect the same amount (or percentage) of faults as before. The only target that could be imagined at that time was to increase the effectiveness within test. The test working group thus set up the target to find more than 92% of all remaining faults in the software before handover to the customer. As a matter of fact this target clearly focused on quality, while elapse time during test was not considered at the first spot.

As a result three key drivers for achieving the downstream targets were singled out and periodically measured in all projects during these processes. The related hypotheses which we tested were as follows:

1. Reducing reading speed during code inspections would improve design defect detection effectiveness and thus reduce normalized fault cost and customer detected faults;

2. Increasing faults found per new or changed statement with module test would improve design defect detection effectiveness and thus reduce normalized fault cost and customer detected faults;

3. Increasing test defect detection effectiveness (i.e. percentage of remaining faults being detected during integration) would reduce normalized fault cost and customer detected faults.

Since the three hypotheses are obviously related, we will try to show the results in one picture. Table 2 provides average values of the different process metrics in the discussed three-year timeframe. They look promising but can not immediately show detailed relations, which as a matter of fact need digging in each project. This is done in fig. 4 which shows the relations or root causes between the different involved process metrics. The three independent variables used in the three hypotheses above are underlined. Correlation coefficients are provided with each link which helps in finding the root causes easier than in a table with all correlation coefficients. Given the 34 investigated projects of this study, a correlation coefficient of above 0.5 has a significance level of below 0.001.

Again delivery accuracy and elapse time of the project had rather low correlations with these variables due to other and here not further treated influencing variables (e.g. project priority or engineers' productivity which varies with a degree of 1:20).

4.2 Effectively Planning Code Reading, Code Inspections and Module Test

The single most relevant techniques for defect detection so far are code inspections and module test. Detecting faults in architecture and design documents has considerable benefit from a cost perspective, however major yields in terms of reliability can be attributed to better code. We therefore provide more depth on these two techniques that help improving quality of code.

There are six possible paths between delivery of a module from design until start of integration test (fig. 5). They indicate the permutations of doing code reading alone, performing code inspections and applying module test. Although the best approach surely is from a mere defect detection perspective to apply inspections and module test, cost considerations and the objective to reduce elapse time and thus improve throughput, suggested to carefully evaluate which path to go in order to most efficiently and effectively detecting and removing faults. To our experience code reading is the cheapest detection technique, while module test is the most expensive. Code inspections lie somewhat in between.

Module test however, combined with C0 coverage targets has highest effectiveness for regression testing of existing functionality. Inspections on the other hand help in detecting distinct fault classes that can only be found under load in the field.

The target is to find the right balance between efficiency (time to be spent per item) and effectiveness (ratio of detected faults compared to remaining faults) by making the right decisions to spend the budget for the most appropriate quality assurance methods. In addition overall efficiency and effectiveness have to be optimized. It must be therefore carefully decided which method should be applied on which work product to guarantee high efficiency and effectiveness of code reading (i.e. done by one checker) and code inspections (i.e. done by multiple checkers in a controlled setting). Wrong decisions can mainly have two impacts:

- Proposed method to be performed is too 'weak': Faults which could have been found with a stronger method are not detected in the early phase. Too little effort would be spend in the early phase. Typically in this case efficiency is high, effectiveness is low.

- Proposed method to be performed is too 'strong': If the fault density is low from the very beginning, even an effective method will not discover many faults. This leads to a low efficiency, compared to the average effort which has to be spent to detect one fault. This holds especially for small changes in legacy code.

In addition faults are not distributed homogeneously through new or changed code [6,8]. By concentrating on fault-prone modules both, effectiveness and efficiency, are improved. Our main approach to identify fault-prone software-modules is a criticality prediction taking into account several criteria. One criterion is the analysis of module complexity based on complexity metrics. Other criteria concern the amount of n/c (new or changed)-code in a module, and the amount of field faults a module had in the predecessor project (see ch. 5).

The main input parameters for planning code inspections are:

1. General availability of an inspection leader: Only a trained and certified inspection leader should be allowed to plan and perform inspections to ensure adherence to the formal rules and achievement of efficiency targets. The number of certified inspection leaders and their availability limits the number of performed inspections for a particular project.

2. Module design effort (planned / actually spent): The actual design effort per module can already give an early impression on how much code will be new or changed. This indicates the effort which will be necessary for verification tasks like inspections.

3. Know-how of the checker: If specific know-how is necessary to check particular parts of the software the availability of correspondingly skilled persons will have an impact on the planning of code reviews and code inspections.

4. Checking rate: Based on the program language and historic experiences in previous projects the optimal checking rate determines the necessary effort to be planned.

5. Size of new or changed statements: Relating to the checking rate the total amount of the target size to be inspected defines the necessary effort.

6. Quality targets: If high-risk areas are identified (e.g. unexpected changes to previously stable components or unstable inputs from a previous project) exhaustive inspections must be considered.

7. Achieving the entry criteria: The inspection or review can start earliest if entry criteria for these procedures can be matched. Typically at least error-free compilable sources have to be available.

The intention is to apply code inspections on heavily changed modules first, to optimize pay-back of the additional effort which has to be spent compared to the lower effort for code reading. Code reading is recommended to be performed by the author himself for very small changes with a checking time shorter than two hours in order to profit from a good efficiency of code reading. The effort for know-how transfer to another designer can be saved.

For module test some additional parameters have to be considered:

1. Optimal sequence of modules to be tested before start of integration test: Start-up tests typically can start without having the entire new features implemented for all modules. Therefore the schedule for module test has to consider individual participation of modules in start-up tests. Later increments of the new design are added to integration test related to their respective functionality.

2. Availability of reusable module test environments: Effort for setting-up sophisticated test environments for the module test must be considered during planning. This holds especially for legacy code where often the module test environments and test cases for the necessary high C0 coverage are not available.

3. Distribution of code changes over all modules of one project: The number of items to be tested has a heavy impact on the whole planning and on the time which has to be planned for performing module test. The same amount of code to be tested can be distributed over a small number of modules (small initialization effort) or over a wide distribution of small changes throughout a lot of modules (high initialization effort).

4. Completion date of planned code reviews and code inspections: Overlap of code reviews or code inspections with module test should be avoided as much as possible in order to ensure high overall efficiency. Obviously it is not reasonable to test in parallel to inspections of the same portion of code, as corrections must be tested again.

5. Achieving the entry criteria: The readiness of validated test lists is a mandatory prerequisite for starting the module test.

The intention is to avoid spending high initialization effort by setting-up module test environments in order to test only a few number of changed statements.

On the other side in cases of existing and reusable module test environments this effort will be small enough to be appropriate. For modules identified as potentially critical (see ch. 5) module test must be performed independent of the effort which is necessary to initialize the module test environment.

During test correction of faults is typically the bottleneck for the project progress (not the detection of faults). It's no problem to add testers to a test phase in order to increase the number of detected faults within a given time schedule, but it's impossible to increase the correction rate by the same time if many corrections have to be made in a small group of modules.

Therefore a criticality prediction performed upfront should help to identify error-prone modules in advance to avoid a small number of designers having to correct the majority of the faults [8,10,11]. For this group of modules early quality assurance activities should be performed preferably to cut peaks for the number of faults in error-prone areas.

The result of a multi-linear discriminant analysis based on complexity metrics for a criticality prediction was taken into account for the planning of code inspections and module tests (especially modules identified as critical had to be inspected and module tested mandatory). It was expected that corrections from Integration Test onwards will be distributed over a larger set of modules. Our experiences clearly demonstrate that the bottleneck in getting corrections could be reduced by performing additional quality assurance activities before start of Integration. Instead of the former 80-20 distribution a 81-40 (that means 81% of the faults are distributed over 40% of the modules), or a 63-20 distribution could be achieved.

4.3 Cost / Benefit Analysis

ROI (return on investment) is a critical and misleading expression when it comes to development cost or justification of new techniques [6,12]. Too often heterogeneous cost elements with different meaning and unclear accounting relationships are combined to one figure that is then optimized. For instance reducing "cost of quality" that include appraisal cost and prevention cost is misleading when compared with cost of nonconformance because certain appraisal cost (e.g. module test) are a component of regular development. Cost of nonconformance on the other hand is incomplete if only considering internal cost for fault detection, correction and redelivery because they must include opportunity cost due to rework at the customer site, late deliveries or simply binding resources that otherwise might have been used for a new project.

We will try to provide insight in a ROI calculation (table 3). The data which is used for calculations results from average values that have been gathered in the *S12* history database. We will compare the effect of increased effort for combined code reading and code inspection activities as a key result of our improvement program. The summary shows that by reducing the amount of code to be inspected per hour by more than a factor three, the efficiency in terms of faults detected increased significantly. As a result the percentage of faults detected during coding increases dramatically. While reading speed reflects only the actual effort spent for fault detection, the effort per KStmt includes both detection and correction, thus resulting in around 3 Ph/Fault which seems stable.

Given an average sized development project and only focusing on the new and changed software without considering any effects of defect preventive activities over time, the following calculation can be derived. The effort spent for code reading and inspection activities increases by 1470 Ph. Assuming a constant average combined appraisal cost and cost of nonperformance (i.e. detection and correction effort) after coding of 15 Ph/Fault, the total effect is 9030 Ph less spent in year 2. This results in a ROI value of 6.1 (i.e. each additional hour spent during code reading and inspections yields 6.1 saved hours of appraisal and nonperformance activities afterwards). Of course not all ROI calculations are based on monetary benefits. Depending on the business goals it can as well be directly presented in improved delivery accuracy, reduced lead time or higher efficiency and productivity.

5 Lessons Learned and Future Work

We have described different techniques for improving reliability during the development of large-scale software systems. Those techniques proved to be liable and efficient once tailored to specific development and release processes. The techniques are described in a way to make them applicable to other development projects. The results of this reliability-oriented part of the software process improvement program can be seen in fig. 6. Field performance in terms of failure rates per operational (i.e. execution time) year are showed over calendar time in months after handover of the project to the network operator for three consecutive years. Achievements towards early defect detection can best be evaluated when going back to fig. 2 and table 2. Before starting the improvement program 17% of all faults were detected at the start integration test, while after 3 years almost two thirds of all faults are detected upfront. Similar observations can be made for intrinsic downtime and other parameters describing field performance of the investigated releases of switching systems.

References

[1] **Tagaki, Y. et al**
Analysis of Review's Effectiveness Based on Software Metrics. Proc. ISSRE '95. IEEE Comp. Society, pp. 34-39, 1995.

[2] **Obara, E. et al**
Metrics and Analyses in the Test Phase of Large Scale Software. J. Systems and Software, Vol. 38, pp. 37-46, 1997.

[3] **Lanubile, F. and G.Visaggio**
Evaluating Predictive Quality Models Derived from Software Measures: Lessons Learned. Journal of Systems and Software, Vol. 38, pp. 225-234, 1997.

[4] **Selby, R. W. and V. R. Basili**
Analyzing Error-Prone System Structure. IEEE Transactions on Software Engineering, Vol. 17, No. 2, pp. 141-152, 1991.

[5] **Shepperd, M.**
Early life-cycle Metrics and Software Quality Models. Information and Software Technology, Vol. 32, No. 4, pp. 311-316, 1990.

[6] **Wayne, M.Z. and D.M. Zage**
Evaluating Design Metrics on Large-Scale Software. IEEE Software, Vol. 10, No. 7, pp. 75 -81, Jul. 1993.

[7] *Generic Requirements for Software Reliability Prediction.* Bellcore GR-2813-CORE, Issue 1, December 1993.

[8] **Ebert, C.**
Experiences with Criticality Predictions in Software Development. In: Proc. Europ. Software Eng. Conf. ESEC / FSE '97, Eds. M. Jazayeri and H.Schauer, pp. 278-293, Springer, Berlin, New York, 1997.

[9] **Siddhartha R.D. and A.A. McIntosh**
When to Stop Testing for Large Software Systems with Changing Code. IEEE Trans. on Software Engineering. Vol. 30, No. 4, pp. 318-323, April 1994.

[10] **Evanco, W.M. and Agresti, W.W.**
A composite complexity approach for software defect modelling. Software Quality Journal, Vol. 3, pp. 27-44, 1994.

[11] **Khoshgoftaar, T.M. et al**
Early Quality Prediction: A Case Study in Telecommunications. IEEE Software, Vol. 13, No. 1, pp. 65-71, Jan. 1996.

[12] **Pfleeger, S.L.**
Lessons Learned in Building a Corporate Metrics Program. IEEE Software, Vol. 10, No. 5, pp. 67 - 74, May 1993.

[13] **Fenton, N. E. and S.L. Pfleeger**
Software Metrics: A Practical and Rigorous Approach. Chapman & Hall, London, UK, 1997.

APPENDIX

No.	Objective	Defect preventive check	Cost	Risk	Status
1.	Performance, Fault tolerance	Consider overload and error cases during design (e.g. buffer size, error conditions in decisions exception handling, default switch cases)			
2.	Maintainability, Reliability	Redesign of top runners of critical modules lists			
3.	Reliability	Apply dedicated inspections and high coverage module test to reused modules that appear on criticality list			
4.	Reliability	Apply dedicated inspections for critical relations in database system			
5.	Reliability	Before starting new variant families ensure that respective parents have been synchronised with open defects			
6.	Testability, Reliability	During architectural and detailed design specify and refine NFR tailored test cases (usage profiles for specific performance conditions with usage frequency, boundary values, error conditions with probability, etc.)			

Table 1: Selected sample defect prevention checklist for reliablity improvement

	baseline	year 1	year 2	year 3
Reading Speed in code inspections [stms/Ph]	183	57	44	30
Faults found in Code Reading or Code Inspections [F/Kstmt]	2	8	12	13
Faults found in Module Test [F/Kstmt]	3	5	9	11
Design Defect Detection Effectiveness	17%	31%	46%	63%
Test Defect Detection Effectiveness	57%	72%	83%	92%
Fault Detection in the Field *	100%	57%	28%	18%
Relative Cost per Fault *	100%	63%	55%	44%
Intrinsic Downttime of Operating Switching Systems *	100%	85%	77%	nya

* Start of Improvement Program taken as 100%

Table 2: Achieving Quality Improvement Targets. Average Values are Given for the Three Year Time Frame

	baseline	**year 1**	**year 2**
Reading Speed [Stmt/Ph]	183	57	44
Effort per KStmt	15	24	36
Effort per Fault	7.5	3	3
Faults per KStmt	2	8	12
Effectiveness [% of all]	2	18	29
***Project**: 70Kstmt; 3150 Faults*			
Effort for Code Reading / Insp. [Ph]	1050		2520
Faults found in Code Reading / Inspections	140		840
Remaining faults after code reading / inspections	3010		2310
Corr. effort after Code Reading / Insp. [Ph] *(based on 15 Ph/F average corr. effort)*	45150		34650
Total correction effort [Ph]	46200		37170
ROI = saved total effort / add. det. effort			**6.1**

Table 3: ROI Calculation of Process Improvements with Focus on Code Reading / Inspections (defect preventive activities are not considered for this example)

CMM Level	Design (TLD/DD)	Design (COR/MT)	Integration (SST - IQT)	Acceptance	Deployment
Defined 3	20%	40%	30%	5%	5%
Initial 1	5%	15%	50%	15%	15%

Figure 1: Typical benchmark effects of detecting faults earlier in the life cycle

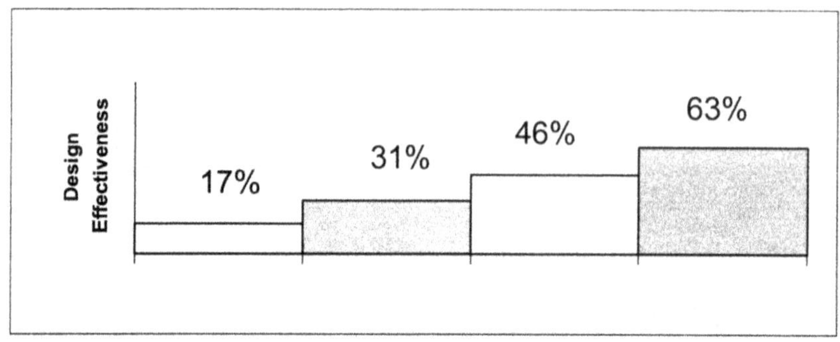

Figure 2: Design defect detection effectiveness improvement over three years. The first bar is the baseline when the software process improvement program was started. The given percentages relate to the sum of the first two bars in figure 1

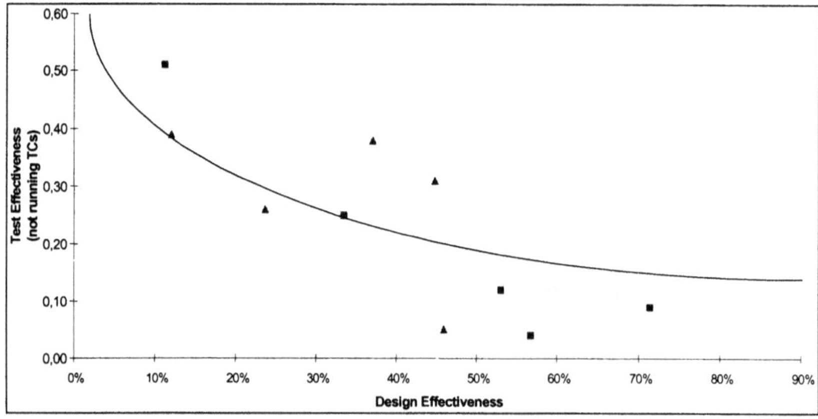

Figure 3: Test Case Effectiveness (in Terms of Unsuccessful Test Cases) vs. Design Defect Detection Effectiveness (in Terms of Defects found before Start of Integration)

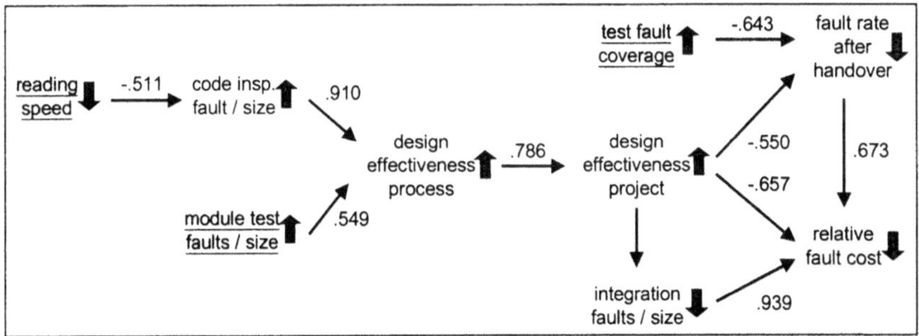

Figure 4: Relations between the Different Measured Variables. Values give the Correlation Coefficients. Underlined Variables are Independent Variables that were Controlled by the improvement Program.

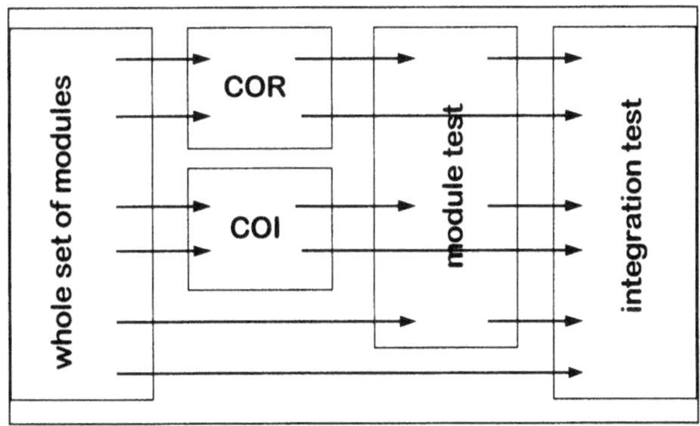

Figure 5: Six possible paths for modules between end of Ccoding and start of integration

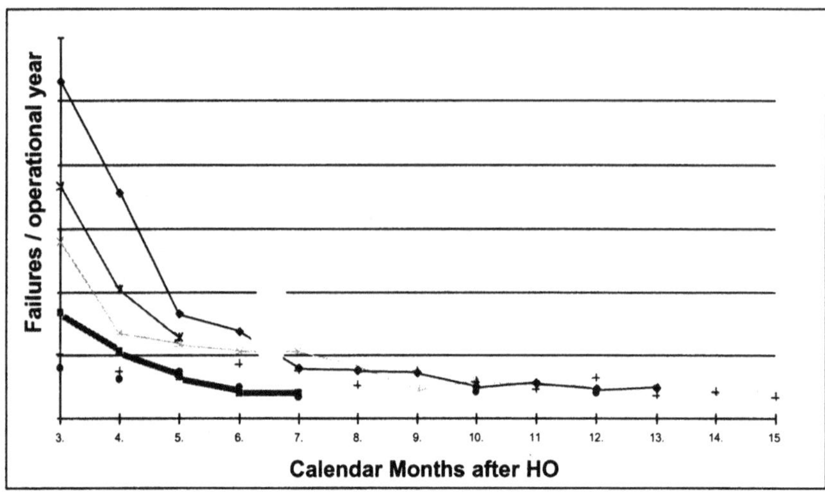

Figure 6: Effects of the described quality improvements in switching software on field performance in three consecutive releases over three years. Failure rates per operational (i.e. execution time) year are showed along months after handover of the project to the network operator.

Prototype of a Software Metrics Database for industrial use

Andreas Schmietendorf, Deutsche Telekom Development Center Berlin (Germany)

1 Introduction

The suitability of using metrics in software projects is now generally acknowledged. There is still, however, a widespread lack of confidence in the interpretation of object-oriented metrics, in concentration on use of only a few metrics and in the processing of large sets of measured values. While in the scientific field a large number of different metrics are generally used, the development of industrial software requires just a few meaningful metrics that can be applied with a minimum of effort. This is exactly the background to the "***metricDB***" project, whose objective is to collect a few significant, mainly object-oriented metrics in a database, largely automatically, in order to enable qualitative statements to be made and effort to be estimated. There must be an extremely easy-to-use interface (Web client) for evaluation purposes, as well as the possibility of complex, highly flexible evaluations, such as is the case, for example, under SPSS or Excel.

The "metricDB" project was launched at the Development Center in Berlin this May. The findings that are described below are principally based on the predefined requirements, on our experiences with the metrics tools used and with a first prototype that is now complete. They also include the results of workshops held jointly with the software measurement laboratory at the Otto-von-Guericke university and a group at France Telekom engaged in research in this field.

2 Initial situation/basis of the project

The "***metricDB***" project builds on the results of the MOSET[1] project carried out at the Berlin Development Center. This project included an examination of the use and potential significance of object-oriented metrics in the development of prototype software. The project resulted in the selection of CAME[2] tools (MetricsONE, RSM, McCabe - still under evaluation), which make it possible to integrate metrics from the object model (UML under Rational Rose) and the implementation (C++ and Java). [7], [9], [6]

Object-oriented effort estimation according to Sneed was recommended for Deutsche Telekom's software applications. In order to determine the

[1] MOSET - German acronym; metrics of object-oriented software development technologies

[2] CAME - Computer Assisted Measurement and Evaluation

Object Points, a defined methodology specifying multiple inclusion of the Object Points at concrete phases of object-oriented software development was developed. The directive for the use of the Object Point method also proposes using the above-mentioned CAME tools to enable at least some of the measurement values needed for effort estimation to be automatically entered. In addition, an initial analysis verified the use of the Object Point method in the field of switching and communications software. [12]

Step by step, the metrics offered by the CAME tool were interpreted and selected, enabling a metrics framework to be set up. The first step was to create Web pages based on HTML[3], which, in the form of input masks, reflect the defined metrics framework. The goal was to collect via mail at a central point metrics that have been defined in object-oriented software projects, for the purpose of incorporating them in a database. The large number of manual interfaces together with the resulting manual evaluation using a tool such as Microsoft Excel meant that this solution only reached low acceptance levels, or was not practicable in the long term due to the effort involved and the achievable results.

Examples of effort in the non-automated use of CAME tools:

- Multiple execution of metrics tool in order to enter measurement values
- Integration of the measurement figures into a database system (e.g. from Excel via ODBC[4])
- In the case of data collected centrally, transfer of measurement values to a Web form
- Simple, statistical analysis of metrics and graphical representations
- Distribution of evaluation results (e.g. HTML file in the Web).

Although this procedure is suitable for use in a brief initial phase, it involves what is in my opinion extremely great effort, and may cause metrics interpretation to be inconsistent. In order to use the existing CAME tools efficiently under the conditions of industrial software production, the need for a standardized database solution became crucial.

3 Requirements analysis

The principle targets in implementing a database prototype for object-oriented metrics are: to collect expertise/experience in the use of a metrics database and to promote discussion on this type of system. As Deutsche Telekom already has

---

3 HTML - Hyper Text Markup Language

4 ODBC - Open Database Connectivity (MS standard for open database interfaces)

other systems for collecting classic metrics and experiences, interoperability and future integration capabilities are the main objectives here. The goal of the metrics database is to take into account the needs of different users and, in particular, to make it easier than before to control the quality and costs of object-oriented software projects. During a workshop with the potential customers (e.g. project managers) for the metrics database, requirements were therefore identified and used as the basis for data and function modeling. The following lists what I consider to be the most important requirements for a metrics database in industrial use:

- The cost of using and supporting /administration of a metrics database must be kept to a minimum, i.e. it must be automated to as great a degree as possible.
- Supporting different user types, e.g. project managers who use ready-made evaluations in order to compare the progress made by their own projects with projects that have already been completed, and consultants who can subject metrics to any type of statistical analysis (including multi-user operations).
- Automatic problem detection in software development on the basis of configurable threshold values that have been exceeded, and offers of alternative solutions.
- Presentation of the progress of metrics and a comparison with other projects by means of graphs and control diagrams. Histograms for graphical representation of e.g. cost related to project phases.
- "Experience database" for project development and control, cost estimation, productivity/efficiency and (indirect) cost control.
- Automation of part of cost estimation (e.g. Object Point) to enable cost estimation and historical estimation at different phases of a project.
- Check of qualitative criteria of modeling or implementation using validated metrics. Examples: maintainability, compliance with the object-oriented paradigm, stability of an object model in the case of change.
- The system must make it relatively easy for users to incorporate new metrics and their interpretations into the database.
- Possibility of integrating evaluations that are not implemented by using the standard functions offered by the application, such as Excel or SPSS evaluations.
- It should also be possible to transfer evaluations to a user's own documents (e.g. Winword, Excel) via such mechanisms as the Windows clipboard.

In my experience, the use of metrics in development projects is only accepted if it produces genuine advantages for project control or when the concentrated use of metrics is called for by top management within the framework of metrics reports. In a software development project, there is little acceptance for effort which involves manual entry and processing. For this reason, the Development Centers at Deutsche Telekom are currently working on the integration of selected object-oriented metrics in their metrics reports, and are also including them in the procedural model for object-oriented software developments, which is itself currently undergoing development. The latter will be dealt with in greater detail in the following section.

4 Integrating metrics into an OO procedural model

Parallel to the introduction of object-oriented metrics, work started at the Development Center on the development of a generic object-oriented procedural model (VM-OO). Based on the general procedural model for software development at Deutsche Telekom (VM base), this specifies details for the phases of object-oriented software development along with the worksteps involved. The project-specific procedural model for each concrete object-oriented software project can then be derived from this procedural model. Object-oriented software development at the Development Center in Berlin is characterized by an iterative procedure, i.e. the development phases concept design, analysis, product design and evolution[5] are repeated several times. Each of the development phases consists of one or more segments, which contain the activities themselves (e.g. identification of classes and objects using CRC[6] cards).

For the first time in this procedural model, we will define how metrics are to be determined. This involves defining fixed measurement points, which enable projects to be compared even when they are still undergoing software generation. In an initial phase, once all activities of a segment have been performed (see description above), relevant metrics are collected. At present, the phases of analysis and design and part of evolution can be measured using the CAME tools already in use. Planning also foresees extending application of the CAME tools to the phases of concept design and maintenance. In the case of concept design, metrics collection primarily involves descriptions and business process models in text format. Metrics planned for maintenance include error statistics, adjustment effort and customer satisfaction.

5 Selecting metrics

The selection of metrics was based on a proposal submitted by [Lorenz 1994] for a metrics form. Selection focussed on metrics which can be included via standard tools (MetricsONE, RSM-Tool, etc.) from models (UML model under

[5] Evolution - Consists of implementation, testing and integration activities

[6] CRC - Class Responsibilities Collaborations

Rational Rose) and implementation (C++ and Java). The objective was to incorporate largely identical metrics from the object model and the implementation, thus enabling us, for example, to check to what extent the model corresponded to the subsequent implementation. In addition to these metrics, project specifications of a general nature are integrated in the database, along with a timestamp to enable unambiguous identification of measurements related to a project phase as defined by the object-oriented procedural model described in the previous section. One important aim was to restrict the number of metrics offered in order to provide a manageable number of suitable metrics. In practice, the following areas are covered, some of which are also to be found in the Entity Relationship Model.

General project details

- Timestamp of measurement related to the project phase reached
- Application type (TMN[7], IN[8], Web application)
- Complexity of graphical interface
- Tools and development languages used
- Description of hardware and software architectures
- Iteration cycle completed, according to VM-OO

Metrics of the analysis object model (UML-compliant from Rational Rose)

- Class metrics (#classes, #attributes, #methods, dependences, legacy depth)
- Use Case metrics (#interaction diagrams referring to Use Cases)

Metrics of the design object model (UML-compliant from Rational Rose)

- Package metrics (#abstract classes, dependence and link metrics)
- Class metrics (#classes, #attributes, #methods, dependences, legacy depth)
- Operation metrics (number of transferred parameters)

---

[7] TMN - Telecommunication Management Network

[8] IN - Intelligent Network

Metrics of implementation (C++ and Java)

- Lines of Code (on all, per method, comments, generated)
- Classes size (#classes, #attributes, #methods,...)
- Object libraries used

Cumulated effort in person days for project phases

- PD[9] required in the pre-project phase (concept design/business process analysis)
- PD required for the analysis and design phases (OO modeling)
- PD required during implementation, developer testing and acceptance test.

Although it is not possible to assign every task in software development unambiguously to one of the above phases of a large-scale project (e.g. performance benchmark of a prototype), the object is to record the effort involved as experience data, meaning that the effort must be characterizable according to its content. An area which should also be considered in this context is that of data protection, as we must preclude tracing data back to individual project staff, as stipulated by the German law on Data Protection.

Not all metrics are accepted for general use. Nevertheless, it may be sensible to store them in a database in order to analyze their value at a later date. For this reason, we considered it suitable to introduce a status for each metric. The status must specify whether the metric is initial (transferred from an external source), verified (currently undergoing verification) or in use (fixed evaluation is possible).

6 General and statistical functions

Based on the use cases of the database and the measurement values it contains, general and statistical functions must be defined for the application. Since, in the case of an industrial metrics database, the academic aspect is not of major importance, we have greatly restricted the statistical and computed functions that are offered as standard evaluations for Web clients in the application.

- Comparison of metrics procedures in different projects,
- Forecasts/trend computations for estimating the course of a project,

[9] PD - person days

- Computations for some object-oriented effort metrics (Object Points according to Sneed),
- Statistical standard functions (arithmetic mean, geometric mean, mean variation, etc.).

Besides these, general information relating to the data contained, such as the project name, the SW/HW platform used, languages used and current project status are output. A standard report of individual metrics with specification of their mean values and threshold values is planned. Planning also foresees the explicit identification of critical values (threshold values that have been exceeded) for metrics from the object model (UML) and the implementation (Java and C++), as well as reaction proposals.

An additional functionality offered to the user involves identifying reusable software components. My experience has shown that there is considerable effort involved in a general consideration of reusable software. Examining software reusability is thus often rejected due to cost pressure. We hope that, by using metrics, it will, at a later stage, be possible to identify reusable software components and to make reuse proposals. In this case, the metrics database should simply serve identification purposes, with an additional application supporting the processing of reusable software components. In an initial phase, identification should relate to the scope of the software component, to dependence on and link values to other objects or components, and to the functionality offered.

7 Architecture and application model

The objective is to develop a Web application consisting of a Web client, a Web server and a relational database. The Web server contains HTML templates and text explanations/help on how to use the metrics database. The database server stores the actual values of the individual metrics, project information and meta information on each measurement. It should also be possible to change the statistical standard functions offered in the application and to integrate new metrics. In future, these administrative tasks will be implemented with a controller application (possibly even an application server).

On the Web clients, HTML pages containing the current contents or complete evaluations from the actual database are read; these are incorporated dynamically in the HTML pages (Active Server Pages) via Store Procedures. Thus, standard evaluations and information on projects are offered but do not permit any interactive work with the data once it is loaded. The application server that we have planned for future versions will be used to integrate automatically triggered statistical evaluations and for database administration in order, for example, to incorporate new types of metrics in the database schema.

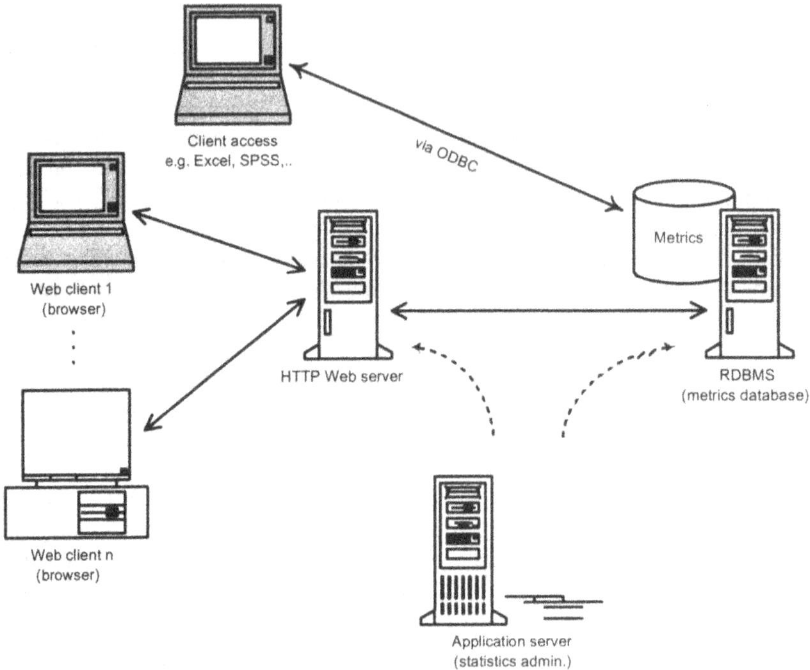

Figure 1: Architecture of the "metricDB" application

Using a relational database makes it necessary to perform entity relationship modeling in order to identify the relations (database tables) and relationships. The ER-Win tool was used for this task, making it possible to fully generate the Data Definition Language required for setting up relations in the database. Triggers were also generated (e.g. Do not delete project if package metrics still exist), which implement consistency conditions in the database. The ER model caters for separate relations for manual (e.g. project data) and automatically integrated data/metrics (e.g. class metrics).

Due to the limited options of the HTML language, the main part of application complexity is stored in the Store Procedures, thus assigning special importance to the design of relevant SQL queries. Unfortunately, the software development technology which is currently used to develop the client does not cater for modeling the required functionality, resulting in a great disadvantage as far as the maintainability of the application is concerned.

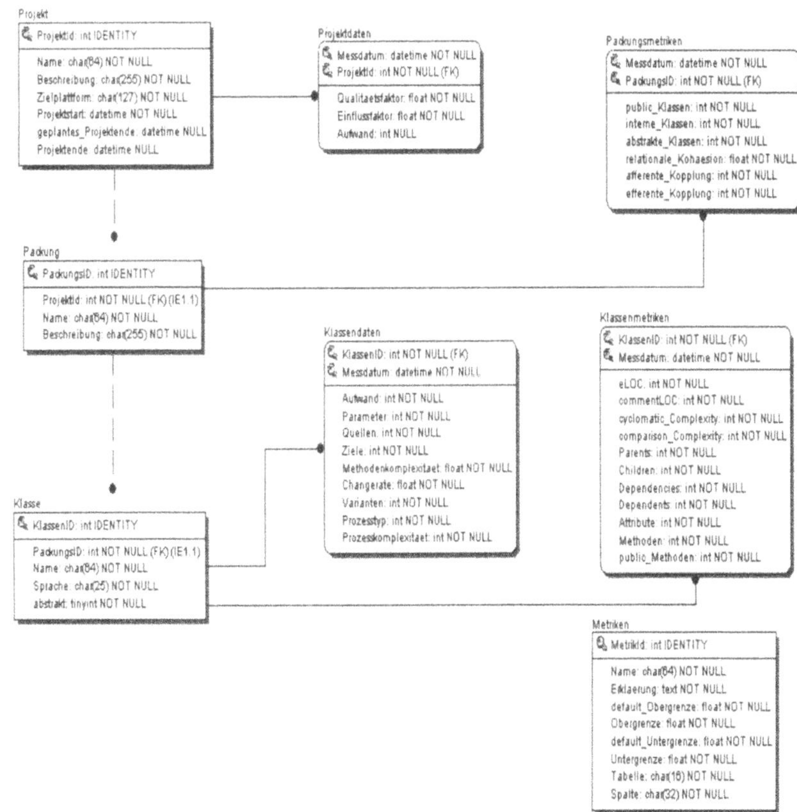

Figure 2: ER model of the metricDB application

8 Implementation of the application

As the staff involved in the project have different levels of previous experience in the use of databases and programming languages, and as there was only a short training period available, we needed tools for implementation that were relatively easy to use. We opted for Microsoft's SQL Server as the relational database management system due to the inhouse administration skills already available. Front Page was chosen for the graphical design of the application, and Microsoft's VISUAL INTERDEV tool for the implementation of Active Server Page components for database queries (incl. Store Procedures) and evaluations, in particular Active Data Objects and the SQL Query Designer. We also use the

Crystal Reports to represent more complex graphics evaluations on the Web pages. The operating system used on the Web server (Internet Information Server V4.0) and the database server is Windows NT Version 4.0.

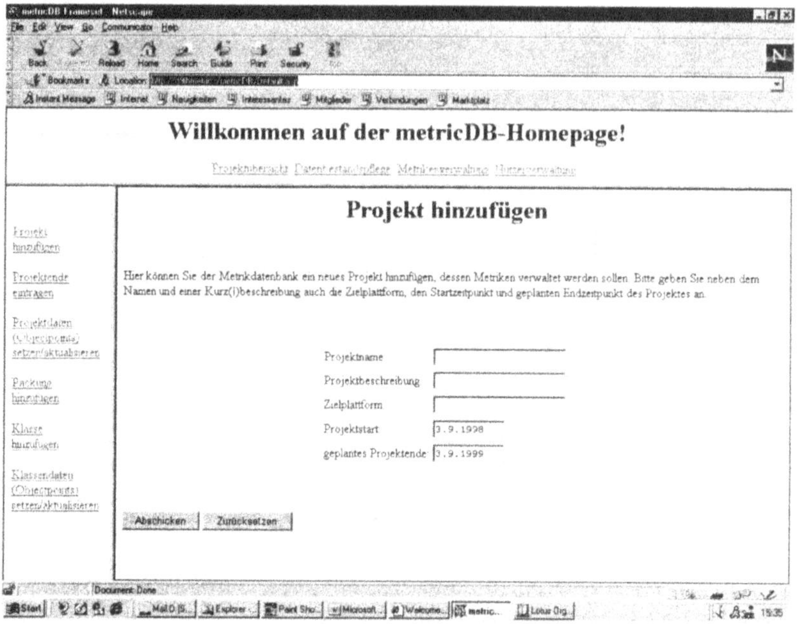

Figure 3: metricDB client interface (early prototype)

These development tools are relatively easy to learn and were selected to avoid increasing the complexity of the task in hand with complicated notations/languages such as UML or C++ or Java. The key factor behind the decision was the limited time available for getting to know the environment and, at the same time, the requirement that a Web application was to be implemented with its typical benefits, e.g. minimization of administrative tasks on the client and the use of widely differing client systems (UNIX, Windows).

The project also focuses on the issue of automating the application, which involves two different tasks. Firstly, after consultation with the customer (clarification of name conventions, file system structures and identification of the project phase reached), models stored in the network and implemented code must be cyclically "measured". Secondly, the standard evaluations offered via Web pages (statistical analyses) must be executed offline for performance reasons. In addition, we must also take into account that securing a consistent database also constitutes a background load.

Even at this early stage, the difficulties involved in automation are clearly definable: I will describe these in more detail using the example of metrics integration from the object model. The MetricsONE (Version 1.0) CAME tool that has been used up to now cannot be usefully executed without the Rational Rose application running: this would seem to make the possibility of automation doubtful. The results of initial analyses for the development of our own parser (source text analysis according to specified rules and criteria) for integrating metrics from the object model can be summarized as follows: although the file format (*.mdl) used under Rational Rose complies with the ASCII standard, making it easy to read, the notations it contains are not officially disclosed by Rational. Nor can the compatibility to new versions of Rational Rose be guaranteed. The only option offered officially, which also requires software maintenance, consists, according to Rational, in using the modeling tool as Rose OLE[10] server (application runs without graphical user interface) and using the Visual Basic-compliant script interface to generate reports under Rational Rose.

9 Support of open interfaces

In addition to restricted read access to the metrics database via dynamic Web pages (Active Server Pages), the project concept has to consider the use of statistics tools such as SPSS, Mathcad and Excel. The options offered by the ODBC interface are currently being examined. This examination focuses not on the tool's possible statistical functions but on the requirement that evaluations, once performed, can be reintegrated into the database. It has already become apparent at this stage that the use of relational systems causes problems. This is due to the question of changes on views of the database and consistent incorporation/transformation to the base relations. The question arises as to whether a relational database management system is the right choice for a metrics database, or whether an object-oriented database system is more flexible in reacting to this kind of requirement. In this context, the possibility of interoperability with other experience or metrics databases must be examined.

In this project, we opted initially for the following solution: evaluations generated by users can be reintegrated into the application and thus made available to other users by storing them as plain HTML files in a kind of discussion forum. The result is that these externally generated evaluations cannot be used for database queries since they are no longer available as structured data. As knowledge of the database schema is imperative for read only access to the database via an ODBC link (there is no write authorization for access to the database outside the actual application), the current version is always available on the metrics database Web site. In addition, any changes to the schema of the database are only admissible via modeling under ER-Win.

[10] OLE - Object Linking and Embedding (Microsoft interface for online data exchange)

10 Summary and outlook

During the course of the project it became apparent that the software development technology we had selected for the client application is only partially suitable. Despite the fact that an application prototype was developed extremely fast, thereby promoting discussion with the potential customer, the use of Active Server Page technology means that many of the requirements involved can only be implemented with difficulty or by using additional technologies (e.g. Java script). In particular, support of interactive functionalities in the application is unsatisfactory. Another problem involves documentation of the source code of the Active Server Pages used in the application. As the HTML source code (incl. plaintext) is subjected to an unstructured mix with the Visual Basic script language, it is not possible to achieve error-free structuring or modularization. It is utterly impossible to model application functionality at an abstract level with structograms or pseudo-code. The Active Server Pages are also limited when it comes to intermediate storage of data on the client side: all the data that is required in one session on the client must be stored temporarily in the form of cookies[11]. In order to eliminate the above deficits, we plan parallel development of the client application with Java.

With the tools we are using, we have not yet achieved the degree of automation defined in the project requirements. One deficiency is that metrics from the object model can only be collected via the existing CAME tools when the modeling application (Rational Rose) is running, and another that the RSM tool only allows some of the required metrics to be determined. For this reason, we are currently evaluating development of our own tools for metrics integration (parsers), and estimating the effort involved.

For comprehensive metrics databases, concentration on object-oriented metrics is definitely not sufficient to prove, for example, that there is an increase in the efficiency in object-oriented development systems as compared with classic paradigms. A solution should offer integration, or the chance of interoperability with other metrics databases and development tools repositories. The objective should be to logically integrate all metrics that can feasibly be included over the entire software lifecycle. I refer here in particular to risk metrics, performance metrics, process metrics and maintainability metrics. In this context, the use of data warehouse technologies and the possibilities offered by multidimensional data analysis (OLAP[12]) are to be examined.

A key requirement is the necessary standardization of usable object-oriented metrics and their inclusion within the framework of integrated software development environments. In my view, success here depends entirely on

[11] Cookies - Way of saving data from an HTML file to the user's system

[12] OLAP - Online Analytica Processing

scientific and industrial institutions cooperating in order to persuade providers to integrate a set of standard metrics in their software development tools.

The effort involved in the "metricDB" project does not include activities for system support and maintenance. It is essential that this effort be included in an operational concept to ensure that new versions of the development tool and user requests are taken into account.

Fig. 4 below summarizes once more the factors that I consider to be critical in influencing the development/introduction of an industrial metrics database, and does not claim to be complete.

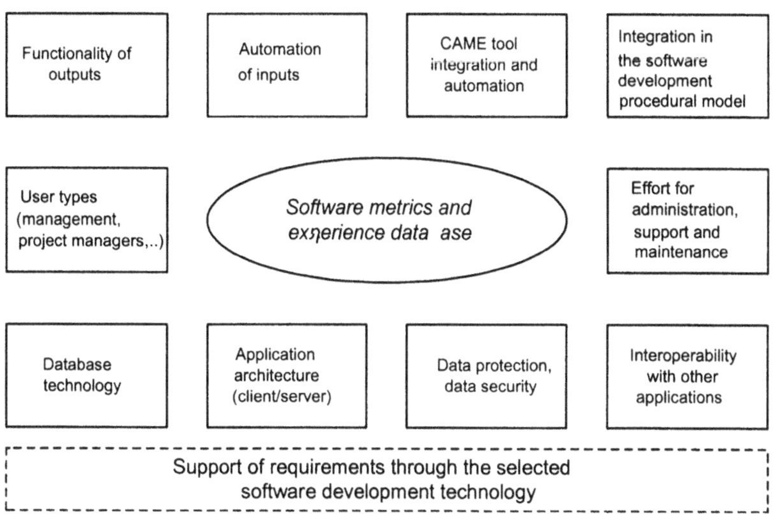

Figure 4: Criteria influencing an industrial metrics database

References

[1] **Dimitrov, Evgeni**
Ein Vorgehensmodell für die Objektorientierte Entwicklung. Internal study, Deutsche Telekom, Berlin: 1998.

[2] **Dumke, Reiner**
Softwareentwicklung nach Maß. Schätzen-Messen-Bewerten. Braunschweig/Wiesba-den: Vieweg-Verlag, 1992.

[3] **Dumke, Reiner; Foltin, Erik; Koeppe, Reinhard; Winkler, Achim**
Softwarequalität durch Meßtools. Braunschweig/Wiesbaden: Vieweg-Verlag, 1996.

[4] **Landais, Gilbert**
Specific Metrics for C++ Programs. France Telecom, FT.BD/CNET/DTL/DLI/98.106.

[5] **Lorenz, Mark; Kidd, Jeff**
Object-Oriented Software Metrics – A Practical Guide. Englewood Cliffs/N.J.: Prentice Hall, 1994.

[6] **McCabe**
Datasheet for McCabe tools, in particular on object-oriented metrics, 1997.

[7] **NumberSIX**
MetricsONE User's Guide Version 1.0, Washington 1997, URL: http://www.numbersix.com.

[8] **Paulisch, Frances**
OO_metriken mit McCabe-Werkzeugen. SIGS publication Objektspectrum 6/97.

[9] Ressource Standard Metrics Version 4.0 for Windows NT, M Squared Technologies, URL: http://www.tqnet.com/m2tech/rsm.htm.

[10] **Schmietendorf, Andreas**
Fallstudie zur Aufnahme von Metriken an einem Visual C++ SQL Prototypen. EZ Berlin, 1997.

[11] **Schmietendorf, Andreas**
Metriken objektorientierter Software-Entwicklungstechnologien. Metric News II/97 (Journal of the GI-Interest Group on Software Metrics), Magdeburg: 1997.

[12] **Sneed, Harry M.**
Schätzung der Entwicklungskosten von objektorientierter Software. Informations Spektrum 19: 133-140, Heidelberg Berlin New York: Springer Verlag, 1996.

[13] **Zuse, Horst**
A Framework of Software Measurement. Berlin, New York: Walter de Gruyter & Co, 1998.

IV. Function Point Foundations and Applications

Comparison between FPA and FFP: a field experience

Jean-Marc Desharnais, SELAM Québec (Canada) and Pam Morris,
Total Metrics (Australia)

Abstract

A requirement for software productivity analysis and estimation is the ability to measure the size of a software product from a functional perspective rather than from a technical perspective. One example of such a functional size measurement (FSM) technique is Function Point Analysis (FPA)[2]. FPA is now widely used in the MIS domain, where it has become the 'de facto' standard in the industry. However, FPA has not had the same acceptance in other domains, such as real-time software. A new technique was proposed by the University of Quebec in Montreal (UQAM) and the Software Engineering Laboratory in Applied Metrics (SELAM) to extend the functional measure to real-time software. The new technique is called Full Function Points.

This article reports on a practical research undertaken in a telecommunications company which compared 5 major applications in the real-time and MIS domains when measured using both FPA and an proposed extension, called Full Function Points (FFP)[1] [4]. This article presents the main FPA and FFP concepts, the description of the types of software, the methodology used in the field tests and the results of field tests. All of the applications are multidimensional and three of them demonstrate the characteristics of real-time software.

The results showed that, when applying the FFP technique for applications at the business user level, both techniques measured an equivalent functional size in term of number of points for MIS applications. However this was not the case, for some of the layered software used within MIS applications.

For applications within the MIS domain, the FFP technique was found to be as effective as the FPA technique, suggesting that it could be of benefit if used within this domain. For real-time applications, the difference in the size measured between the two techniques was significant. This was expected for the real-time applications since the FFP technique was designed to ensure that the functional characteristics of real-time are taken into account when measuring this type of software.

1 Introduction

Measures can be used to quantify the software product as well as the process by which it is developed. Once these measures are obtained, they can be used, for example, to build cost estimation models, productivity models [3] and cost-benefit models. One important measure is the size of a software product. There are basically two kinds of size measures: technical measures and functional measures. Technical measures are used to measure software products and processes from a developer's point of view. For example, they can be used in efficiency analysis to improve the performance of the designs. In comparison Functional measures, on the other hand, are used to measure software products and services from a user's perspective. Being independent of technical development and implementation decisions, functional measures can therefore be used to compare the productivity of different techniques and technologies. In this context, major organisations frequently use functional size measurement techniques to measure the software products identified within their outsourcing contracts.

Function Points Analysis (FPA), first introduced by Allan Albrecht of IBM in 1979 (Albrecht, 1979), is an example of a functional size measure. FPA measures the size of software in terms of its delivered functionality, measuring such objects as inputs, outputs and files[1]. Since FPA was developed for an MIS[2] environment, its concepts, rules and guidelines are adapted to software that is oriented toward that environment. Consequently, FPA has gained a wide audience in this specific area of software applications and is now being used extensively, among other things, to analyse productivity and to estimate project costs. However, FPA has not obtained the same acceptance in other areas of software and also still struggles to measure some types of software used in MIS organisations that we refer to as layered software in this document.

2 FFP technique

The technique which extends Function Point Analysis (FPA) to take into account functional characteristics specific to real-time software, is called Full Function Points (FFP) [4] [17] [18]. FFP was designed with the objective of retaining the beneficial measurement qualities of FPA including instrumentation, repetitiveness and applicability. This extension takes into consideration current industry practices in the design of real-time software and the design of what is currently documented regarding the user requirements from a functional perspective. Our approach, from the functional perspective instead of user view gives to this measure the possibility of considering functionality at different levels (not just the business user level). For this reason, the FFP technique, when applied, could be also linked with the concept of layers (as synonym of levels) described in more detail in part 6 of this document (layered software).

The FFP rules were developed based on the observation that real-time software has the following specific transactional and data characteristics:

1 Readers unfamiliar with Function Points (FP) are referred to Box A for an overview.

2 MIS: Management Information Systems.

Transactions: The number of sub-processes of a real-time software process varies substantially. In the MIS domain, on the other hand, processes of the same types have a more stable number of sub-processes. Data: Existence of a large number of single control data elements, that is, data characterized by the fact that there is one and only one occurrence of the data element in the whole application. This data is used to control, directly or indirectly, the behavior of the application or mechanical devices.

New data and Transactional function types were therefore introduced to take into account these characteristics: four control Transactional function types (Entry, Exit, Read and Write) and two Control data function types (Updated Control Group and Read-Only Control Group).

To verify if FFP met its stated objective of measuring the user functional requirements and desired qualities of measurement methods, preliminary field tests were conducted. The results of the field tests were positive: according to the real-time specialists who assisted in the tests. The FFP technique has met its stated objective of adequately measuring the user functional requirements [13]. The analysts also found that the FFP rules and procedures could be applied easily to software whose functional requirements had been documented according to common current practices.

To verify the effectiveness of FFP to measure the functionality of real-time software compared to FPA, additional field tests were conducted using both techniques to measure the same applications. All field tests were conducted on major existing applications within one organization. These supplementary field tests lead to the introduction of the concept of layers (already recognized in ISO 14143-5). The concept of layered software provided the opportunity of extending the FFP measures to other types of software which has proved difficult to fully measure with FPA.

3 FPA and FFP concepts

This section compares the differences between the basic concepts of FPA and FFP. FFP was developed by the University of Quebec in Montreal (UQAM) and the Software Engineering Laboratory in Applied Metrics (SELAM) to take into account functional characteristics specific to real-time software [8] [9] [11] [15] [20]. However its concepts have been found to be equally applicable to other types of software particularly where the primary users are not human.

3.1 FPA concepts

FPA was designed and refined for Business applications software, which usually constitutes about 70% - 80% of a commercial organisation's software portfolio. This section describes the basic concepts of FPA, which have contributed to it being able to be used to effectively measure Business Applications software over the past 20 years. Full details of the rules for applying FPA can be found in the IFPUG Counting Practices Manual 4.0 [10].

The FPA technique measures functionality by quantifying the software's processes (inputs, outputs, enquires) and data files (internal and external). It is based on the following fundamental principles:

1. Functional size is the measure of the functionality delivered to the end business user [5]. Only processes that send or receive data to, or from, the external user boundary are included in the measurement of functionality delivered to the user.

2. A process is required to have a predominant role of *either* inputting *or* extracting data. This predominant role determines the process type (input, output or inquiry).

3. The functional size of a process is directly related to the amount of data, which crosses the external user boundary of the software during the execution of the predominant side of the process.

4. An extremely complex process of a particular type can only be assigned a numeric functional size that can be almost double the assigned functional size of the simplest process of that type.

5. Functionality delivered by stored data is a significant contributor to the overall functional size of the software.

6. Functionality changed is recorded as being the measure for the whole function irrespective of the proportion of the process being changed.

3.2 FFP concepts

The FFP technique measures functionality of the software by quantifying the software's sub-processes within each process and control data (internal and external). It is based on the following fundamental principles:

1. It measures functional size from the functional perspective instead of the external user view. I.e. measures the functionality *required* to be delivered

by a process to the user of the process not just the functionality experienced directly by the user. Sub-processes that read and write the data to and from data groups are included in the measurement of functionality in addition to the sub-processes required to receive data (entry) and extract data (exit).

2. A process is not required to have a predominant role *per se* (only an entry or only an exit). In order to measure size it is only necessary to identify all the entry, exit, read and write sub-process types.

3. The functional size of a process is determined by measuring the size of individual sub-processes, which are not limited to those which only accept (entry) or extract (exit) data. The predominant role of a process to either extract or accept data does not influence its size.

4. An extremely large process of a particular type can be sized accordingly by awarding proportionally more points. In theory, there is no limit to the number of points awarded for one specific process.

5. Functionality delivered by stored data is a less significant contributor (in number of points) to the overall functional size of the software, than functionality delivered by the processes.

6. Functionality changed is recorded at the level of the sub-processes. Only a part of the process (identified by the sub-processes) is credited for the change.

The FFP technique has taken into consideration current industry practices in the design of real-time software and the design of what is currently documented regarding the user requirements from a functional perspective. It introduces new concepts for measuring data and transactional function types, which cater for the characteristics of non-business applications software [17] [18] [19].

Overview of FFP Technique

FFP, like FPA, measures functional size by evaluating transactional processes and logical groups of data. However unlike FPA, the transactional processes are evaluated at sub-process level. I.e. the sub-processes within a process are identified, classified and assessed. Points for functional size are awarded at sub-process level. The sub-processes within each transactional process can be categorised into one of four types:

- External Control Entry (ECE)
- External Control Exit (ECX)
- Internal Control Read (ICR)
- Internal Control Write (ICW)

The data groups, which contribute, to the overall size fall into two categories.

- Multiple record data groups, which can be either updated or only, read by the processes. These are similar to the Internal Logical files and External Interface files counted for FPA.
- Single Record (single occurrence) data groups. These data groups may be maintained by the processes (Updated Control Group - UCG) or only read by the processes (Read-only Control Group - RCG). The single occurrence data groups contain all instances of single control values used by the processes. There may be only one instance of a UCG or RCG per application.

4 Types of Software

Software that is usually included within the scope of the MIS organisation can be categorised based on the types of service by software such as illustrated in Figure A and described in the following sections.

<table>
<tr><td>Business</td><td colspan="2">Business Application Software</td><td colspan="2">Embedded or Control Software</td></tr>
<tr><td rowspan="2">Infra-structure</td><td>Utility Software</td><td colspan="2">Users Tools Software</td><td>Developers Tools Software</td></tr>
<tr><td colspan="4">Systems Software</td></tr>
</table>

Figure A

4.1 Business Applications Software

These applications deliver functionality that supports the organisation's core business.

The users are primarily human business users, however a small proportion of the functionality may also be delivered to, or triggered by, other Business Applications. This type of software is typically business or commercial (MIS) software and would include Payroll applications, Accounts Receivable or Fleet Management systems.

4.2 Embedded or Control Software

These applications also deliver functionality which supports the organisation's core business.

The users are primarily other software applications embedded in equipment. This type of software typically operates under strict timing conditions and is often referred to as Real-time software. Examples would include Equipment monitoring Systems, Telephone Switching Systems.

4.3 Utility Software

These applications deliver software that provides the infrastructure to support the Business Applications Software. The users are primarily Business Applications, which trigger the operation of the utilities but may include the developers or business administration people as the administrative users. Examples would include backup utilities (to ensure the data reliability of the Business Application) or archiving utilities (to optimise the performance of the Business Application). Other examples are installation and conversion software.

4.4 Users Tools Software

These applications are tools used by administrative users to create the functionality delivered by the Business Applications Software.

The users are primarily Business Applications Software, which utilise functionality delivered by the tools to enable them to deliver functionality to the business. Administrative human users of these tools may be from either the Business or IT. Examples would include Report Generators, Spreadsheets, and Word processors.

4.5 Developers Tools Software

These applications are tools used by developers to create the functionality delivered by the Business Applications Software. The users are primarily other applications, which are either generated by, or used as input to, the tools operation. Human Users may also include IT developers as administrative users. Examples would include, Code Generators, Testing software, New Product Generators etc.

4.6 Systems Software

These applications enable all other types of software to operate and deliver functionality. The users are primarily other applications with a limited interface to human IT operational staff. Examples would include operating systems, printer drivers, protocol converters, and presentation software.

5 FPA and real-time processes

FPA does not adequately capture the functionality delivered by the last five types of software (from 4.2 through 4.6). Since, the characteristics of these types of software tend to resemble those of real-time software.

The size of real-time processes varies substantially, and therefore the size also varies substantially.

They have no predominant function type for inputting or outputting data; therefore a process could have both an input (entry) part and an output (exit) part. This dual role causes a problem when trying to consistently categorise the process into an FPA single function type.

For example when measuring the functional size of a compiler. A compiler has many processes each of which has few or many sub-processes. A process may be initiated by the entry of non compiled code (sub-process(es) for the entry) and complete with the exit of compiled code (sub-process(es) for the exit). FPA rules make it difficult to determine whether the process is an External Input (EI), an External Output (EO) or an External Enquiry (EQ). The process does not satisfy the requirement of an EQ (input and output side of an EQ) because the compiled code is derived. If categorised as an EI, then the definition of an elementary process is violated, e.g. the definition of an elementary process, within the CPM Guide 4.0, is that the process must be 'self-contained' (be 'complete' from the user view and leave the business in a consistent state). In this case, the process is only complete when the code is compiled. Just measuring the non-compiled code as the External Input or the compiled code as an External Output, is inconsistent with the FPA definition of an elementary process.

6 The layered applications

If the characteristics of the different types of software are considered, then they can be identified as being on a different level to that of the business user applications and to each other. In fact, they constitute different layers: the business user will see the utility software as providing the technical features of their software, while the user of utilities could consider the developer tools as the technical means of providing their software. The lowest layer in the non-inclusive list is the operating systems software.

Within an organisation, especially within a telecommunications organisation, it is possible to identify additional types of software. For this reason, it is necessary to find definitions and rules helping the person measuring the software to identify the different layers of the software. The functionality delivered by software at one layer is not of the same type of functionality delivered by software at a lower layer. Trying to compare them is not straightforward. It is like comparing different types of building.

6.1 Definition of a layer

An item of software is typically structured in horizontal "layers" [16]. Each layer is a world unto itself. A layer does not need to know how its inputs (entry) are generated. It is just required to deal appropriately with the input when it is received. A layer perceives the layer below it as a set of primitives. Each layer "sees" the layers below but cannot see the layers above. Similarly, what happens to data output (exit) from a layer is irrelevant to the producer once that output has been dispatched. The internal operation of one layer does not need to be known by any other layer. Indeed, it is preferable that internal details be protected from outside alteration. Making one layer dependent upon internal organisation of another is very undesirable. Such dependency restricts the ability to maintain (i.e. change or enhance) the layer which is depended upon. This is the basic principle of information hiding. For example, the organisation ought to be able to entirely re-construct a server layer without impacting clients, which use its primitives, so long as the software retains the same interface. For this reason, the organisation usually prevents a client layer from directly using the services of any subordinate layers except the one immediately below it.

6.2 Rules for identifying a layer

The following are the recommended rules for identifying a subordinate layer from a superior layer:

A. A subordinate layer is considered as a technical implementation by the superior layer.
B. A subordinate layer does not recognise the superior layer and has no functionality by itself to communicate with the superior layer.
C. A subordinate layer could work without the assistance of a superior layer. If the superior layer is not working properly, this will not affect the subordinate layer.
D. A subordinate layer is independent of the technology used by the superior layer.
E. A subordinate layer provides services to the superior layer and could be used by the superior layer.
F. A superior layer could not fully work if the subordinate layer is not working properly.
G. A superior layer does not necessarily use all the functionality of the subordinate layer.
H. A subordinate layer could be a superior layer from the perspective of a layer below it.

I. A layer always delivers functionality
J. A layer is software, not a piece of equipment. The software could be embedded, within the equipment.
K. From one layer to another the data has distinct information content and value for users at the respective layer level.

7 Field Test Methodology and results

7.1 Methodology

One counter was responsible for all the counts to ensure consistency and avoid different interpretations [6] [7] [14]. The counter was experienced in functional measurement (12 years), IFPUG-certified and co-author of the FFP technique.

FPP and FPA were used in parallel to measure 5 applications and 10 sub-systems within those applications. Of these 10 sub-systems, 5 could be described as real-time while the remaining 5 were mostly MIS (B, C2, C3, D1, D2). Both measurement techniques were used for 7 sub-systems. Due to time constraints, the remaining 3 sub-systems were measured using only FPA (these sub-systems were entirely MIS type: C3, D1, D2) under the presumption that the FFP measured functional size should be comparable with that obtained using FPA. In our methodology we also used the concept of "layer" which is not a part of the actual IFPUG rules.

The existence of layered software is related to the infrastructure of IT organizations. The users of the layered software were not directly the business users but the business users still took advantage of the infrastructure software because, without it, their applications would be useless. This is comparable to having all the electrical wiring in a house but no power. In the context of outsourcing an IT organization, measuring software only from a user perspective hides a good part of the reality as shown with application C. This is why it is necessary to understand the importance of the layers and their contribution to adequately measure the functionality delivered by software (Figure B).

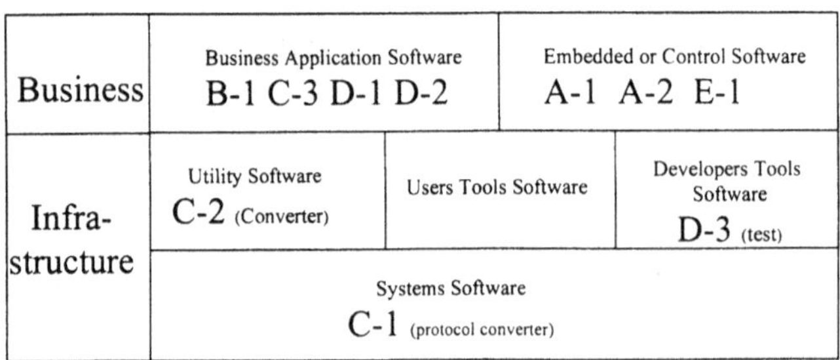

Figure B

7.2 Results

As expected, our results show a large difference between the measured size of the same applications when they are measured using the two techniques. Table 1 shows that the total FPA counts for all applications was 4067 points and the total FFP counts for all applications was 8372 points. The difference is nearly 50%. Whist we are not proposing that FFP points and FPA function points are directly comparable, we believe that difference is still significant for the following reasons:

- When measuring typical MIS applications with both techniques, the results were similar. "This is demonstrated by the results from Application B1 and to a lesser extent by Application B2
- Some applications could not be measured at all using FPA because, the functionality they delivered could not be reliably categorized into Function types, nor did they fit with the definition of an elementary process. This was the case for D3 and both real-time applications, A and E. The example of the compiler in Section 5 explained this problem.
- When measuring real-time applications, which have complex processes, the difference is always significant. Application A was a typical example.

App	Type Layer	FPA	FFP	Diff.	Diff. %	Type
A	A1- L1	210	794	584	74%	Real-time
	A2- L2	115	183	68	37%	Real-time
B	B1-L1	764	791	27	3%	Mostly MIS
C	C1-L3	272	676	404	60%	MIS[3]
	C2-L2[4]	878	896	18	2%	MIS
	C3-L1	1273	N/C[5]	0	0%	MIS
D	D1-L1	727	N/C	0	0%[6]	MIS
	D2-L1	110	N/C	0	0%[6]	MIS
	D3-L2	0	2604	2604	100%	Real-time
E	E1-L1	43	318	275	86%	Real-time
		4067	**8372**	**3980**	**51%**	**FFP total[6]**

Table 1

[3] This system could be considered a batch system.

[4] We had difficulty identifying each process as input, output or inquiry. In the end, the count did not change.

[5] N/C = Not counted

Application C is layered software. Four layers were identified but it was decided to regroup the two top layers (C1). One of the layers is a Report Generator. The two layers below (C2 and C3) were considered to be the same application from the FPA point of view by field experts even if they are technically very different. C3, at the lowest level, is an application that automatically captures data from many different applications and constructs an ASCII file. C2 converts the ASCII file data to be read by a specific database (Eg: Oracle). It was difficult to categorize these processes as EIs, EOs and EQs. However the final result was not impacted since the number of points allocated by the IFPUG CPM 4.0 counting rules are the same for EI and EQ and with a difference of only 1 point for EO.

If we oversimplified, from a user perspective, both applications could be seen as one batch application that provides data to a Report Generator. When applying the concept of layers, we discovered two different applications with independent data. This is the reason why, in C1, the number of FPA points is low compared to the FFP points. Almost all the FPA points from C1 were points from the measurement of the data.

8 Issues

Implementing a new measurement technic, and trying to compare it with an existing measure, is not a trivial exercise. It has highlighted the need to address the following questions through more research:

8.1 The concept of layers versus the concept of boundaries

FPA does not address the issue of layers. It measures functionality delivered to the business user level. If some part of the information provided to the user comes from another layer, then with FPA the functionality delivered by the layer is usually considered to be a technical feature of the software. With layered systems important parts of the functionality are then totally ignored which will have impacts in the estimating, the productivity rates, etc.

With application C and D3, it was necessary to address the issue of layers because the purpose of the measure was to address all the functionality within a system, not just the functionality related to the business user view. For example, an outsourcing contract could cover more than just the business user view. FPA practitioners could argue that infrastructure is "technical" as opposed to functional. In our opinion, this is a question of perspective. The business user view is just one perspective. Within an organisation, there are many users, each one using the functionality delivered by the software. An operating system also has functionality, which is useful for the developer of an application. Using the concept of layers helps the person measuring the software address this software functionality which was considered rather as a technical issue in the FPA measurement meta-model. The first rule (section 6-2 A) for identifying layers (states: "A subordinate layer is considered as a technical implementation by the superior layer". It is then possible to count all the functionality of different types of systems using the concept of layers.

FPA practitioners could also argue that infrastructure software is in the Black Box and is taken into consideration in their measurement. The reasoning used is that if they measure by the infrastructure functionality, then the size of different applications can be compared because, implicitly, the infrastructure functionality is incorporated in the measure.

This approach is valid when all the applications counted are related to the same type of infrastructure. However, this was not the case in the organisation in which we conducted the research. It is necessary to make a distinction between the real measured functional size and an extrapolation of the functional size. Considering the infrastructure as an extrapolation of the functional size can be useful in some cases but not all.

Do we have a potential conflict between FPA and FFP when mixing the two types of measures? In our opinion, this is not a conflict since they should not be mixed, unless the measures are conducted at the same level, and distinct labels on the measurement results should be used whenever they are compared or reported. For example, in the construction or in the leasing industry, they specify very clearly the types of measures they used: square metres (with the outside walls); square metres net (excluding the walls; square metres excluding public spaces such as stairs, elevators, office space floors, versus parking space floor and infrastructure.

8.2 User view versus functionality

The purpose of the measurement is very important, regardless of the functional size measurement technique used. In the context of a productivity measure, it is necessary to separate what could be measured. Inside an IT organisation, the construction of an application, and its maintenance, is only part of the job. There is also the development, maintenance and support of the entire infrastructure software to help develop and maintain those applications. The trend in the IT industry is to construct better infrastructure functionality to improve the development and the maintenance of software applications. Considering only one perspective of the user view means that the measurement activity focuses only on the business applications, without taking directly into account the additional functionality delivered by the infrastructure software.

When people measuring software consider the infrastructure as technical "overhead", there is a potential problem when the purpose is not only to measure and maintain the applications, but also to provide and account for the infrastructure. This is the case, for example, in a large IT outsourcing contract.

8.3 Verification method with correct proportions at the intermediate level

For FPA, there is a technique to audit the resulting functional size measures using the comparison of the measure being tested to that of other valid measurements. This audit technique uses the relative distribution of function points contributed by different function types, based on historical database of hundreds of projects already measured[6]. For FFP, such an 'audit' procedure is in progress and a first draft has been prepared.

A similar analysis on the results obtained from FFP measurements needs to be conducted. This would compare measures of layers, different types of layers, and across different domains of infrastructure - MIS and real-time for example, without presuming that they would be equivalent if there is no reasonable basis to make such assumptions.

8.4 Construction of a productivity model for FFP

From preliminary data collection we have observed that:

- the cost per FFP could be higher for a subordinate layer than for a superior layer
- the cost to develop of real-time software is higher than the cost to develop MIS software but there is not yet actual supporting evidence of this.

We are still unaware if it is possible to compare:

- the cost per FFP to develop one layer with that of another layer
- the cost per FFP to develop software in one domain (real-time) with that of another domain (MIS infrastructures).

[6] The intermediate counting is the one identifying each Function Type (EI, EO, EQ, ILF and EIF). There is also a lower level of count when identifying the number of DETs (Data Elements Type), the number of RETs (Record Elements Type) and the number of FTRs (File Type Reference) for each Function Type. For FFP, the intermediate level is the identification of the processes and sub-processes and the lower level is the identification of the number of RETs. There are no DETs and FTRs with FFP.

Box A: Function Point Analysis (FPA) [10] Overview

FPA is a measurement technique to measure the functional size of a software product. It was introduced in 1979, and, in 1984, the International Function Point User Group (IFPUG) was set up to clarify the rules, set standards and promote their use and evolution. Since then, four major releases of the rules and standards have been published. In this article, all references to FPA definitions and measurement rules will be based on the most recent version (IFPUG, 1994).

The first step in calculating FPA is to identify the counting boundary, that is, the border between the application being measured and the external applications, or the user domain. A boundary establishes *what* functions are included in the function point count.

The next step consists in determining the unadjusted function point (UFP) count which reflects the specific measurable functionality provided to the user by the application being measured. Calculation of the UFP begins with counting five components or *function types* of the application: Internal Logical Files - ILF (files as conceived by the user, not physical files), External Interface Files – EIF (files accessed by the application but not updated), Inputs (e.g., transactions types), Outputs (e.g., reports) and Enquiries (e.g., on-line enquiries). These function types are classified into two groups: data function types (ILF and EIF) and transactional function types (Inputs, Outputs and Enquiries). The complexity of these function types is then classified as relatively low, average or high, according to a set of prescriptive standards based on the Data Element Types – DET (comparable to fields), File Types Referenced – FTR (files used by the function types) and Record Element Types – RET (Record types of a file). After making this classification for each of the five function types, the UFP is computed using predefined weights.

The last step involves assessing the environment and processing complexity of the project or application *as a whole*. The impact of fourteen general systems characteristics is rated on a scale from 0 to 5 in terms of their likely effect on the project or application. The value adjustment factor is obtained which will adjust the UFP by a maximum of ±35% to produce the *Adjusted Function Points (AFP)*.

A complete description of the FPA including definitions, procedures, counting rules and examples is found in the *Function Point Counting Practices Manual, Release 4.0*, published by the IFPUG (IFPUG, 1994).

References

[1] **Alain Abran, Marcela Maya, J.-M. Desharnais, Denis St-Pierre**
Adapting Function Points Analysis to Real-time Software. American Programmer, Fall, 1997.

[2] **Albrecht, A.J. (1979)**
Measuring Application Development Productivity. Proceedings of Joint Share Guide and IBM Application Development Symposium, October, 1997, pp. 83-92.

[3] **Desharnais, J.-M.**
Statistical Analysis on the Productivity of Data Processing with Development Projects using the Function Point Technique. Université du Québec à Montréal. 1988.

[4] **Desharnais Jean-Marc, St-Pierre Denis, Maya Marcela, Abran Alain, Bourque Pierre**
Full Function Points: Counting Practices Manual. Technical Report 1997-04 UQAM and SELAM, Montreal, September, 1997.

[5] **Desharnais J.-M., St-Pierre D., Abran A., Gardner B.**
Definition of When Requirements Should be Used to Count Function Points in a Project. The Voice, International Function Point Users Group, July, 1996.

[6] **Desharnais** J.-M.
Validation Process for Industry Benchmarking Data. Invited Paper, Conference on Software Maintenance, IEEE, Montreal, September, 1993, pp. 371-372.

[7] **Desharnais J.-M., Morris P.**
Post Measurement Validation Procedure for Function Point Counts. Position Paper Forum on Software Engineering Standards Issues, October, 1996.

[8] **Galea, S. (1995)**
The Boeing Company: 3D Function Point Extensions. V2.0, Release 1.0, Boeing Information and Support Services, Research and Technology Software Engineering, June, 1995.

[9] **IEEE, (1990)**
IEEE Standard Computer Dictionary: A compilation of IEEE Standard Computer Glossaries. IEEE Std 610-1990, The Institute of Electrical and Electronics Engineers, Inc., New York, NY, 1990.

[10] **IFPUG (1994)**
Function Point Counting Practices Manual. Release 4.0, International Function Point Users Group - IFPUG, Westerville, Ohio, 1994.

[11] **Illingworth, V. (1991) (editor)**
Dictionary of Computing. Oxford University Press, 3rd edition, 1991, 510 pages.

[12] **Jacquet, J.-P. and Abran, A. (1997)**
From Software Metrics to Software Measurement Methods: A Process Model. presented at the Third International Symposium and Forum on Software Engineering Standards, ISESS '97, Walnut Creek (CA), 1997.

[13] **Maya M., Abran A., Oligny S., St-Pierre D., Desharnais J.-M.**
Measuring the functional size of real-time software. ESCOM-ENCRESS 98, Rome, May 1998, 10 p.

[14] **Morris P., Desharnais J.-M.**
Validation Procedure for Function Point Counts. IFPUG, April 1996.

[15] **Reifer, D. J. (1990)**
Asset-R: A Function Point Sizing Tool for Scientific and Real-Time Systems. Journal of Systems and Software, Vol. 11, No. 3, March, 1990, pp. 159-171.

[16] **Rules, Grant**
Function Point Counting Practices for Highly Constrained Systems – Release 1.0. United Kingdom Software Metrics Association (UKSMA), March 1993, UK.

[17] **St-Pierre, D., Maya, M., Abran, A. and Desharnais, J.-M. (1997a)**
Full Function Points: Function Points Extension for Real-Time Software - Concepts and Definitions. Software Engineering Management Research Laboratory, Université du Québec à Montréal, Technical Report 1997-03, March, 1997, 18 pages.

[18] **St-Pierre, D., Maya, M., Abran, A. Desharnais, J.-M. and Bourque, P. (1997b)**
Full Function Points: Function Points Extension for Real-Time Software - Concepts, Definitions and Procedures. Software Engineering Management Research Laboratory, Université du Québec à Montréal, Technical Report 1997-04, September, 1997, 43 pages.

[19] **St-Pierre, D., Abran, A., Araki, M. and Desharnais, J.-M. (1997c)**
Adapting Function Points to Real-Time Software. IFPUG 1997 Fall Conference, Scottsdale, AZ, September 15-19, 1997.

[20] **Whitmire, S. A. (1992)**
3-D Function Points: Scientific and Real-Time Extensions to Function Points. Proceedings of the 1992 Pacific Northwest Software Quality Conference, June 1, 1992.

Function Point Counts Derived from SAP Business Scenario Requirements

Maya Daneva, Clearnet Communications Inc., Ontario (Canada)

1 Introduction

Recent years have witnessed a very high level of interest in the SAP technology and the Function Points Analysis (FPA). The motivation for implementing the SAP R/3 business application suite is twofold. On one side, SAP provides the information technology infrastructure for business process re-engineering [2] and a component-based concept for R/3 implementation which benefits the most from software reusability. On the other side, SAP has protected its customers from the Year 2000 problem and, in addition, has brought internet capabilities to the R/3 application suite. Simultaneously, Function Points (FP) have been becoming widely accepted as the standard metric for software controlling and planning.

Given the heightened attention on both SAP technology and FPA, it is surprising that little research has been conducted to examine the linkages between these two concepts in depth and to integrate them properly.

This paper presents how FPA fits with the SAP technology. Specifically, we explore the use of Function Points to help with SAP business scenario requirements. Our work proposes an approach to deriving Function Points from SAP *scenario process models* and *business object models*. The paper discusses some size and complexity attributes pertinent to the SAP business requirements and suggests a set of components to be counted together with a set of rules which specify how to obtain the SAP size and complexity numbers.

2 The Approach

2.1 Background

Our approach is based on two major sources: (1) Jones's framework for applied software measurement [8] and the existing FP counting practices promoted by both the industry and the academy [1, 6], and (2) our previous work [4, 5] in the area of Process Model Benchmarking which obtained a set of measurable complexity attributes for business process models represented by means of the SAP standard modelling language.

The approach presented in this paper refers to two basic problems: *how to link the SAP modelling concepts to the FPA concepts*, and *what procedure to follow in order to get FP counts*. The following sections discuss these two issues.

2.2 Mapping the SAP modelling concepts into FP components

SAP uses business processes and business objects in order to describe the business content of the R/3 business application components. The SAP business requirement documents specify business scenarios that are usually represented in terms of event-driven process chains [3]. This modelling language comprises three basic elements: *processes, events, and logical connectors* (*and, or*, and *exclusive or*). The *processes* are considered as time-consuming business transactions that use, update or create business objects. The *events* are both conditions for the execution of processes, and results. The events referred to points in time and are defined as data items that should be available at the start and at the end of the process' execution. Events trigger, or drive, the process flows that follow. Logical connectors describe the logical relationships between events and processes. The connectors define alternative or parallel work flows through the process chains.

The processes included in the scenario have business objects, business object models and data entity types assigned to them. A business object is a set of entity types that share a common external interface [9]. A business object usually consists of a source entity type and all those entity types that are hierarchically dependent on it. The underlying data model used to describe the internal structure of the business objects is based on a semantic entity-relationship representation language. It includes the concepts of specialization, generalization and aggregation.

Following the FPA [7], we assume that the complexity of a process would depend on the number of the business objects whose instances are created, updated or used during the process' execution. Next, the size and the complexity of a business object could be determined by analyzing the structure of the object (e.g. the inclusion of aggregations), as well as, the attributes of the source entity and these of the hierarchically dependent entities. Fortunately, this analytical task can be supported by using the SAP R/3 Business Engineer, a navigation tool that helps identifying all the business object models and data entities assigned to a specific process [9].

To identify linkages between the SAP modelling concepts and those of the FPA, we compared the concept definitions and their interpretations. This effort resulted in formulating four classes of mapping rules: (1) *boundary identification rules*, which refer to the scope of the enterprise area being measured, (2) *component identification rules*, which help identifying items subjected to FP counting, (3) *component classification rules*, which suggest how to classify the components being counted, and (4) *complexity assessment rules*, which refer to the assignment of complexity factors to the components. An extraction of the *component identification rules* is given in Tab. 1.

FP concept	*Relevant SAP concept*	*Mapping Rule*
Logical File	Business Object	Consider the source entity of each business object from the Input/Output assignment diagram as a candidate for a logical file.
Logical File	Data Entity	If the Input/Output assignment diagram contains a data entity without reference to a business object, then consider the entity as a candidate for a logical file.
Logical File	Master Data File	Do not consider the master data files as logical files. Consider the master files as a physical implementation technique.

Table 1.

2.3 The sizing procedure

We propose the following procedure to count FP:

1. Identify the application boundary based on the SAP business scenarios that are discussed in the business blueprint. Define multiple boundaries if the business blueprint covers scenarios pertinent to different SAP application components.
2. For each business scenario, identify processes and business objects that can be mapped into transactional types and data types.
3. Classify the processes and the business objects. Divide the processes in three classes: external inputs, external outputs and external inquiries. Group the business objects in two sets: internal logical files and external interface files.
4. Assess the complexity of each process and each business object.
5. Calculate the Unadjusted FP counts as per the UFPUG manual [7].

3 Application

The sizing procedure has been applied to three SAP R/3 implementation projects. The Phase I implementation has referred to 12 scenario processes related to 4 R/3 application components (Financial Management, Controlling, Asset Management, Project System, and Material Management). The Phase II project has been focused on 8 scenario processes and 5 R/3 components (Financial Management, Controlling, Sales and Distribution Material Management and Service Management). Finally, the Phase III project scope has covered 6 scenarios and 2 components (Sales and Distribution, and Material Management). For each project, multiple boundaries have been determined. Four types of documents have been used as an input to the sizing procedure: the business blueprint document, the customer-specific scenario process models, the business process questionnaires filled out by the business process owners, and the business object model.

Our three case studies have demonstrated the applicability of the procedure in the Business Requirements/Blueprinting phase of the SAP R/3 implementation cycle.

4 Major Results

The main points embodied in this paper are:

- An approach to deriving FP from SAP business scenario models and business object models was proposed. It involves four sets of rules for mapping the SAP modelling concepts into the FPA terms together with a procedure for sizing the SAP R/3 business requirements. The approach provides a guidance on what we believe to be effective FP counting. In this sense, it can serve as a prescriptive, not only as a descriptive, counting model.
- The Function Point metric can be successfully used as a controlling tool during the business blueprinting stage of the R/3 implementation. The applicability of the counting procedure was examined, what lead us to identify potential problems and new research opportunities.

References

[1] **Abran A., P. Robillard**
Function Points Analysis: an Empirical Study of its Measurement Process. IEEE Transactions on Software Engineering, vol. 22, pp. 895-909.

[2] **Brenner, W., G. Keller**
Business Reengineering mit Standard-Software. Campus Verlag, Frankfurt/Main, 1995.

[3] **Currant, T., G. Keller**
SAP R/3 Business Blueprint. Prentice Hall, New Jersey, 1998.

[4] **Daneva M.**
The Role of Benchmarking in the IS Development. Proceedings of the International Conference on Computer-aided Information System Engineering (CAiSE'96), May 22-25, Crete, Greece, 1996.

[5] **Daneva, M., R. Heib, A.-W. Scheer**
Benchmarking Business Process Models. Veröffentlichungen des Instituts für Wirtschaftsinformatik der Universität des Saarlandes, Nr. 136, Saarbrücken, Germany, October 1996.

[6] **Garmus, D., D. Herron**
Measuring the Software Process. A Practical Guide to Functional Measurement, Yourdon Press, Prentice Hall PTR, New Jersey, 1997.

[7] **IFPUG**
Function Point Counting Manual. Release 4.0. Westerville, Ohio, 1994.

[8] **Jones, C.**
Applied Software Measurement. McGraw Hill, 1996.

[9] **SAP AG**
R/3 System. SAP Business Objects, Walldorf, Germany, 1997.

"Information Engineering und IV-Controlling"

Herausgeber: Prof. Dr. Franz Lehner

GABLER EDITION WISSENSCHAFT

Michael Bosch
Management internationaler Raumfahrtprojekte
1997. XX, 226 Seiten, 92 Abb.,
Broschur DM 89,-/ ÖS 650,-/ SFr 81,-
ISBN 3-8244-6611-2
M. Bosch entwickelt am Beispiel der internationalen Raumstation ALPHA ein computergestütztes Projektführungssystem, das das Management auf jeder Ebene bei der Projektplanung und -steuerung unterstützt und die beteiligten internationalen Institutionen und Unternehmen integriert.

Martin Hölz
Anwendungssystem-Planung im Großunternehmen
Bestandsaufnahme und Entwicklungstendenzen
1997. XX, 345 Seiten, 59 Abb., 26 Tab.,
Broschur DM 118,-/ ÖS 861,-/ SFr 105,-
ISBN 3-8244-6553-1
Der Autor bietet eine detaillierte Analyse des aktuellen Stands der industriellen Anwendungssystem-Planung und entwickelt sein Rahmenkonzept „IV-Bebauungsplanung“ zur ganzheitlichen, systematischen Planung und Gestaltung.

Thomas Jaster
Entscheidungsorientierte Kosten- und Leistungsrechnung
Ein Rahmenkonzept für das Controlling von Software-Entwicklungen
1997. XVI, 261 Seiten, 30 Abb.,
Broschur DM 98,-/ ÖS 715,-/ SFr 89,-
ISBN 3-8244-6595-7
Anhand von praxisrelevanten Situationen wird theoretisch fundiert gezeigt, daß eine entscheidungsorientierte Bewertung in allen Phasen des Software-Lebenszyklus wertvolle Informationen für eine Wirtschaftlichkeitsanalyse bietet.

Franz Lehner u. a. (Hrsg.)
Multimedia in Lehre und Forschung
Systeme - Erfahrungen - Perspektiven
1998. VIII, 198 Seiten, 74 Abb., 2 Tab.,
Broschur DM 98,-/ ÖS 715,-/ SFr 89,-
ISBN 3-8244-6602-3
Der Band bietet einen Überblick über Aktivitäten und Projekte zum Thema Multimedia an der Universität Regensburg. Das Spektrum reicht von der Medizin über die Geisteswissenschaften, den Unterhaltungsbereich und den Unterricht bis hin zur Namenforschung und zur Psychologie.

Franz Lehner et al. (eds.)
Software Metrics
Research and Practice in Software Measurement
1997. VIII, 232 Seiten, 68 Abb.,
Broschur DM 98,-/ ÖS 715,-/ SFr 89,-
ISBN 3-8244-6518-3
This volume presents the findings of the 6th International Workshop on Software Metrics. Consequently continuing the Workshop's tradition the focus is on the combination of theoretical and practical contributions.

Franz Lehner (Hrsg.)
Softwarewartung und Reengineering
Erfahrungen und Entwicklungen
1996. VII, 352 Seiten, Broschur DM 118,-/ ÖS 861,-/ SFr 105,-
ISBN 3-8244-6294-X
In diesem Tagungsband werden Erfahrungen, Lösungen, Konzepte sowie Werkzeuge präsentiert, die den aktuellen Stand auf dem Gebiet der Softwarewartung und des Reengineering in Theorie und Praxis dokumentieren.

Franz Lehner/Schahram Dustdar (Hrsg.)
Telekooperation in Unternehmen
1997. X, 379 Seiten, Broschur DM 89,-/ ÖS 650,-/ SFr 81,-
ISBN 3-8244-6433-0
In dem Sammelband sind aktuelle Beiträge über rechnergestützte Zusammenarbeit von räumlich verteilten Personen und Organisationen zusammengefaßt, die den Stand der Technik bewerten, Erfahrungen dokumentieren und Perspektiven für die Zukunft aufzeigen.

www.ingramcontent.com/pod-product-compliance
Lightning Source LLC
Chambersburg PA
CBHW071411050326
40689CB00010B/1834

9783824468768